Behind the Crisis

Marx's Dialectics of Value and Knowledge

Historical Materialism Book Series

More than ten years after the collapse of the Berlin Wall and the disappearance of Marxism as a (supposed) state ideology, a need for a serious and long-term Marxist book publishing program has arisen. Subjected to the whims of fashion, most contemporary publishers have abandoned any of the systematic production of Marxist theoretical work that they may have indulged in during the 1970s and early 1980s. The Historical Materialism book series addresses this great gap with original monographs, translated texts, and reprints of "classics."

Haymarket Books is proud to be working with Brill Academic Publishers (www.brill.nl) and the journal *Historical Materialism* to republish the Historical Materialism book series in paperback editions. Current series titles include:

Alasdair MacIntyre's Engagement with Marxism: Selected Writings 1953–1974, edited by Paul Blackledge and Neil Davidson

Althusser: The Detour of Theory, Gregory Elliott

Between Equal Rights: A Marxist Theory of International Law, China Miéville

The Capitalist Cycle, Pavel V. Maksakovsky, translated with introduction and commentary by Richard B. Day

The Clash of Globalisations: Neo-Liberalism, the Third Way, and Anti-Globalisation, Ray Kiely

Critical Companion to Contemporary Marxism, edited by Jacques Bidet and Stathis Kouvelakis

Criticism of Heaven: On Marxism and Theology, Roland Boer

Criticism of Religion: On Marxism and Theology II, Roland Boer

Exploring Marx's Capital: Philosophical, Economic, and Political Dimensions, Jacques Bidet, translated by David Fernbach

Following Marx: Method, Critique, and Crisis, Michael Lebowitz

The German Revolution: 1917–1923, Pierre Broué

Globalisation: A Systematic Marxian Account, Tony Smith

The Gramscian Moment: Philosophy, Hegemony and Marxism, Peter D. Thomas

Impersonal Power: History and Theory of the Bourgeois State, Heide Gerstenberger, translated by David Fernbach

Lenin Rediscovered: What Is to Be Done? in Context, Lars T. Lih

Making History: Agency, Structure, and Change in Social Theory, Alex Callinicos

Marxism and Ecological Economics: Toward a Red and Green Political Economy, Paul Burkett

A Marxist Philosophy of Language, Jean-Jacques Lecercle, translated by Gregory Elliott

Politics and Philosophy: Niccolò Machiavelli and Louis Althusser's Aleatory Materialism, Mikko Lahtinen, translated by Gareth Griffiths and Kristina Köhli

The Theory of Revolution in the Young Marx, Michael Löwy

Utopia Ltd.: Ideologies of Social Dreaming in England 1870–1900, Matthew Beaumont

Western Marxism and the Soviet Union: A Survey of Critical Theories and Debates Since 1917, Marcel van der Linden

Witnesses to Permanent Revolution: The Documentary Record, edited by Richard B. Day and Daniel Gaido

Behind the Crisis

Marx's Dialectics of Value and Knowledge

Guglielmo Carchedi

Haymarket Books
Chicago, IL

First published in 2011 by Brill Academic Publishers, The Netherlands
© 2011 Koninklijke Brill NV, Leiden, The Netherlands

Published in paperback in 2012 by
Haymarket Books
P.O. Box 180165
Chicago, IL 60618
773-583-7884
www.haymarketbooks.org

ISBN: 978-1-60846-196-7

Trade distribution:
In the US, Consortium Book Sales, www.cbsd.com
In Canada, Publishers Group Canada, www.pgcbooks.ca
In the UK, Turnaround Publisher Services, www.turnaround-psl.com
In Australia, Palgrave Macmillan, www.palgravemacmillan.com.au
In all other countries, Publishers Group Worldwide, www.pgw.com

Cover image of *Non-Objective Composition (Suprematism)*, 1916,
by Olga Rosanova. Cover design by Ragina Johnson.

This book was published with the generous support of Lannan Foundation
and the Wallace Global Fund.

Printed in Canada by union labor.

10 9 8 7 6 5 4 3

Library of Congress Cataloging-in-Publication data is available.

Contents

Foreword: On Marx's Contemporary Relevance

As these pages are being written, we are witnessing a deep crisis of the Western capitalist civilisation – overlapping environmental, energy-, and economic crises, social exclusion, and famines. The roots of these as well as other evils should be sought in an economic system whose basic aim is production for profit, and that therefore requires human and environmental exploitation, rather than the production for the satisfaction of everybody's needs in harmony with each other and thus with nature. The thinker, whose work offers the sharpest tools for an analysis of the root causes of these and other social ills, is undoubtedly Marx. Much has been written since *Capital* was first published, and more recently after the demise of the Soviet Union and the consequent triumph of neoliberalism, about the irrelevance, inconsistency, and obsoleteness of Marx. This book goes against the current. It argues that Max's work offers a solid and still relevant foundation upon which to further develop a multi-faceted theory highly significant to understand the contemporary world, both its present condition and its possible future scenarii.

More specifically, this book is about the present crisis. But it is also and perhaps mainly about what lies behind the crisis. In this, it differs from other works on this topic, whose focus is essentially the economic causes and consequences of crises. The basic thesis is that, to understand the crisis-ridden nature of this system, one needs to develop Marx's own method of enquiry, that is, to rescue it from the innumerable attempts to see Marx through an Hegelian lens. This is the task of Chapter 1, which provides a specifically Marxist interpretative template, a distinctive dialectical method of social research extracted from Marx's own work rather than from Hegel's. The starting point is the conceptualisation, through the application of a clear and workable notion of dialectics as a method of social research, of social phenomena as the unity-in-determination of social relations and social processes. This method rests on three fundamental principles: that social phenomena are always both potential and realised, both determinant and determined, and subject to constant movement and change. On this basis, the capitalist economy is seen as being powered by two opposite rationalities: one is the expression of capitalism's tendency towards its own supersession and the other is the expression of the counter-tendency towards reproduction, even if through crises as potential moments of supersession. In other words, the dialectical method reveals the dynamics of capitalism, namely, why and how it attempts to supersede itself while reproducing itself. From this perspective, the economy and thus society do not and cannot tend towards equilibrium. The notion that the economy is in a state of equilibrium, or is tending towards it, which is the mainstay of neoclassical economics and of almost all other economic theories, are, it will be argued, highly ideological and scientifically worthless. The thesis that capitalism tends not towards equilibrium and its own reproduction but towards its own supersession requires the introduction of a novel distinction, that between concrete and abstract individuals and thus between individual and social phenomena. Central to society's contradictory movement and tendency towards its own supersession is the dialectical interplay of individual and social phenomena and thus of subjectivity and objectivity. This subjectivity is informed by the internalisation by each individual of a double and contradictory rationality in its endless forms of manifestation: capital's need for human exploitation and labour's need for human liberation.

It follows that subjectivity and more generally knowledge, both individual and social, are contradictory because class-determined. Of great significance is the question as to whether this principle holds only for the social sciences or whether it can be valid for the natural sciences and techniques as well. To anticipate, Chapter 4 examines both similarities and differences between the dialectics of society in Marx on the one hand and Engels's dialectics of nature on the other hand. While there are many common features, one basic difference stands out: for Marx, all knowledge is class-determined and thus has a class-content. This includes also the natural sciences and techniques. Not so for Engels, even though it would be difficult to find in Engels a clear statement to this effect. Therefore, the difference between the two great thinkers revolves around the class-determination, as opposed to class-neutrality, of the natural sciences and techniques and thus of the forces of production. The importance of the implications of this issue for a theory of social change cannot be overestimated. Finally, social analysis on the basis of the above-mentioned three principles of dialectics cannot avoid the question of the use of a dialectical logic as opposed to formal logic. Section 6 in the first chapter considers the basic features of formal logic and its relation to dialectical logic. On this basis, it distinguishes between formal-logical contradictions (mistakes) and dialectical contradictions, those which arise from the contradiction between the realised and the potential aspects of reality. The conclusion is reached that the rules of formal logic (rather than formal logic itself, whose class-content is inimical to labour) apply to the realm of the realised (which without the potentials is a static reality) and that only dialectical logic (which incorporates the rules of formal logic but not formal logic itself) can explain movement and change. Substantiation for this approach comes from Appendix 3, a re-examination of Marx's mathematical manuscripts. Contrary to all commentators of the manuscripts, the thesis of this appendix is that the manuscripts' real importance resides in providing key insights into, and support for, the notion of dialectics submitted here as being an explicit rendition of Marx's own implicit notion.

Each work bears the imprint of the scientific debates within which it is formed. At present, Marx's work is deemed to be, even by many Marxist authors, logically inconsistent and thus useless as a guide for social action, unless corrected and modified. The charge goes far beyond the dusty walls of academia. It challenges no less than Marxism's claim to be labour's theoretical compass in its struggle against capital. Chapter 2 examines, on the basis of the method developed in Chapter 1, whether the charges of inconsistency hold water. Specifically, Chapter 2 focuses on and introduces the reader to the debates about whether labour is the only source of value, whether abstract labour is material, whether the average profit-rate tends to fall, and whether the transformation of values into prices is logically (in)consistent. These are the four major charges purportedly showing that Marx's theory is in need of a major overhaul. This chapter's basic argument is that the debates have been misled by an exclusive focus on the quantitative and formal-logical aspects, thus disregarding those basic traits of Marx's method, including the temporal dimension, that reveal the internal consistency of his work. From this perspective, labour is indeed the only source of value, abstract labour is indeed material, the average rate of profit does indeed tend to fall (through the zigzags of the economic cycle), and Marx's procedure to transform values into prices is indeed perfectly logically consistent. In the end, the issue of consistency in its four aspects should be seen as part and parcel of a wider theory of radical social change and discussed within this perspective. Finally, the double and contradictory rationality inherent in the capitalist system and internalised by the individuals and social agents is contrasted with the rationality of *homo economicus*, which is the basis of neoclassical theory and neoliberal policies. The latter is shown to be ideological rather than scientific, a rationalisation of the status quo.

The debates sketched in Chapter 2 touch upon only a few elements of, and are propaedeutic to, a theory of crises. Chapter 3 deals with what it argues to be Marx's crisis-theory in greater detail by examining the crisis that exploded in 2007 and that, at the time of writing, is far from having found its resolution. It evaluates the most influential theories of crises and sets them against Marx's theory of the falling average profit-rate. It discards the former theories and substantiates the latter on both theoretical and empirical grounds. It stresses that the financial and speculative bubbles did not cause the crisis in the real economy but rather were an expression of the tendential fall in the average profit-rate in the productive spheres. It then focuses on the specific features of the present financial crisis and examines the possibilities for Keynesian policies to jump-start the economy again. The conclusion is reached that Keynesian policies are as impotent as neoliberal policies and that, short of a radical change in the economy's social structure, the crisis will peter out only after sufficient capital will have been destroyed, only to re-emerge again later on, more virulently and destructively.

A work on the crisis that focuses only on its objective causes and operations, without considering how this contradictory objectivity emerges at the level of individuals and social consciousness, is only half the story. The other half requires the development of a theory of knowledge consistent with Marx's wider theoretical opus, suitable to be developed to account for those aspects left unexplored by Marx, in tune with contemporary reality, and appropriate to foster radical social change. Chapter 4 relates the objective working of the economy to the subjectivity of the social agents, that is, to the subjective manifestations of the contradictory objective foundations of the economy. Within this framework, two areas of a Marxist theory of knowledge are explored. The first one concerns the relation between the crisis-ridden nature of the capitalist economy, on the one hand, and the subjective and necessary manifestations of these objective developments at the level of social consciousness. This requires the development of a theory of individual and social knowledge and especially of how classes express their own view of reality through the mental products of concrete individuals. In the process of providing answers to these questions, other debated issues are explored, as for example, whether and when the production of knowledge is production of value and surplus-value. This is of great importance because of the twin widespread mistaken notions that in contemporary capitalism the economy rests more on the production of knowledge than on objective production (mistakenly called material production) and that the production of knowledge (mistakenly considered to be immaterial) is not production of value and surplus-value.

This chapter's second area of research deals with the question as to whether the knowledge produced under capitalist relations is suitable to be applied to a period of transition towards a socialist society. This discussion is highly relevant for a theory of transition. The conclusion is that a radically different type of society will both require and produce a qualitatively different type of knowledge, including the natural sciences and techniques. This is the thesis of the class-determination of knowledge which is contrary to what is held by the great majority of the commentators, according to whom knowledge (and especially the natural sciences and techniques) is not class-determined and has no class-content. But, if knowledge is not class-determined, then the working class does not produce its own view of reality and thus of the crisis-ridden nature of this system. This, in turn, deprives the working class of the theoretical guidance in its struggle against capitalism. The thesis of the class-neutrality of knowledge has thus devastating effects on the struggle for a radically alternative form of society.

Drawing on the modern philosophy of science, epistemology, economics and sociology, this work retraces Marx's original multi-disciplinary project and aims at developing it into a modern instrument capable of understanding and challenging contemporary capitalism.

I would like to thank Elliott Eisenberg and Peter Thomas for the patience and thoroughness with which they read the manuscript. They helped me to avoid some mistakes, but, due to my stubbornness, could not rectify all of them.

Chapter One
Method

1. **The need for dialectics**

As is well-known, Marx did not explicitly write a
work on dialectics. Nevertheless, in a letter to Engels,
he wrote 'I should very much like to write 2 or 3
sheets making accessible to the common reader the
rational aspect of the method which Hegel not only
discovered but also mystified'.[1] There are different
ways to carry out Marx's suggestion. Traditionally,
commentators have tried to force Marx into conformity with Hegel.[2] Marx was certainly influenced by
Hegel. The point here is not the perennial question
of the relationship between the two thinkers. Rather,
the Hegelian tradition seems to be the very opposite of what Marx had in mind, as indicated by his
well-known remark that 'My dialectical method is
not only different from the Hegelian, but is its direct
opposite'.[3] Hegelian Marxism seeks its way to dialectics not in Marx but in Hegel, where all the major features of Marx's theory (the determination in the last
instance of the ownership relation, class and class-
struggle, temporality, etc.) are missing. It does not

---

[1] Marx 1983b, p. 248.
[2] One of the last attempts is Arthur 2004b. For a critique, see Chapter 2 of this
work.
[3] Marx 1967a, p. 19.

pay any attention to Marx's own remark that 'Here and there, in the chapter on the theory of value, [I] coquetted with the mode of expression peculiar to him [Hegel]'.[4] This work takes that remark seriously and thus departs from that tradition. Emphasis will be placed here on the clarification of the originality of Marx's contribution. This work will also not follow the tradition established by Engels, who grounded dialectics in the law of development immanent in nature.[5] Rather, it will submit a notion of dialectics as a method of social research focused exclusively on social reality.[6]

What follows does not claim that the approach to be submitted below is applicable to all modes of production. It is sufficient to claim that it can be applied to the capitalist mode of production. Nor will it provide ready-made formulae for social analysis. Rather, it will offer some principles of social research whose validity must be constantly verified in terms of their fruitfulness for the analysis of the incessant mutations in social reality and for their application to fresh fields of research. But these results, in their turn, will have to be tested in terms both of logical consistency and of their consistency with the class-content of Marx's theory. Finally, no attempt will be made to show that this notion of dialectics is what Marx's had in mind, even though evidence will be submitted that the present approach is supported by Marx's quotations.[7] However, the question is not fidelity to quotations but consistency (in its two-fold sense) and explanatory power. It is in *this* sense that the notion of dialectics to be submitted below can be argued to be Marx's own. Earlier versions of the method to be described below have proven their fruitfulness in dealing with the transformation of values into prices,[8] with the law of the tendential fall of the profit-rate,[9] with a theory of knowledge,[10] with a class-analysis of the European Union[11] and with a theory of social classes.[12] This chapter sets out that method in more detail thus providing a broader conception of dialectical logic as a method of social research.

---

[4] Marx 1967a, p. 20.
[5] See Section 5 below.
[6] For a similar view, see Paolucci 2006b, p. 119.
[7] For such an attempt see Paolucci 2006a, p. 76.
[8] Carchedi 1984; Freeman and Carchedi 1996.
[9] Carchedi forthcoming.
[10] Carchedi 2005a.
[11] Carchedi 2001.
[12] Carchedi 1977; 1983; 1987; 1991.

2. Dialectical logic and social phenomena

The starting point, as it occurs in Marx, is empirical observation. Empirical observation is, of course, filtered through a previous interpretative (theoretical) framework. Nobody, except perhaps a new-born baby, is a *tabula rasa*. This apparent chicken-and-egg dilemma (what comes first, empirical observation or the interpretative filter?) will be dealt with and resolved in Section 6 of this chapter. Here, it only suffices to mention that, no matter what the interpretative framework, society appears to our senses as a kaleidoscope of continuously changing relations and processes. Let us define them.

Relations are interactions among people. Every time a relation arises, or changes into a different type, or ends, there is a change in the social fabric (whether perceptible or not). For example, if two people engage in a relation of friendship, the rise of such a relation changes (even though minimally) social reality. The same holds in the case when an enterprise is started (or goes bankrupt), a family is formed (or breaks up), a political party is founded (or is dissolved), etc. *Processes* are transformations people carry out in the context of those relations (for example, two friends might go fishing together). Let us call *phenomena* the *unity-in-contradiction of relations and processes*.[13] Phenomena are the basic unit of social reality and as such the starting point of the enquiry. The analogy with Marx's method in *Capital* should be clear. Marx starts the enquiry into economic life with a class-determined analysis of commodities conceived as the unity in contradiction of use-value and exchange-value. The present work starts the enquiry into social life with a class-determined analysis of phenomena as the unity-in-contradiction of relations and processes. Phenomena can be either social or individual. This section deals with social phenomena. The next section will introduce the notion of individual phenomena and clarify their difference and interplay with social phenomena. For the purposes of this section, an intuitive notion of social phenomena is sufficient: they are relations and processes in which people are considered as members of social groups rather than in their individuality. Social phenomena are enquired into on the basis of three fundamental principles. No *a priori* justification of these principles can be provided. Only the validity of the theory based upon them,

---

[13] Subsection 2.2 and Section 3 below will clarify why this unity is a contradictory one.

a judgement that can be given only after the whole theory has been set out, can verify their selection.

2.1. *First principle: social phenomena are always both realised and potential*

As mentioned above, the starting point is empirical observation. The notion of potential existence is intuitively evident. Observation tells us that everything is what it is and at the same time can be something different. This applies to ourselves since, at any given moment, we are what we are (have become) and at the same time are potentially different, due to the potentialities inherent in ourselves; it applies to an institution, like the state that is both the actualised state and a potentially different state, since it can evolve, due to its contradictory social nature, in many different directions and take many different shapes; it applies also to knowledge, which – as we shall see in Chapter 4 – is subjected to a constant process of change (realisation of its potentiality), etc. Thus, reality has a double dimension, what has become realised and what is only potentially existent and might become realised at a future date. In Marx, the existence of, and the relation between, the realised and the potential is fundamental, even if usually disregarded by Marxist commentators. A few examples are: gold as a measure of value, being a product of labour, is potentially variable in value;[14] money is potentially capital;[15] the labourer is only potentially so, she becomes actually a labourer only when she sells her labour-power;[16] 'by working, the [worker – G.C.] becomes actually what before he only was potentially, labour-power in action';[17] unemployment increases with capital's potential capacity to develop itself;[18] the bodily form of the inputs contain potentially the result of the production-process;[19] in a state of separation from each other, labourers and means of production are only potentially factors of production;[20] a commodity is only potentially such as long as it is not offered for sale;[21] the part of capital that is not turned

---

[14] Marx 1967a, Chapter 3.
[15] Marx 1967a, Chapter 4; 1967c, Chapter 21.
[16] Marx 1967a. Chapter 7.
[17] Marx 1967a, p. 177.
[18] Marx 1967a, Chapter 25.
[19] Marx 1967b, Chapter 1.
[20] Ibid.
[21] Marx 1967b, Chapter 6.

over every year is only potentially capital;[22] money earmarked for the purchase of labour-power is a constant magnitude, potential variable capital; it becomes a variable magnitude only when labour-power is purchased with it;[23] commodities are only potentially money, they become such only upon sale;[24] surplus-value is potential capital;[25] hoarded money is only potentially money-capital;[26] labour-power, as long as it is not employed in the production-process, is only potentially able to create surplus-value;[27] a commodity is only potentially money-capital;[28] the money spent in purchasing land is potential capital because it can be converted into capital.[29]

Particularly important for our purposes is the notion of value. Upon its completion, a commodity contains value, crystallised human labour in the abstract. This is its individual value, a realised substance. But this is not the value that the commodity realises upon its sale, its social value. 'The real value of a commodity, however, is not its individual, but its social value; that is to say, its value is not measured by the labour-time that the article costs the producer in each individual case, but by the labour-time socially required for its production.'[30] As I argue in Chapter 2, tendentially, a commodity realises the socially-necessary labour-time. If it has cost more labour, the producers lose value. They gain extra value in the opposite case.

Thus, the commodity can realise more or less than its value contained or even nothing at all, if it is not sold. The *individual* value is then a *potential social* value. The same holds for the use-value of the commodity. It is present in the commodity right after production as the specific features that configure its future use. But it is a *potential* use-value, an object whose use must be socially validated through sale (if it is considered useless, it will not be sold) and consumption.[31] Another example of a potential phenomenon is that of tendencies, for example that type of tendency which realises itself cyclically (the fall in the average rate of profit): the rise (counter-tendency) is potentially

---

[22] Marx 1967b, Chapter 13.
[23] Marx 1967b, Chapter 20.
[24] Ibid.
[25] Marx 1967b, Chapter 21.
[26] Marx 1967c, Chapter 19.
[27] Marx 1967c, Chapter 23.
[28] Marx 1967c, Chapter 30.
[29] Marx 1967c, Chapter 47.
[30] Marx 1976a, p. 434.
[31] Marx 1967c, p. 279.

present in the fall (the tendency) when the latter becomes realised and the fall (the tendency) is potentially present in the rise (the counter-tendency) when the latter becomes realised.[32] In short, the 'properties of a thing do not arise from its relation to other things, they are, on the contrary, merely activated by such relations'.[33] But what is activated can only be what is potentially present. Therefore, each realised phenomenon contains within itself a realm of potentialities.

Three points follow. First, since a phenomenon is potentially different from what it is as a realised phenomenon, a phenomenon is the *unity of identity and difference*. As a realised phenomenon, it is identical to itself but also different from itself, as a potential phenomenon. It is only by considering the realm of potentialities that the otherwise mysterious unity of identity and difference makes sense. Second, a phenomenon is also the *unity of opposites*, inasmuch as the potential features of a phenomenon are opposite (contradictory) to its realised aspects. Disregard of the potential leads to absurd conclusions. For example, Lefebvre asserts that life and death are 'identical' because the process of ageing starts when a living organism is born.[34] But life and death are opposites rather than identical. Life is a realised phenomenon and death is a potential within life itself that starts becoming realised the moment an organism is born. Contrary to Lefebvre,[35] the unity of contradictions is not identity. Third, a phenomenon is the *unity of essence and appearance* (in the form of the manifestation of the essence): its potential aspect is its own essence, that which can manifest itself in a number of different realisations, while its realised aspect is its (temporary and contingent) appearance, the form taken by one of the possibilities inherent in its potential nature.[36] Notice, however, that the essence is not immutable but subject to continuous change. Notice also the temporal dimension: at a certain moment, a realised phenomenon contains within itself a realm of potentialities and *subsequently* those potentialities manifest themselves as (a different) realised form. The realised phenomenon

---

[32] See next section and Chapter 2.
[33] Marx, quoted in Zelený 1980, p. 22.
[34] Lefebvre 1982, p. 164.
[35] Lefebvre 1982, p. 172.
[36] A phenomenon's realisation cannot be its essence because it excludes from that phenomenon's essence those potentialities that have not become realised.

is temporally prior to the realisation of the potential one. This first principle, then, contains within itself a *temporal dimension*.

The notions of realisations and potentials should now be clarified. Potentials are not, as in physics, elements of realised reality (particles) waiting to be discovered. Potentials are not, as in the Hegelian tradition, empty forms waiting to receive content the moment they realise themselves. This is particularly important for the debates discussed in Chapter 2. Potentials are not, as in formal logic and inasmuch as they play any role in formal logic, attributes of realised reality in a suspended state.[37] Potentials are not fantasies but actually-existing aspects of objective reality, even though not yet realised. Their number is neither 'infinite'[38] nor finite because it is impossible to quantify something that has not realised itself, something formless. Rather, potentials are *real* possibilities because they are contained in realised phenomena and, simultaneously, they are *formless* possibilities because they take a definite form only at the moment of their realisation. For example, the knowledge needed by an author to write an article exists in that author as a formless possibility. It takes a definite form only when that article is written or the author has clearly conceived that article in her head.

Three final considerations follow. First, realised phenomena contain potential phenomena within themselves, but not the other way around. A shapeless whole cannot, by definition, contain within itself a definite form, while a definite form can contain within itself a range of shapeless possibilities. Realisation is thus the transformation of what is potentially present into a realised form. It is the formation of something formless into something with a definite form. It is transformation. Second, potentials, being formless, can never be observed because observation implies realisation. However, some realised phenomena, for example social relations, are unobservable as well. Consequently, it would seem that observation is not the criterion to distinguish potentials from realisations. But the question revolves around *direct* observation. A realised phenomenon can be unobservable directly, but observable indirectly through

---

[37] Bradley and Swartz 1979, p. 5, submit that a man is a runner not because he actually runs but because he has the capacity, potentiality, to run. But this potentiality is simply an attribute, that man is already a realised runner, whether at any given moment he runs or not. The question is whether he can become a cook or a mountain-climber.

[38] Ibid.

other social phenomena. If social relations cannot be observed as such, directly, what people do when engaging in those relations (that is, when they carry out social processes) *can* be observed. In other words, social processes are the form of manifestation of social relations, of something which has already left the realm of potentialities and has already become realised (the actual inter-action among people). This is not the case for the potential aspects of social reality, including those social relations that have not manifested themselves yet. Or, to give another example which will be dealt with in detail in Chapter 2, abstract labour is only potentially value. It becomes value only under capitalist production-relations. Value cannot be observed, only labour can. Yet, value becomes realised as labour is expanded. Third, as Chapter 2 will argue, what is potential within a certain sphere of reality (at a certain level of abstraction) can be realised in another sphere (at another level of abstraction). Thus, we shall see that the individual value of a commodity as an output of a certain production-process is the labour actually expanded for its production. This realised entity (individual value) is a potential social value at a different level of abstraction, after this value is modified through the process of price-formation. This social value, once realised, is the potential money-value, the ultimate realisation of value as far as that process of value-production and distribution is concerned. This money-value becomes again an individual value if that commodity becomes an input of the next production-process.

2.2. Second principle: social phenomena are always both determinant and determined

Here, too, the starting point is empirical observation. We can observe that all elements of social reality are interconnected (people can live and repro-duce themselves only through reciprocal interaction) into a whole (groups, families and thus finally society), that this whole changes continuously (even though some changes might be minimal or even unobservable), that this change can be continuous or discontinuous, and that the whole's intercon-nected parts can be *contradictory, that is, the reproduction of some phenomena might imply the supersession of some other phenomena and vice versa.* The precise definition of supersession will be given later on in this chapter. For the time being, an intuitive notion such as abolition will be sufficient. This apparently chaotic movement is given a conceptual structure by the notion of dialectical determination.

To begin with, dialectical determination should be rooted in class-analysis. Our species has potentialities that set it apart from other living creatures, as, for example, the capacity to create our own means of production[39] or of creating and communicating through complex languages.[40] These potentialities are not unchangeable. Society moulds them; it not only gives them a historically-specific form but penetrates them and adapts them to itself. That society changes those potentialities is something that is becoming increasingly clear as shown by the possibility created by biotechnology to shape human life-forms in ways functional for profit-making. The speed of this development is terrifying. In 1997, the cloning of the sheep Dolly at the Roslin Institute opened the way to the cloning of human beings.[41] In 2000 the English Parliament approved the creation of, and experimentation on, human embryos for profit-purposes.[42] Finally, in the same year, patent EP 380646 was given by the EU Patent Office to the Australian enterprise Amstrad for the creation of so-called 'Mischwesens', that is, beings made up of human and animal cells, to be precise cells of mice, birds, sheep, pigs, goats, and fish.[43] This is the very opposite of notions, such as utility, that are supposed to be a-historical

> To know what is useful for a dog, one must investigate the nature of dogs. This nature is not itself deducible from the principle of utility. Applying this to man, he who would judge all human acts, movements, relations, etc. according to the principle of utility would first have to deal with human nature in general, and then with human nature as historically modified in each epoch. Bentham does not trouble himself with this.[44]

It is within these socially-given boundaries that humans try to develop those potentialities to the utmost. Under capitalism, these boundaries are ultimately demarcated by the *ownership-relation*. What is specific to this relation is that the producers have been expropriated of the means of production. The ownership-relation is considered to be here the *real ownership-relation* and not the juridical one, meaning that the real owners of the means of production are those who can decide *what to produce, for whom to produce, and how to produce.*

---

[39] Marx and Engels 1970a, p. 42.
[40] Geras 1983, p. 48.
[41] McKie 1997.
[42] *Corriere della Sera* 2000.
[43] Guidi 2000.
[44] Marx 1967a, p. 609.

'What to produce' means is that, under capitalism, it is commodities that have
to be produced, namely the unity of use-values and (exchange-) value. 'For
whom' means that surplus-value must be produced for the owners of the
means of production, that is, it means that the labourers must be exploited.
Finally, 'how to produce' means that the owners, through their scientists and
technicians (see Chapter 4), choose the process of production. The *production-
relations* consist of the different forms taken by the ownership-relation when
the owners decide, and the non-owners have to accept, what to produce, for
whom to produce it, and how to produce it.

Notice that the final and specific outcome of the decision as to what to produce, for whom and how, is the result not of an absolute power of the owners
over the non-owners of the means of production, but of the class-struggle
between these two fundamental classes.[45] In fact, under capitalism, the development of the capitalists' potentialities is shaped by their need to deal with the
labourers as the source of the maximum feasible quantity of unpaid labour.
On the other hand, the development of the labourers' potentialities is shaped
by their need to resist and abolish their alienation, not only from their own
products (which they must alienate to the owners of the means of production) but also from themselves (because they are not free to fully develop their
potentialities). Thus we have both a class's objective need to exploit another
class, together with the objective need the latter class has to resist and abolish
that exploitation; both the need to thwart human development and the need
to expand it to the maximum. The former class needs an egoistic and exploitative behaviour, the latter altruistic and solidaristic behaviour. For the former,
one's well-being must be based upon the others' misery, for the latter, one's
well-being must be both the condition for, and the result of, the others' well-
being. The satisfaction of the former need is functional for the reproduction
of the capitalist system; the satisfaction of the latter need is functional for the
supersession of that system.[46]

Given that the reproduction of the system implies exploitation, inequality
and egoism, the supersession of the system implies cooperation, solidarity and

---

[45] Of course, there are more than the two fundamental classes, there are also the
old and the new middle classes but the focus on these two classes is sufficient for the
present purposes. For an analysis of the economic identification of the two fundamental
classes as well as of the old and new middle class, see Carchedi, 1977.
[46] That individual labourers do not behave as mentioned above is no objection to
this thesis. See Chapter 4.

equality. *This double rationality is the contradictory social content of the capitalist ownership-relation and thus of the capitalist production-relations.* It is this content (its being based on exploitation, inequality and egoism *as well as* on the resistance against them, which implies solidarity, equality and cooperation) that the capitalist ownership-relation transfers to all other relations and processes in an endless variety of individual and social phenomena. *It is in this sense that the ownership-relation is ultimately determinant.* In some of these phenomena, the reproductive rationality is *dominant* and the supersessive rationality is *secondary* (in the sense that those phenomena contribute to the reproduction of the system due to their reproductive rationality, in spite of their supersessive rationality, thus reproducing society in a contradictory way) while, in other phenomena, the opposite is the case.

This should not be understood as if capitalist oppression were historically and socially specific while the need to resist it were an ahistorical need for self-development. The need for self-development, the development of human potentials as its own goal, is common to all humans in all societies. Under capitalism, the capitalists strive for their own self-development at the cost of the labourers, while the labourers strive to achieve their own self-development by resisting their oppression and exploitation. To a specific form of oppression there corresponds a specific form of resistance: both are the historically and socially specific ways to strive for self-development, an ahistorical need that must take a specific social form. The slaves' resistance against their oppression is specific to slave-society just as the workers' resistance against their oppression is specific, even if multifaceted, to capitalist society.

The choice of the production-relations and thus of the ownership-relation as the ultimately determinant phenomenon is not arbitrary. It is argued for by Marx as follows:

> In all forms of society there is one specific kind of production which predominates over the rest, whose relations thus assign rank and influence to the others. It is a general illumination which bathes all the other colours and modifies their particularity. It is a particular ether which determines the specific gravity of every being which has materialised within it.... Capital is the all-dominating economic power of bourgeois society.[47]

---

[47] Marx 1973a, p. 10.

Or, in more detail:

> The conclusion we reach is not that production, distribution, exchange and
> consumption are identical, but that they all form the members of a totality,
> distinctions within a unity. Production predominates not only over itself, in
> the antithetical definition of production [this is the contradictory nature of
> the capitalist ownership and thus production-relations – G.C.], but over the
> other moments as well. The process always returns to production to begin
> anew [after what has been produced in one period has been distributed,
> exchanged and consumed, a new production-process starts *in the following*
> *period* – G.C.]. That exchange and consumption cannot be predominant is self-
> evident.... A definite production thus determines a definite consumption,
> distribution and exchange as well as *definite relations between these different*
> *moments*. Admittedly, however, *in its one-sided form*, production is itself
> determined by the other moments. For example if the market, that is, the
> sphere of exchange, expands, then production grows in quantity and the
> divisions between its different branches become deeper [this, again, implies
> that exchange can influence the production of the following period – G.C.].
> Mutual interaction takes place between the different moments.[48]

Temporality is essential to understand the passage above. *Given a certain*
time-period, production is prior to distribution and consumption (only what
has been produced can be consumed). The former contains potentially the
latter within itself. Therefore, only the former can be determinant of the latter.
Distribution and consumption can temporally precede production, but this is
the production of the *following* period. If production is temporally prior to the
realisation of the distribution and consumption inherent in it, within a certain
period the former can only be determinant and the latter determined.

The adjective 'ultimately' implies that there are social phenomena that are
determinant even if not ultimately so. In fact, the other phenomena are far
from being simple copies, reflections, of the ownership-relation. Given that
each phenomenon is an element of society and is thus connected directly or
indirectly to all other phenomena, each phenomenon – due to the double
rationality it has received from the ownership-relation, either directly or indirectly, through other social phenomena – is the condition of existence and/or

---

[48] Marx 1973a, p. 100.

reproduction and/or supersession of all other phenomena and thus of society.[49] This is the *contradictory social content* of realised phenomena, their being conditions of existence, and/or reproduction, and/or supersession of society. Through their reciprocal interaction, phenomena modify reciprocally their contradictory social content. And, since their form is the form of appearance of their content, that form undergoes a change as well. This holds also for the ownership-, production-, relations whose form of appearance changes due to their interaction with the rest of society, even though their social content (their double rationality) does not change. Each phenomenon's social content is specific to it because it is the result both of its determination in the last instance by the ownership-relation and of its being both determinant of and determined by all other phenomena. It is in this sense that each social phenomenon is *relatively autonomous* from, because indirectly determined by, the ownership-relation.

It is only in this sense that it becomes possible to understand why society is *causa sui*, that is, how it can both determine itself and be determined by itself. It becomes also possible to define the *volume* of social life, as the quantity of social relations, and the *intensity* of social life, as the number of intersections of social relations. These remarks are sufficient to take distance from both a theory that negates the mutual interconnection of all (social and individual) phenomena and focuses only on the (ultimately) determining role of the ownership-, and thus production-, relations and from a theory focusing only on that mutual interconnection with no ultimately determinant role for the ownership-, and thus production-, relations. For example, in commenting on the above quotation in which Marx states that 'production predominates not only over itself ... but over the other moments as well', Resnick and Wolff hold that the specific sense of 'predominates' is that of 'serving as ... the entry-point and the goal point of [their – G.C.] strictly non-essentialist theoretical process'.[50] The authors see social phenomena as constituting themselves in the process of mutual determination but deny any determination in the last instance.[51] The problem with this approach is that they, following Althusser, by disregarding

---

[49] A phenomenon is a condition of existence *or* of reproduction *or* of supersession of *some* other phenomena only if a section of reality is considered. See the last paragraph of this sub-section.
[50] Resnick and Wolff 2006, p. 29.
[51] Resnick and Wolff 2006, p. 132.

the ultimately determining role of the ownership-relation, disregard the system's tendency towards its own supersession.[52] Notice that this complex process of determination is not the whole story, because no account has been taken yet of the role played by individual phenomena in the determination of social phenomena. A complete account will be possible only in Sections 3 and 4 below in this chapter.

Two objections can be levelled against this approach. First, it can be held that it is consumption-relations which are ultimately determinant of production-relations, because people realise their potentialities through consumption rather than through production.[53] But the point is not whether people realise their potentiality through production or through consumption (both production and consumption are needed to realise those potentialities). The point is that a phenomenon can transfer its social content to another only if the former pre-exists the latter (see above). *Given a certain time-period*, production is prior to distribution and consumption (only what has been produced can be consumed). Therefore, only the former can be determinant of (transfers its social content, its double rationality and thus its possibility to reproduce and/or supersede to) the latter. Distribution and consumption can precede temporally production but this is the production of the *following* period rather than of their own period.

Second, it is held that other exploitative relations, like racism or gender-relations, have the same contradictory social content as the capitalist ownership-relation. Thus it is they that could be determinant. My response is that the capitalist ownership-relation is the only constant feature of capitalism, while other exploitative relations are not and could disappear without imperilling capitalism's survival. It could be replied that other exploitative relations, for example racism, can be observed under different exploitative systems and that therefore it is racism which could be regarded as determining all these systems, including capitalism. But the point is that, if it is capitalism that we are analysing, the focus must be on what is constant and therefore specific to that system, thus determinant, that is, the capitalist ownership-relation. If it is racism that is being analysed, it must be analysed under different social systems. In the words of Nick Dyer-Witheford, 'sexism and racism do not in-

---

[52] For an assessment, see Carchedi 2008b, p. 13.
[53] Holton 1992, p. 174.

and-of themselves act as the main organising principle for the worldwide production and distribution of goods... key issues of sexuality, race and nature
[are compelled – G.C] to revolve around a hub of profit'.[54]

It is thus the capitalist ownership-relation that is determinant of both the
reproduction and the supersession of capitalism and thus of itself. *Reproduction* refers to capitalism undergoing changes while retaining its basic feature,
the real ownership-relation. *Supersession* refers to its changing radically the
social content of the ownership-relation, thus disappearing possibly to be
replaced by a radically different societal form.[55] It is the ownership-relation
that explains why capitalism can continue to reproduce itself while maintain-
ing its exploitative nature; why it can also self-destruct, as with the prospect
of nuclear wars, the destruction of our natural habitat, and so forth indicate;
why it can change into a different type of exploitative society; and why it can
develop into a society which is the very opposite of capitalism, one based
on cooperation, solidarity and equality as opposed to exploitation, inequality
and egoism.

We can now specify in what sense social phenomena are determinant and
determined. As determinant, phenomena call into realised existence the determined elements which are already present in the determinant phenomena as
their potential development. In this sense, the determinant phenomena are
the condition of existence of the determined ones. As determined, phenomena are the conditions of reproduction or supersession of the determinant
ones. Thus, a *relation of mutual determination, or a dialectical relation, is one in
which the determinant phenomenon calls into realised existence the determined one
from within its own potentialities through its interaction with other phenomena.* Or,
the determinant phenomenon calls into existence the determined one as its
own conditions of reproduction or supersession. The determined phenomenon, in its turn, becomes the realised condition of the determinant phenomenon's reproduction or supersession. For example, the ownership-relation
calls into realised existence one of its potentialities, the accumulation of capital, and the latter becomes the realised condition of capitalism's (extended)
reproduction.

---

[54] Dyer-Witheford 1999, p. 15.
[55] This refers to society as a whole. As we shall see below, for social phenomena,
supersession means either a radical change in their social content or their becoming
individual phenomena, their disappearing from the realised social context.

The question then is: how can the determined phenomenon be the condition of reproduction or supersession of the determinant one? Given that the determined phenomenon is potentially present in the determinant one, and given that the determinant (realised) phenomenon has a specific contradictory social content which it received ultimately from the ownership-relation, if the determinant phenomenon calls into existence the determined one it thereby *transfers* to it its own contradictory social content, which is modified by the contradictory social content of the phenomena with which it interacts. Due to its contradictory nature, the determined phenomenon's social content *reacts upon* and possibly changes the determinant phenomenon's social content so that the determined phenomenon becomes the realised condition of reproduction, or of supersession, of the determinant phenomenon. This can be stated in more traditional terms, as the 'negation of the negation'. A contains B and determines the realisation of B as its own condition of supersession. A negates itself in B, the realised negation of A. Then, B reacts upon and changes A thus negating itself in A. However, the outcome is *a new A* rather than the reproduction of an unchanged A.

We now have all the elements with which to consider mutual, dialectical determination in more detail. Given two phenomena, A and B, A is said to be determinant of B in the sense that A is the condition of the realised existence of B and transfers its contradictory social content to B. In its turn, B is said to be determined by A because it owes its realised existence to A. But B, in its turn, determines A because, having received its contradictory social content from A, it becomes the condition of reproduction or supersession of A. Thus, the sense in which A determines B is different from that in which B determines A. This mutual determination between the determinant and the determined instances takes place within a temporal setting. In fact, first A determines B and then B determines A. Reality is a temporal process of determinations in which some phenomena, the determinant ones, become actualised prior to other phenomena, the determined ones. Only previously existing phenomena can determine the actualisation of other phenomena, because the latter are initially only potentially present in the former. Notice that the stress on the time-dimension does not imply that all phenomena realise themselves in a temporal succession. Some might become realised together with some others (see Sections 3 and 4 below). However, this does not imply that reality should be conceptualised as if time did not exist, as if everything happened simultaneously. The contraposition between a temporal view of reality and a simultaneous view of reality will play a fundamental role in the next chapter. A concise and formal representation of this process can be found in Appendix 1.

Dialectical determination is usually confused with that of mutual interaction. But determination is a very specific form of interaction, it is an interaction with a very specific internal structure, that between determinant and determined phenomena.[56] Also, dialectical determination is usually confused with the relation of cause and effect, as in formal logic. The relation between formal and dialectical logic will be dealt with in Section 6 of this chapter. Here, it suffices to mention that, in formal logic, A and B are *either* the cause *or* effect of each other. In dialectical logic, conceived within the context of the whole, they are *both* determinant *and* determined. However, social analysis can consider only one sector of reality, no matter how large. In this case, it is possible for phenomena to be either determinant or determined, according to the section of reality and thus to the *level of abstraction* considered. For example, at a certain level of abstraction, if only distribution and consumption are considered, distribution determines consumption. But, at another level of abstraction, if also production is considered, distribution is itself determined by production. And, if a certain period is considered, production is itself determined by the distribution and consumption of the previous period. Distribution, being determined by production, is a condition for the continuation of the same type of production (possibly in a different form) or for its radical change in the following period. But, even if we consider a certain level of abstraction at which A is only determinant and B only determined, both A and B are *both* 'cause' and 'effect' of each other. A 'causes' B by being B's condition of existence and is the 'effect' of B, because B is the condition of A's reproduction or supersession. Vice versa for B which is the 'cause' of A, by being A's condition of reproduction or supersession, and the 'effect' of A, because A is the condition of B's existence. For formal logic, at most, A can be the cause of B within a certain context and B can be the cause of A within a different context. But, once the context has been delimited, A can be only cause and B only effect.

---

[56] According to Ollman, 'in any organic system viewed over time, each process can be said to determine and be determined by all others. However, it is also the case that one part often has a greater effect on others than they do on it' (Ollman 1993, p. 36). The problem here is that the reader is kept in the dark about what exactly 'greater' means.

To the contrary, for dialectical logic, A and B are always both the 'cause' and 'effect' of each other.

2.3. *Third principle: social phenomena are subject to constant movement and change*

This principle follows from the empirical observation that reality is in constant movement. This movement can now be interpreted according to the two principles submitted above. A realised phenomenon can change only because this is potentially possible, because its potential nature changes through its interaction with other realised phenomena and thus with their potential nature, because of its potential nature and of the potential nature of the other realised phenomena it determines and by which it is determined. Without this potential reality, realised phenomena would be static, they would be what they are, but not also what they could be. Their potential nature makes possible not only their change but also delimits the quantitative and qualitative boundaries of that change. Phenomena are always both what they are (as realised phenomena) and potentially something else, in the process of becoming something else. Thus, *movement* is the change undergone by phenomena from being realised to being potential and vice versa and from being determinant to being determined and vice versa.

Movement has five specific features. First, it is *temporal*, that is, it is a temporal succession of potential phenomena becoming realised and then going back to a potential state and of determinant phenomena becoming determined and then going back to a determinant state. Second, it is *contradictory*, because phenomena, due to their inner contradictory social content, reproduce or supersede themselves and become realised or potential in a contradictory fashion. Third, movement is not chaotic, but has its own specific features, namely it takes place within the confines posed by specific social and historical *laws of movement*. Marx refers to these laws as those that are 'the same under all modes of production'[57] and thus as those that 'cannot be abolished'.[58] This is an ahistorical definition, no doubt correct, but of little help for an understanding of capitalism's laws of movement. It is precisely their historical and

---

[57] Marx 1967c, p. 790.
[58] Marx 1969a, p. 419.

social specificity as social forms of ahistorical elements common to all modes of production that makes these phenomena essential elements for the social system's reproduction, so that their supersession is a necessary condition for the supersession of the system.[59] It is in this sense that these specific social forms of natural laws acquire the force of social laws, of laws of movement of socio-economic systems. For example, the wealth produced in any society must be distributed for that society to reproduce itself. Under capitalism, wealth is produced as (surplus-) value in the form of money. The distribution of wealth is thus the distribution of labour's product between labour and capital, as wages and profits. Due to their importance, the laws of movement set the framework within which other (non-essential) phenomena are subject to change. Other phenomena are non-essential, in the sense that their own reproduction or supersession, while contributing to the reproduction or supersession of the whole, is not *essential* for the reproduction or supersession of the system.

Fourth, the laws of movement are *tendential*, the whole moves and changes in a tendential manner. We have seen that a determinant phenomenon (A) determines a determined phenomenon (B). But A can and does determine not only one but several phenomena (B and C). Given A's contradictory nature, some phenomena (B) are conditions of reproduction of A (because this is their dominant rather than their secondary feature) and some other (C) are conditions of supersession of A (because this is their dominant feature). Then, at any given moment, if B is dominant, A reproduces itself in spite of C, which is the supersessive force, that is, *it reproduces itself in a contradictory way*. If C is dominant, A supersedes itself in spite of B, the reproductive force. *It supersedes itself in a contradictory way*. However, the contradictory reproduction of A, through the dominant force of B over C, is only temporary because C, the supersessive force, eventually gains the upper hand. The same is true for A's supersession. Thus, A's contradictory movement towards reproduction or supersession is the result of contradictory forces that make A's movement oscillate between its contradictory reproduction and its contradictory supersession. In short, and this is the fifth feature, A's movement is *cyclical*

---

[59] This is consonant with Antonova's view that Marx denied the possibility to ground social phenomena in natural phenomena (Antonova 2006, p. 172). See Section 5 of this Chapter.

and the cyclical movement is made up of a contradictory reproductive phase (movement) and of a contradictory supersessive phase (movement). The alternative position that there are no objective laws of motion will be criticised and rejected in Chapter 2.

At this juncture, the question becomes: why is a certain movement the tendency and another movement, to the contrary, the counter-tendency? Anticipating a result to be reached later on, for Marx, the capitalist system tends not towards equilibrium but towards its supersession. Then, in its laws of movement, *the tendency must be the determined phenomenon that hinders the reproduction of the determinant phenomenon.* The counter-tendency is then the determined phenomenon that favours the reproduction of the determinant phenomenon. Let us apply this principle to the three types of cyclical movements that can be discerned from a close reading of Marx's work.

Consider labour-mobility. At this level of abstraction, it is the determinant factor. It determines both an average wage-rate (because labourers move to where – geographical areas, institutions like trade-unions, etc. – they are guaranteed the same rights and thus the same wage-rates) and wage-rates different from the average, because labourers move from (lower-than-) average wage-rates to higher ones and, unwillingly, also in the opposite direction. The movement towards the average wage-rate hinders the reproduction of labour-mobility, while the movement towards wage-differentials favours the reproduction of labour-mobility. Thus, the former is the tendency and the latter the counter-tendency. This is an example of a cyclical movement of *the first type*, because empirical observation shows the realisation of *both* the tendency *and* the counter-tendency *at the same time.*

Consider technological competition among capitals. This is the determinant factor which determines both a decrease and an increase of the average rate of profit. On the one hand, technological innovations replace people with

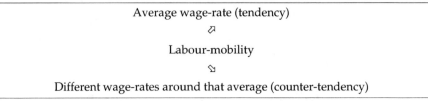

Figure 1. Cyclical movement of the first type

Decrease in the average profit-rate (tendency)

↗

Technological innovations

↘

Increase in the average profit-rate (counter-tendency)

Figure 2. Cyclical movement of the second type

machines, thus decreasing the (surplus-) value produced per unit of capital invested. On the other, they increase the surplus-value produced (for example, if technological innovations reduce the value of the means of production, thus reducing costs and decreasing the organic composition of capital).[60] The fall in the average rate of profit is the tendency because it hinders the reproduction of technological innovations. In fact, the smaller the total surplus-value produced, the smaller the total surplus-value available for society as a whole for new investments (technological innovations). An increase in the average rate of profit is the counter-tendency. This is an example of a cyclical movement *of the second type* because empirical observation shows the realisation of *either* the tendency *or* the counter-tendency, because it shows the alternation of the tendency and of the counter-tendency.

Consider capital-mobility across branches. By constantly trying to overtake each other in terms of profitability, individual capitals scatter around an average profitability-level. No average rate of profit is empirically observable under conditions of capital-mobility because, the moment a capital moves to a different sector, its capital invested and profit-rate change too, thus changing the average. The average rate of profit can be computed only if we assume that the movement of capital stops, but not under the conditions of its own movement. Nevertheless, the average rate of profit is a realised

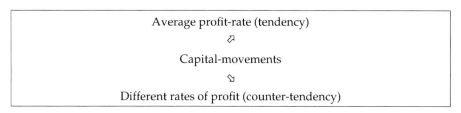

Average profit-rate (tendency)

↗

Capital-movements

↘

Different rates of profit (counter-tendency)

Figure 3. Cyclical movement of the third type

[60] Carchedi 1991, Chapter 5.

social phenomenon, even if not observable in its movement, because, follow-ing the criterion submitted above, it is indirectly observable through the real (realised) movements of capital. The average rate of profit is the tendency because it hinders the reproduction of the determinant phenomenon (capital-mobility), and the counter-tendencies are the different profit-rates because they favour that capital-movement. This is an example of a tendency *of the third type* because empirical observation shows the realisation of *only* the *counter-tendency*. In the case of capital-immobility (e.g. due to obstacles to capital-movement), the average rate of profit becomes a static quantity set-ting the limits to static profit-rates. The scatter is frozen. Without movement, there is neither a tendency nor a counter-tendency. Yet there is an average rate of profit. Capital-mobility is necessary to explain the movement of the average rate of profit, but is not necessary to explain its static existence. The average rate of profit exists independently of capital-movement. But, of course, in the real world, capital is mobile even though there are obstacles to capital-mobility of various kinds.

3. The dialectics of individual and social phenomena

As Engels once said: 'History does nothing…history is nothing but the activ-ity of man pursuing his aims.'[61] Paraphrasing Engels, we can say that social phenomena do nothing, they are nothing but the activity of people pursuing their aims. However, there is a difficulty here: the categories 'people' or 'man' are too generic. Social phenomena are relations and processes among people considered as members of social groups rather than in their individuality. But, in order to act, people require will and consciousness which are attri-butes of individuals, not as undifferentiated members of social groups but of individuals thinking and acting as specific and unique individuals. How can the undifferentiated dimensions of human agents as social agents be rec-onciled with their individual specificity? Put differently: if social phenomena are relations and processes among real people, and if social phenomena can exist also potentially, how can real, and thus, by definition, realised, people engage in potential (formless) relations and processes?

---

[61] Marx and Engels 1975a, p. 92; emphasis in the original.

The answer hinges upon a new distinction, between *concrete and abstract individuals*. This distinction is implicit in Marx: 'here individuals are dealt with only insofar as they are the personifications of economic categories, embodiments of particular class relations and class interest...the individual [cannot be made – G.C.] responsible for relations whose creature he socially remains, however much he may subjectively raise himself above them.'[62] This distinction is similar to the one Marx makes between concrete and abstract labour and plays the same fundamental role here as Marx's distinction does in his value-theory.

Individuals can be considered in their uniqueness, as unique individuals. As such, they are referred to as *concrete* individuals. But they can also be considered as possessing some common features (for example, they are all Catholic), irrespective of the specific, individual, forms taken by those common features (for example, somebody's specific way of being a Catholic). It is because of these common features that individuals are considered to be members of a certain group. From this angle, they are considered not in their individuality and specificity but as members of a group who share certain characteristics. As members of social groups, individuals are *abstract* individuals, since abstraction is made of their specific features, of their concrete forms of existence. The basic difference between abstract and concrete individuals is that the former are replaceable (on account of their common features), while concrete individuals, being unique, are not. This is in line with Marx's notion of commodities as replaceable due to their common social substance, abstract labour: 'As *values*, the commodities are expressions of the *same unity*, of abstract human labour.... Their *social relationship* consists exclusively in counting with respect to one another as expressions of this social substance of theirs which differs only quantitatively, but which is qualitatively equal and hence replaceable and interchangeable with one another.'[63] *In reality*, individuals are *always both* concrete *and* abstract. I am a teacher in the abstract because I belong to the group of teachers and, at the same time, I am a teacher with features that are only my own. However, *analytically*, individuals are *either* concrete *or* abstract. If we consider their unique features, we disregard their common features, and vice versa. While concrete features differentiate, general features unify.

---

[62] Marx 1967a, p. 10.
[63] Marx 1967c, pp. 28–9; emphasis in the original.

As concrete individuals, people engage in individual relations and processes, that is, in *individual phenomena*. Individual phenomena depend for their inception, continuation, transformation or termination only on the uniqueness of those individuals and on their capacity and will to engage (either freely or not) in that relation. This should not be interpreted as if other 'external' factors did not play a role – they do, but only inasmuch as they change the specific and unique features of those individuals and thus of their individual relation. On the other hand, as abstract individuals, people engage in social relations and processes, that is, in *social phenomena*. Social phenomena are relations and processes among abstract individuals, that is, individuals seen from the point of view of some common features and, as such, replaceable in those phenomena. Thus, concrete individuals determine individual phenomena because the former, due to their specificity, contain within themselves the latter as a potentiality, thus being the latter's condition of existence. In their turn, individual phenomena are the conditions of reproduction or supersession of concrete individuals, because concrete individuals can reproduce themselves only thanks to those relations and processes. Similarly for abstract individuals and social phenomena.

In individual phenomena, concrete individuals, being unique, are not replaceable. For example, two friends engage in an individual relation because they are unique, and thus irreplaceable. If a friend were replaced by another one, a relation would be replaced by another one, rather than a specific and unique individual being replaced by another one within the same relation. One can speak of friendship in general, but this is a merely verbal category that disregards the specific, irreplaceable, characteristics of each relation of friendship. It does not indicate a social relation in which friends are replaceable. In social phenomena, on the other hand, individuals are replaceable. Therefore, social phenomena can *continue* to exist and reproduce themselves *irrespective* of the concrete individuals who, as abstract individuals, carry those specific social relations and engage in those processes.

The categories of concrete and abstract individuals (individual and social phenomena) are not simply categories of thought, they pertain to the same social reality. These categories find their objective basis in the fact that there are really two dimensions in social reality: that of the concrete individuals (individual phenomena) and that of the abstract individuals (social phenomena). There is no third dimension. There is no location of individuals outside these two dimensions. Individuals exist only in relation to each other, and these relations (and processes) constitute the social space. The social space is not something that exists even in the absence of social and individual phenomena. Relations and processes *do not fill* a social space, they *are* the social space. It follows that it is futile to ask whether relations and processes pre-exist individuals or the other way around. It is as futile as asking what existed before the Big Bang. Neither is the social space something static. It exists only because social phenomena exist in their mutual determination, it is an ever-changing entity. But there is mutual determination not only among social phenomena but also between social and individual phenomena. Let us see how.

Similarly to social phenomena, individual phenomena are both potential and realised. Realised individual phenomena can become realised social phenomena if those individuals engaging in them become substitutable. This would be the case of two friends setting up an enterprise in which they, as economic agents, become substitutable. This implies that the realised social phenomenon (the enterprise) was already potentially present in the realised individual phenomenon (the relation of friendship) as one of its potentialities. Vice versa, social phenomena can go back to a potential state if those agents become irreplaceable. It follows that *individual phenomena are potentially present in the individuals engaging in those relations and processes and that those potential individual phenomena, upon their realisation, as realised individual phenomena, become potential social phenomena* (just as, for Marx, individual values are potential social values). It follows that *concrete individuals are potentially abstract individuals.* It is now possible to answer the question posed at the beginning of this section, namely: if social phenomena are relations and processes among real people and if social phenomena can exist also potentially, how can real, and thus, by definition, realised people engage in potential (formless) relations and processes? The answer is that real people can engage in potential social phenomena because they, as *concrete individuals, engage in realised individual phenomena which are formless potential social phenomena* (a relation of friendship can originate an array of social relations and processes), that is, because concrete individuals are potential abstract individuals.

These two dimensions of reality are different. What holds in one dimension does not hold in the other, due to their radical differences. However, they are related to each other, rather than being unbridgeable. The bridge is constituted by the potential aspects of individual and social phenomena. Within the dimension of individual phenomena, social phenomena are internalised by concrete individuals and become potential individual phenomena, that is, are reduced to a potential state. This internalisation is part of the process of mental (knowledge) production to be discussed in Chapter 4. It is because of this, that upon their realisation, these individual phenomena become potential social phenomena. Within this dimension, individual phenomena determine social phenomena because the latter are contained potentially within the former. This is the bridge from the individual to the social dimension of society. But, within the dimension of social phenomena, it is realised social phenomena that determine individual phenomena. Realised social phenomena must manifest themselves in a personal, concrete form (see point 2 below). Thus, they contain within themselves a variety of personal forms, depending upon the specific features of those individuals. Social phenomena determine individual phenomena as potential social phenomena and not in their individual specificity. And this is the bridge from the social to the individual dimension. Thus, the mutual determination (and thus connection) between realised individual and realised social phenomena takes place through their potentials. It is the realm of the potentials, rather than that of the realised, that connects the two dimensions of social reality. Some points implicitly present in the above can now be explicitly stated.

(i) It has been submitted above that phenomena are contradictory unities in determination of relations and processes. First, let us see why relations determine processes. We have seen that the criterion for attributing the determining status is that only what has already realised itself can be the condition of existence of the potentialities inherent in itself. Determination implies temporality. It follows that relations must be temporally prior to processes, if they must be determinant and processes determined. It could be argued that, for certain phenomena, it might be impossible to determine whether the relation is determinant, because the transformations inherent in that relation might start as soon as people engage in that relation: the capitalist can hire a labourer and set her immediately to work. But this disregards the fact that the capitalist is already the owner of the means of production before hiring the labourer and setting her to work. The production-process presupposes as its condition of existence the ownership-relation (or the labourers would not produce surplus-value for the capitalist) and is the condition of further reproduction of the ownership-relation. If this holds for the ultimately determining social phenomenon, it must also hold for all other social and individual phenomena. This is why phenomena are *unities-in-determination*. Given that a unity-in-determination can supersede itself if there is contradiction between the determinant (relation) and the determined (processes) element, a phenomenon is also a *contradictory* unity-in-determination.

(ii) We can distinguish among four types of transformations: (a) relational transformations, the transformation of the relation itself; (b) objective transformations, the transformations of reality outside of our perception of that transformation; (c) personal transformations, the transformations of the persons engaging in that relation; and (d) mental transformations, the transformations (production) of knowledge, which issue into the transformation of our perception of objective transformations.[64]

(iii) Given that, in reality, individuals are always abstract and concrete (they live in two dimensions contemporaneously), when they engage in social phenomena they inevitably give a personal, concrete form to those phenomena. In other words, concrete individuals are the specific *personification* of abstract individuals. For example, the capitalist is nothing but the 'personified capital endowed with a consciousness of its own and a will.'[65] From this angle, *the personal is the form of appearance of the social.* The notion of capital as a process without a subject but with a purpose is nonsensical and similar to Durkheim's notion of social structure without people. If there is a purpose, there must be subjects, concrete individuals who, through their purposefulness, become carriers of either of capital's or of labour's rationality.

(iv) Given that we can observe a relation only by observing what people do when they engage in a process, a *process is* also the specific, *empirically observable form taken by that relation.* As argued above, social relations are the non-observable and yet realised part of social phenomena.

---

[64] The usual terminology is material versus mental transformations. However, as argued in Chapter 4, all transformations are material, including the mental ones. The proper distinction is between objective and mental transformations.

[65] Marx 1967a, pp. 289–90.

(v) Given that relations determine processes and given that processes are transformations, that is, movement, *relations determine their own movement by determining their own processes*. The relation of dialectical determination developed above applies not only to different phenomena but also within phenomena, between relations and processes.

(vi) A process, being determined, might change either only the form or also the social content of its determining relation. In the former case, that relation undergoes a *formal* transformation, in the latter case a *radical transformation* (that is, it changes from being a condition of reproduction to being a condition of supersession or vice versa). In the former case, the relation is superseded.

(vii) We have seen that abstract individuals are replaceable. However, substitutability implies only the *possibility* to be replaced in an actually-existing relation and process. An actual substitution does not have to take place.

(viii) The mutual interaction (determination) of realised phenomena changes their potential nature (their essence). In turn, these changes must result in changes of their form of appearance, in the specific form taken by those phenomena. But these changes in their potential nature emerge in new forms of realisation.

(ix) People's substitutability among and within processes requires standardisation of tasks. Tasks should not change because of the unique features of the concrete individuals. Rather, individuals must adapt their behaviour to those tasks. In a standardised process, their behaviour must be standardised and coerced, it must be imposed by customs, laws, house-rules, norms and values, etc. If this were not the case, individuals could choose to perform those tasks as they wished and the performance of tasks would depend upon the specific features and willingness of individuals, that is, upon their features as concrete individuals. External coercion does not exclude psychological acceptance through internalisation and thus willingness to perform coercive tasks.

(x) It is in this sense that 'in the social production of their life men enter into definite relations that are independent of their will, relations of production which correspond to a definite stage of development of their material productive forces'.[66] It is concrete individuals who enter into relations that are independent of their will (social and principally production-relations) and that correspond to a definite stage of development of society.

(xi) Given that individuals are always both concrete and abstract, individuals as abstract individuals are the agents through whom those phenomena manifest their social content while attaching to them, as concrete individuals, their own personal meaning and purposefulness. However, this personal meaning is not the social content of those phenomena.

(xii) It follows that both abstract and concrete individuals possess *a social nature*: the former because they are the actual carriers of social relations and agents of social processes; the latter because they, due to the internalisation of social phenomena, are potential carriers of social relations and agents of social processes (their potential social nature). Thus, individuals are always, and at the same time, both actual carriers of social relations and agents of social processes (as abstract individuals); both potential carriers of social relations and potential agents of social processes (as concrete individuals). And, as concrete individuals, they are always both the actual carriers of individual relations and actual agents of individual processes, along with being potential carriers of social relations and potential agents of social processes.

(xiii) Not all realised individual phenomena become social phenomena. Only some of them become actualised social phenomena.

(xiv) An *individual relation*, while presupposing the unique features of the concrete individuals engaging in it, also presupposes something those individuals have in *common*. If this were not the case, there could be no relation at all. A relation of friendship, for example, implies that both individuals share a need for, say, companionship. But the fact that this feature (need) is common to two or more people (or possibly to everybody) is not sufficient reason for that feature to be the basis of a social relation. That relation is individual because, for the people involved, the relation presupposes only those specific individuals in their unique features, that

---

[66] Marx 1977.

is, because in that relation, those individuals are not replaceable. The same applies to processes.

(xv) The existence of certain common characteristics shared by people creates only the possibility for those individuals to become abstract individuals on the basis of those characteristics. Those features must have acquired a *social significance,* that is, they must be used (for whatever purpose) to define social groups. For example, in a sexist society, women are abstract individuals not because of their biological specificity but because their biological features are used in a process of discrimination against women by men, that is, because the object of discrimination are women as women and not women with their specific and unique features. But each woman, as a concrete individual, experiences sexism in her own specific way and is a specific concretisation of a sexist social relation.

(xvi) It would be a mistake to assume that relations can exist without people. For example, for Durkheim 'When the individual has been eliminated, society alone remains.'[67] This view is based on the failure to distinguish between individual and social relations. While individual relations cannot pre-exist the concrete individuals engaging in them, social relations usually do pre-exist the abstract individuals who become their carriers. Social relations and processes must abstract from concrete individuals, but obviously imply abstract individuals, that is, individuals seen not in their uniqueness but inasmuch as they share some characteristics. These common characteristics are the basis for their being categorised into a group, thus making those individuals replaceable. The fact that individuals are substitutable does not mean that relations can exist without individuals. It is *social relations,* which, disregarding their concrete form of manifestation, can exist without individuals *as concrete individuals.*

(xvii) A relation can be *spurious.* This is the case of one agent having a social relation with another who has an individual relation with the former. For example, in a relation between a charismatic leader and her followers, to the extent that the followers are substitutable (so that the movement can continue irrespective of the specific personal features of the followers),

---

[67] Durkheim 1966, p. 102.

the relation is a social one. But, insofar as the leader is concerned, she is not substitutable (the movement would collapse without her) so that the relation is an individual one.

(xviii) Relations and processes can be in a *transitional* state, that is, from an individual state to a social one and vice versa or from a spurious state to either a social or an individual state and vice versa. In the example above, a spurious relation could be in a transitional state to a social one, if that social group produces a number of leaders whose substitutability might ensure continuity to that group.

(xix) Individuals engaging in a relation do not necessarily, and usually do not, continuously interact with each other. Friends alternate periods of contact with periods of separation, labourers work only part of the day, and so on and so forth. The actual interaction can be *suspended* without breaking that relation. The interacting persons agree, either formally (that is, legally) or informally, either freely or under coercion, either explicitly or implicitly, either by personal or by common consent, to resume their interaction. Their specific processes are suspended too.

4. Class-analysis and the sociology of non-equilibrium

We have seen that social phenomena can emerge both from other social phenomena and from individual phenomena. In a different manner from a potential social phenomenon that is contained in a specific realised phenomenon and which becomes a condition of reproduction or of supersession of that realised phenomenon, individual phenomena are called into existence by *all* the social phenomena that have gone into the concrete individuals' internalisation and are transferred to any individual phenomenon and, from there, to any social phenomenon. This is why any realised social phenomenon can emerge from any individual phenomenon (within the limits posed by that concrete individual's internalisation), and this is why, upon their realisation as social phenomena as conditions of reproduction or of supersession of *any* social phenomenon, they can reproduce or supersede any social phenomenon. Several points follow.

(i) The determinant phenomenon calls into realised existence the determined one (a) from within its own potentialities, (b) in its interaction (determination) with other social phenomena, (c) as well as in its interaction with individual phenomena as potential social phenomena.

(ii) *Social reality*, seen from a dialectical perspective is a temporal flow of determining and determined contradictory individual and social phenomena, in which social phenomena continuously emerge from a potential state (as either contained in some realised social phenomena or as realised individual phenomena) to become realised and then returning to a potential state as individual phenomena, due to the contradictory social content of all phenomena.

(iii) The *dialectical research-method* inquires into (a) a social phenomenon's origin, present state and further development within this view of reality, and (b) tests the results of this enquiry in terms both of formal logic and of their class-content (see Sections 6 and 7).

(iv) The relation between the realised determinant and realised determined *social* phenomena is society's *social structure*. Continuity in social life requires types of relations and processes which are independent of, and thus both pre-exist and survive, *concrete* individuals. Without social phenomena, society would collapse and disintegrate.

(v) Due to the dynamic nature of determination, the social structure is not static but dynamic. Without the relation of dialectical determination among its constituent parts, society could neither continue to exist in a changed form, nor change radically, nor (possibly) cease to exist. Society's movement is the change undergone by realised social phenomena and thus by society as a whole.[68] *Any contraposition between structure and movement is artificial.*

(vi) There is thus no need, as for example in the neoliberal view, to ascribe the cohesive factor holding society together to the self-regulating and equilibrating function of the market, that is, to the fact that the market, if not tampered with, tends towards equilibrium. *Reproduction is not equilibrium*, neither static nor dynamic. Reproduction is a *countertendency* in which the reproductive forces dominate the supersessive forces; it is a *phase* of the cyclical process that tends towards supersession (see below). Supersession is the tendency and reproduction is the counter-tendency.

---

[68] This is shown in relation (δ) in Appendix 1.

(vii) Given the two opposite rationalities emanating from the capitalist owner-ship-relation, behaviour according to capital's rationality facilitates and is a condition for the reproduction of the system; behaviour according to labour's rationality hinders that reproduction and is a condition for its supersession. The two rationalities co-exist in each phenomenon and the realisation of one or the other is the consequence of an internal struggle, of movement. In line with the third principle of dialectics submitted above, this movement is not only contradictory but also tendential.

(viii) Some social phenomena can be functional only for the reproduction of capitalism, while other social phenomena can only be for its super-session, and yet still others are amenable to their social content being radically changed through a radical transformation. Those social phe-nomena that cannot be radically changed can only be superseded by being reduced to a potential state, that is, to an individual state. Thus, the *supersession* of a realised social phenomenon is the *radical transfor-mation of its social content and, if that is not possible, its disappearance from the realm of the realised and thereby becoming an individual, that is, potential social phenomenon.*

Conclusions in many ways similar to those submitted here are reached by Resnick and Wolff.[69] Their work builds upon Lukács, Gramsci and especially Althusser. Its specificity is its focus on contradiction, class, and overdetermi-nation as the three basic coordinates of analysis. For these authors, *overdetermi-nation* holds that each process is the cause and at the same time the effect of all other processes, and that processes are constituted through this interconnec-tion.[70] This is society's dialectical movement. No process exercises 'any more determinant influence on the others than any of those others do on it'.[71] This, the authors hold, is contrary to essentialism, the view that 'one aspect of capi-talist society…functions…as an essence, that is, the determinant of the other social aspects'.[72] *Class* is defined in terms of production and appropriation of

---

[69] Resnick and Wolff 2006.
[70] Resnick and Wolff 2006, p. 36.
[71] Resnick and Wolff 2006, p. 30.
[72] Resnick and Wolff 2006, p. 106.

surplus-labour.[73] The fundamental class-process is based on the production of surplus-labour and the subsumed class-processes are 'based on the distribution of the already appropriated surplus'.[74] Finally, *contradiction* arises from overdetermination, from the fact that each process is pulled and pushed 'in all directions with varying force'.[75]

It is instructive to compare these authors' approach to the one submitted in this work. Consider, first, the differences. First, as in Althusser, overdetermination focuses on social processes as each other's condition of existence, but undertheorises their being also each other's condition of supersession. Second, if each process is constituted by an infinity of other processes with no ultimately determinant factor, one falls into infinite regression. Resnick and Wolff agree that all explanations are necessarily and inherently partial and subject to infinite regression. However, they hold that their theory is not an explanation but rather an 'intervention', or 'position', or 'story'.[76] But the infinite regression implied in overdeterminism applies no matter how one characterises what an explanation is. Third, since no factor is ultimately determinant, any social process or notion of it can be the 'entry point' into analysis. 'No reductionism is possible here, no ranking of the relative effectivity of one vs. another process'.[77] The authors' preferred entry-point is class as the production and appropriation of surplus-labour. However, if each theory has its own entry-point, and if each entry-point is the 'conceptual tool to make sense of this infinity of social processes',[78] and, furthermore, 'the concept that will distinctively shape the asking of all questions',[79] then each entry-point is the concept of what each theorist believes is specific to social reality. This applies also to class. But the process that is specific to social reality and from which the theorists must begin their analysis is actually the ultimately determinant process, if not in reality at least in theory. The authors are aware of this objection: if the theorist must 'focus on but some aspects pertinent to the explanation of any event...will not that focus amount...to a kind of explana-

---

[73] Resnick and Wolff 2006, p. 21.
[74] Resnick and Wolff 2006, p. 77.
[75] Resnick and Wolff 2006, p. 71.
[76] Resnick and Wolff 2006, p. 86.
[77] Resnick and Wolff 2006, p. 132.
[78] Resnick and Wolff 2006, p. 49.
[79] Resnick and Wolff 2006, p. 265.

tory essentializing of those aspects?'.[80] Their negative answer is that this is only 'a momentary' essentialist moment and that each subsequent essentialist moment *changes the relation posed in the initial essentialism'*.[81] However, the essentialism inherent in the first moment (stage of the analysis) disappears only to reappear enlarged in the next moment. A finite sequence of essentialist moments is an enlarged essentialist moment. In short, Resnick and Wolff are correct in stressing that social phenomena constitute themselves, in their specificity, in their mutual interaction. But this can be combined with the determination in the last instance. Without determination in the last instance, not only can infinite regression not be avoided, but also the inherently contradictory nature of social phenomena remains unexplained.

In spite of these differences, the authors' work is to be recommended because of a number of achievements. Among these, one should mention the rejection of empiricism, that is, the view that considers facts as conceptually neutral;[82] the stress on dialectics (even though this is synonymous with overdetermination) as the foundation of social analysis, together with the dynamic approach to social reality which is seen as a complex of continuously changing processes;[83] and the stress on contradiction as the characteristic of social processes and the concept of class as a process.[84] Moreover, there are two points of fundamental importance shared by the authors and the present approach. First, a non-equilibrium theory of capitalism deriving from the point that 'Overdetermination entails rejecting...order for disorder',[85] and that a deep instability describes capitalism's functioning.[86] Second, the *scientificity* of a 'partisan reading' of reality due to an opposition to capital and a preference for communism.[87] Even though the authors do not connect this latter fundamental insight to the presently ongoing discussion between equilibrium and non-equilibrium Marxism,[88] their work is a welcome departure from a formal-logical reading of a theory whose vital core cannot but be dialectics.

---

[80] Resnick and Wolff 2006, p. 82.
[81] Resnick and Wolff 2006, p. 83; emphasis in the original.
[82] Resnick and Wolff 2006, p. 16.
[83] Resnick and Wolff 2006, p. 24.
[84] Resnick and Wolff 2006, p. 78.
[85] Resnick and Wolff 2006, p. 51.
[86] Resnick and Wolff 2006, p. 239.
[87] Resnick and Wolff 2006, p. 62.
[88] This will be one of the major themes of the next chapter.

5. A dialectics of nature?

The above has dealt with the notion of dialectics, both as a view of social reality and as a method of social research. A full appreciation of this approach requires that similarities and differences be addressed with regard to Engels's notion of the dialectics of nature as well as to formal logic. This section deals with Engels's dialectics of nature, the one that follows will deal with a comparison between formal and dialectical logic.

For Engels, the 'most general laws of dialectics' can be reduced to three. First, 'the law of the transformation of quantity into quality and vice versa'. Second, 'the law of the interpenetration of opposites'. Third, 'the law of the negation of the negation'.[89] These laws are reflections in thought of reality and are therefore 'real laws of development of nature...valid also for theoretical natural sciences'.[90] There is some correspondence between the present approach and Engels's notion of dialectics. Engels's first law (the transformation of quantity into quality and vice versa) corresponds to the transformation of an aggregation of individual phenomena (potential social phenomena) into realised social phenomena and vice versa (see Section 3). Engels's second law (the interpenetration of opposites) corresponds to the relation between determinant and determined phenomena, if the latter are conditions of supersession of the former (see Section 2). And Engels's third law (the negation of the negation) corresponds to that aspect of mutual determination (see Section 2) in which the determinant phenomenon calls into realised existence the determined one as its own condition of supersession (negation). The realised determined phenomenon then supersedes the determinant one (negation of the negation). In short, the determinant phenomenon negates itself into the determined one and the latter negates the former. Another possible point of convergence is the notion of potential reality. Engels does not theorise potential reality explicitly, but it could be argued that that notion is inherent in his view. Water can become steam if boiled at 100 degrees centigrade. Or,

> The plant, the animal, every cell is at every moment of its life identical with itself and yet becoming distinct from itself,...by a sum of incessant molecular changes...even in inorganic nature identity as such is in reality non-existent.

---

[89] Engels 1987, p. 356.
[90] Engels 1987, p. 357.

> Every body is continuously exposed to mechanical, physical and chemical
> influences, which are always changing it and modifying its identity.[91]

Thus, it could be submitted that, for Engels, change is due to the reciprocal
interaction of realised instances (e.g. molecules) but these changes are already
potentially present before their realisation. In terms of the present approach,
at any given moment, something is identical to itself (as a realised entity)
and potentially different from itself.

Although Engels's concept of the dialectics of nature has been called into
question because of an inherent lack of compatibility with social reality, per-
spectival and processual similarities might be adduced that seem to appear
between the social and natural reality. I will indicate several possible examples below. For instance, just as we do not see the objects but only the light
reflected by them, we do not see relations but only the processes determined
by those relations. Or, just as the force of gravity is the result of the effect
of the gravitational field upon objects immersed in it, so is the ownership-
relation the 'gravitational field' in which other relations are immersed and
towards which they are attracted. Or, just as there is no absolute location of
things in space, but only the relative location of objects, that is, relative to one
another – in other words, just as space is the relation between dynamic objects –
so there is no absolute location of individuals in the social space, but only
individuals in ever changing relations to one another. Or, most importantly
for the temporalist approach to be argued for in Chapter 2, just as in nature,
space and time can only be described together, in the present approach social
space cannot be analysed disjointed from time. Or, finally, just as 'Statistical
mechanics and thermodynamics... allow us to make some predictions in spite
of the fact that we don't know the exact movement of *all* the macroscopic
variables',[92] forecasts in the social sciences are possible in spite of the fact that
not all determinants of change are known (see Section 7 below).

There is, however, a fundamental difference between the two approaches.
The three principles of dialectics on which this book is based differ from
Engels's dialectics because they are extracted from Marx's work and thus
from a *class*-analysis of *social* reality and apply only to that reality, rather then
to nature. Social phenomena are not only the objective transformations and

---

[91] Engels 1987, p. 495.
[92] Rovelli 2006, p. 52; emphasis in the original.

the relations in which people engage when performing those transformations. They are also the knowledge (mental transformations) of those objective transformations and the relations into which people enter when producing that knowledge. Thus, knowledge has a social content, a class-content. This applies to all knowledge, including the natural sciences and techniques. While there is no explicit denial of the social determination of the natural sciences in Engels, for him, natural sciences seem to develop according to their own internal logic: progress in these sciences consists in overcoming errors and attaining an increasingly correct insight into the laws of nature.[93] This presupposes that the development of natural science is not class-determined (it is class-neutral), whereas it can be argued that, for Marx, knowledge, all knowledge, is class-determined and has a class-content. The apparent advantage of grounding dialectics in nature was that socialism became grounded in the objective laws of nature, thus becoming inevitable. On the other hand, placing dialectics outside nature was, and still is, seen as subjectivism and thus an individualistic approach.[94] But there is also a third option, dialectics as a class-determined method of analysis of the social world, that is, of both the objective and the mental transformations and relations.[95]

This topic will be developed in Chapters 3 and 4. Here, it suffices to say that the myth of the neutrality of science has led to the myth of the neutrality of the productive forces which, thanks also to Engels, was accepted by the great majority of Marxists, including Lenin. It became possible, then, for the Bolsheviks, and for Lenin in particular, to accept the class-neutrality of Taylorism and therefore of the conveyor-belt. More generally, it became possible to accept the neutrality of the productive forces and hence to think that it would have been possible to build socialism by using the *capitalist* productive forces, that is, productive forces with a capitalist class-content. Chapter 4 will develop this thesis. It is sufficient here only to mention that this was indeed the fundamental weakness of the Soviet Union and the ultimate reason for its

---

[93] Engels 1987, p. 361. See also Kircz 1998.

[94] See, for example, Gerdes 1985, p. 122.

[95] Notice that Engels discusses almost exclusively the natural sciences, a practice followed by commentators up to the present day. Engels has been criticised because he did not consider the most advanced developments in the natural sciences of his time. The critics, however, should show that, had his knowledge been more up to date, he would have had to reject or modify his notion of dialectics. This is unproved. Lacking this proof, the critique is irrelevant within the context of this work.

demise.[96] The course of history might have been different had the productive forces, and thus knowledge, been seen as social phenomena with a definite class-, that is, capitalist, content.

But a proper understanding of dialectics is essential also within the contemporary social context. Take, for example, the class-content of neoliberalism. Neoliberalism is founded on an economic theory that, as argued in Chapter 2, Section 6, is based on the notion of *homo economicus*, an economic agent whose rationality is supposed to be natural, that is, the manifestation of human nature, rather than being the embodiment of capitalist rationality. Consequently, economic policies deriving from the supposed class-neutrality of economics cannot but favour capital at the expense of labour. The practical, political and social implications of different views on dialectics are thus far-reaching and all-important.

6. Formal logic and dialectical logic

The mainstream social sciences make use of traditional formal logic. This work has set out three principles for the analysis of social reality from a dialectical, and hence from a class-, perspective. The question is whether formal and dialectical logic exclude each other or whether they can coexist. This section will consider only traditional formal logic for two reasons. First, this is the type of logic used in the social sciences. Second, and most importantly, for the purposes of this work, that is, the comparison between formal and dialectical logic, both types of formal logic share the same drawback, the impossibility to explain contradictions in a constructive way. For example, for Bradley and Swartz, 'if any proposition ascribes truth to both members of a pair of contradictories, then that proposition is one which has a contradiction within itself'.[97] This applies both to traditional and to modern formal logic. Therefore, in what follows, formal logic will be taken to mean traditional formal logic.

Formal logic also rests on three basic laws. *The law of identity* states that something is equal to itself, that is, A = A. It is well-known that this is nothing more than a truism. As such, it cannot generate any knowledge about A and

---

[96] See Carchedi, 1983, 1987, 2005.
[97] Bradley and Swartz 1979, p. 18.

thus about its change. *The law of the excluded middle* states that A=A is either true or not true, that is, either A=A or A ≠ A. There is no third possibility. The *law of non-contradiction*, states that two contradictory propositions cannot both be true. A proposition, A=A, and its denial, A ≠ A, cannot both be true.

As just pointed out, A=A is a truism. To be a meaningful statement, it must also be possible for A to be different from A, that is, A ≠ A. In this case, we can enquire into the conditions for A=A and for A ≠ A, that is, why and how A=A and why and how A ≠ A. This is what dialectical logic does. For dialectical logic, A is at the same time both itself and different from itself, because of both its realised and of its potential nature. Given that both the realised and the potential are two aspects of the same phenomenon, A as a realised phenomenon is equal to itself, but at the same time is different from itself because of the potentialities it contains.[98] If A^r indicates A as a realised phenomenon and A^p indicates the potentials inherent in A^r, A=A because $A^r = A^r$ and at the same time A ≠ A because $A^r \neq A^p$. Formal logic is blind to the realm of potentialities, so that a realised phenomenon is always equal to itself. Thus, given that phenomena change continuously because of their contradictory potentialities, change is banned from this view. Most importantly, to focus only on the realm of the realised while disregarding the realm of potentialities, that is, to state that A is always equal to A, implies a timeless dimension. The exclusive application of formal logic leads necessarily to simultaneism. In other words, a temporal approach needs dialectical logic. This allows us to distinguish dialectical contradictions from logical mistakes.

Case 1. Formal logic contradictions (mistakes)

If only realised reality, A^r, is considered, only $A^r = A^r$ holds and $A^r \neq A^r$ is a logical mistake. What has become realised can be only what it is, as a realised phenomenon. An eight-hour working day is just that ($A^r = A^r$) and to

---

[98] Blunden 1984 stresses the interest shown by Marx in the *Mathematical Manuscripts* 'in the differing roles of the left and right sides of the equals sign.... [and that Marx] had previously studied the equivalence relation... in relation to the exchange of commodities'. The author draws the conclusion, concerning the law of identity, that 'this law is a useless tautology which leads nowhere – except in so far as "A on the left" is not the same, but the opposite of "A on the right"...the meaning of the law is the identity of opposites – the statement that every single concept contains two opposite sides'. But Marx examines the exchange of two real and different use-values, A and B, and argues that they are equal only because of a *third* factor, because they contain the same substance, (exchange-) value. See Chapter 2 below and Appendix 3.

assert that a working day is also not an eight-hour working day $(A^r \neq A^r)$ is a formal logical contradiction, a mistake. Thus, *in the realm of the realised, which is formal logic's only domain,* 2=2 and 2=1 is a mistake. It follows that, since the contradiction between the realised form of social phenomena and their potential nature is disregarded, formal logic applies *only to cases in which the premises are not contradictory.*

Case 2. *Meaningless contradictions*

If we consider both realisations and potentials, $[A^r = A^r$ and $A^r \neq A^p]$ is a meaningless contradiction *if A^p is not contained as a potentiality within A^r.* In fact, it is meaningless to assert that a realised phenomenon is different from what it cannot potentially be. This can be the case either because A^p dos not exist in reality or because it is excluded by definition by A^r. For example, a realised eight-hour working day cannot be different from a potential twenty-five-hour working day because the latter does not exist, because the same forces that fix the length of the working day at eight hours cannot fix it at twenty-hours. For this reason, this type of contradiction cannot, by definition, explain change. This type of contradiction is *meaningless from the standpoint of a theory of (social) change.*

Case 3. *Dialectical contradictions*

If we consider both the realised and the potential, $[A^r = A^r$ and $A^r \neq A^p]$ is *not* a logical contradiction *if a contradictory potentiality, A^p, is contained potentially within A^r,* that is, if A^p is a real possibility because it belongs to the potential realm of reality contained in A^r. In this case, we a have a real, or dialectical, contradiction. That a realised eight-hour working day is different from a potential ten-hour working day is a dialectical contradiction, because a ten-hour working day is a real possibility, indeed the same forces that fix the length of the working day at eight hours can also change it to ten hours, thus explaining (the possibility of) its change. *A dialectical contradiction is a contradiction between what has become and what can become, as contradictory to what has become.* Far from being a logical mistake, a dialectical contradiction is what allows for, and explains, change. In dialectical logic, a temporary lack of change is explained not in terms of lack of movement but in terms of opposing forces temporarily unable to override each other, as, for example, an unchanged average rate of profit is the result of the tendency being unable to override the countertendency (or vice versa). On the other hand, for formal logic, *all* contradictions are a mistake. This is different from saying that something can both be (exists) and not be (does not exist). This is not dialectical logic, but absurd nonsense deriving from disregarding the existence of the potential. Formal logic cannot explain change. Formal logic reduces to a succession of static moments what is a temporal flow of determining and determined contradictory phenomena continuously emerging from a potential state to become realised and continuously going back to a potential state.

It follows that formal logic, seen from the standpoint of its class-content, is ideological because it rules out dialectical contradictions, and thus movement and change. An *ideology* is a form of knowledge that defends, implicitly or explicitly, the interests of a class *as if they were the interests of all classes*, sometimes by denying the existence of classes. This is the case for formal logic as well. It was born in a slave-society and was functional for the reproduction of that society. It was a static view of reality, a rationality in which radical change was absent. By extension, it was the status quo that was rational. It continued to be accepted in subsequent societies, including capitalism, because it can perform the same reactionary function in societies which, however different, share the common feature of being class-divided societies and in which it is in the interest of the ruling classes to use and foster this implicit rationalisation of the status quo. This accounts for the resilience of formal logic. Formal logic is ideological not so much because of what it says but because of what it does *not* say. Acceptance of formal logic as *the* method of social analysis excludes the analysis of social change. The banning of dialectics cannot but result in a static and thus conservative view. Formal logic and dialectical logic do not complement each other; they exclude each other because of their opposing class-content. On this point, the present approach differs substantially from that of Engels and of many Marxists after him. For Engels, 'Metaphysical categories' which for him are the same as the categories of formal logic 'retain their validity' but only 'for everyday use, for the small change of science'.[99] This notion is unsatisfactory, not only because it does not provide a clear-cut principle as to when dialectical logic is applicable as opposed to formal logic.

---

[99] Engels 1987, p. 494.

Also, and more importantly, formal logic explains neither everyday change nor the small change of science.

Nevertheless, if the class-content of formal logic is the opposite of, and excludes, that of dialectical logic, the *principles* of formal logic can and should be applied *within* dialectical logic as an *auxiliary* method because *the rules of formal logic apply to the realm of the realised* (which without the potentials is a static reality) *and only to that realm*. While exclusive focus on the realised disregards the potential and thus cannot account for dialectical contradictions, movement and change, consideration of the realised as a *partial step* in the analysis is acceptable and necessary, if one chooses as a level of abstraction only the realm of the realised within a view of reality stressing both the realised and the potential. The rules of formal logic, if immersed in a dialectical interpretative scheme, do not deny dialectical contradictions, movement and change but complement their understanding. To ban dialectical contradiction, movement and change from analysis (as in formal logic) means to adhere to a specific class-content of the analysis. But to temporarily disregard these features of dialectical logic, and thus A^p, to analyse separately $A^r = A^r$ and $A^r \neq A^p$ as a technique within a dialectical framework, is methodologically possible and, indeed, necessary. A similar conclusion is reached by Zelený in his analysis of the relation between modern formal logic and dialectical logic: 'In Marxian analysis, elementary induction and deduction...[that is, induction and deduction as in formal logic – G.C.] play a legitimate role in so far as one is entitled and required by the relative *stability* of the essence and the universal to treat that stability as fixed within certain limits.'[100]

For example, Marx analyses the subdivision of the working day into necessary and surplus labour-time by holding the length of the working day constant. The premise is $A^r = A^r$, that is, 8 hours are 8 hours, that is a premise that deals only with what has been realised. Thus the rules of formal logic hold. The purpose is to focus on the movement within A^r: the greater the necessary labour-time, the smaller the surplus labour-time and vice versa. However, a full comprehension of A^r requires an insight into A^p and thus into $A^r \neq A^p$, that is, into how the same forces that determine the subdivision within a working day of a certain length (A^r) can determine also a potential change in A^r. By considering the reasons why a realised eight-hour working day is different

---

[100] Zelený 1980, p. 100. See next section.

from a potential ten-hour working day, we hypothesise the possibility of a change in the length of the working day. This does not negate the results obtained by taking an eight-hour working day as a constant, but enriches the analysis by *transforming that constant into a potential variable*. Formal logic cannot encompass dialectical logic because the former shuns contradictions, which it considers to be mistakes.[101] But dialectical logic does encompass the formal rules of reasoning (but *not* formal logic with its class-content) even though these rules cannot explain dialectical contradictions and thus contradictory change, that is, the change in a phenomenon's social content. To explain quantitative change within the realm of the realised, one needs the rules of formal logic and thus induction, deduction and verification, as in formal logic. But, to explain the quantitative change arising from the contradiction between the realised and the potential or the change in a phenomenon's contradictory social content, in short, to explain dialectical contradictions, one needs induction, deduction and verification, as in dialectical logic. This is the theme of the next section.

7. Induction, deduction and verification

Deduction can test whether some conclusions follow from some premises. These premises have been arrived at by a previous process of induction. This method applies to both formal and dialectical logic. However, there are fundamental differences.

7.1. *The specificity of dialectical induction and deduction*

This is the first difference between formal and dialectical logic.

> It seems to be correct to begin with the real and the concrete, with the real precondition, thus to begin, in economics, with e.g. the population, which is the foundation and the subject of the entire social act of production. However, on closer examination this proves false. The population is an abstraction if I leave out, for example, the classes of which it is composed.

---

[101] It would seem that Marx engages in what is nowadays called controlled experiments, holding some variables constant and letting others vary, thus accepting this positivistic method. But a change between two different quantities of the same realised phenomenon could not take place if this were not a real possibility.

These classes in turn are an empty phrase if I am not familiar with the elements on which they rest. E.g. wage labour, capital, etc. These latter in turn presuppose exchange, division of labour, prices, etc. For example, capital is nothing without wage labour, without value, money, price etc. Thus, if I were to begin with the population, this would be a chaotic conception [*Vorstellung*] of the whole, and I would then, by means of further determination, move analytically towards ever more simple concepts [*Begriffe*], from the imagined concrete towards ever thinner abstractions until I had arrived at the simplest determinations.[102]

For Marx, then, induction starts with observation, the 'chaotic conception of the whole', for example, 'population'. He discerns that it would be wrong to consider population as the foundation of production. Rather, this foundation should be sought in classes. This first narrowing of the scope of the analysis is also the first step in the process of dialectical induction. In this process, the more complex (population as a realised phenomenon) is reduced to the less complex (classes, also as a realised phenomenon), so that the more complex (population) is reduced to a potential state contained in the less complex (classes). Or, the less complex (classes) is seen as containing within its potentialities the more complex (population). In this way, classes as a realised phenomenon are seen to contain potentially within themselves the population, thus becoming the condition of existence of the population. In reducing population from a realised to a potential state (within classes), that is, in compressing population into classes, the concreteness and complexity of the realised population is lost, because the realised population is more than realised classes. It is in this sense that the latter (classes) are a 'thinner' concept (abstraction) than the former. Given that only what is realised can determine what is potentially existent within itself as a condition of its own existence, if the realised population is reduced to, compressed into, a potential population contained within realised classes, in this conceptual process (induction) population is determined by classes. But classes, too, are a realised phenomenon that can be reduced to a yet-simpler realised phenomenon, for example, the ownership-relation. Again, the more complex (classes) is reduced to a potential state contained in the realised less-complex

---

[102] Marx 1973a, p. 100.

(the realised ownership-relation), so that the latter becomes determinant of the former. At a certain level of abstraction of the analysis, that is to say, if a certain slice of social reality is considered, the population is contained potentially in and determined by classes; at another level of abstraction, classes are contained potentially in and determined by the ownership-relation. In short, dialectical induction is a process that, through different phases (levels of abstraction), compresses the richness of phenomena into simpler, 'thinner' states (thus reducing them to a potential state) until it reaches the ultimately determining phenomenon, the ownership-relation.

At this point, induction terminates and deduction begins. The excerpt above continues as follows: 'From there the journey would have to be retraced until I had finally arrived at the population again, but this time not as the chaotic conception of a whole, but as a rich totality of many determinations and relations'. This is what Marx calls the 'concrete in thought'.[103] The 'retracing' phase is the dialectical deduction, the unfolding (reconstruction in thought) of more-and-more concrete, detailed, and articulated notions of reality derived from their potential state. Each step in the unfolding is a (temporary) conclusion, but also the premise for the following step in the chain of deductions. The realised phenomenon (population) that was compressed into its potential state and made to become the potential inherent to another realised phenomenon (classes) is now unfolded from its potential state contained in the determinant phenomenon (classes) into its realised state, the realised population, the notion of population which is not 'chaotic' any longer but structured through the process of induction and deduction. There is no chicken-and-egg dilemma here, for any initial observation is perceived through a previous process of induction and deduction and is unstructured ('chaotic') only relative to a further conception that is the outcome of a further process of induction and deduction. The search for an observation not influenced by a previous theoretical framework, no matter how primitive, is senseless. Stated differently, to start from empirical, observed reality is not an empiricist standpoint. Marx's starting point of induction is indeed empirical reality, but there is no *empiricism* in his method. The reason is that the inductive phase, the observation of reality, begins on the basis of a previously developed theoretical conception, in Marx's case, a class-analysis, which is the outcome of a pre-

---

[103] Marx 1973a, pp. 100–1.

vious phase of deduction. If Marx begins with the real concrete, empirical observation, he begins with an observation which has already been filtered through a previous process of induction and deduction. It might be useful to recall that the notions developed in the process of induction and deduction (knowledge-formation) are not a reflection in thought of objective reality, but class-determined conceptualisations.

7.2. *Contradictory premises*

The second difference is that, in formal logic, the premises should not be contradictory. If they are so, the conclusions cannot but be ambiguous and undetermined. For example, we shall see in Chapter 2 that technological innovations can *both* increase the (surplus-) value produced (for example, if they decrease the value of the means of production per unit of capital invested) *and* decrease it (for example, if they replace people with machines, given that only human labour can produce value and surplus-value). From this contradictory premise, it is impossible for formal logic to conclude unambiguously whether the new value produced increases or decreases as a result of technological innovations, so that the movement of the average rate of profit is seen as indeterminate. On the other hand, dialectical logic deduces from this contradictory premise a tendential (not an indeterminate) movement, a movement exhibiting tendencies and countertendencies, a contradictory movement. This is not a logical mistake but a rendition of a real contradictory movement. The same holds if we start from two mutually contradictory premises. This does not imply that deduction, as in formal logic, should be discarded. It allows us to distinguish correct from incorrect statements about social phenomena if only non-contradictory premises are considered, that is, if they are separated from their movement and change and thus from the contradictory relations with other phenomena. For example, if only the premise of labour-reduction is considered, the average rate of profit can only fall as a consequence of 'labour-saving' technological innovations. Within this partial approach, deduction as in formal logic applies. However, it is only one aspect of the analysis of tendential and contradictory movements. In formal logic, results following from contradictory premises are called paradoxes. For example, 'John is a New Yorker, John says that all New Yorkers are liars'. If John is telling the truth, all New Yorkers are liars including John, who however tells the truth. Thus, John both tells the truth and lies. This conclusion follows from contradictory premises.

7.3. *The scope of the premises*

The third difference concerns the scope of the premises. Deduction, as in formal logic, requires the explicit enunciation of all the premises that are needed in order to necessarily reach an unambiguous conclusion. This is impossible in dialectical logic, and more generally in the social sciences, because all elements of reality are interconnected.[104] For example, in considering the movement of the rate of profit, one has to choose among a vast array of real contradictory causes, the premises that can explain contradictory movements. Then, one models in thought the real, contradictory and tendential movement. And, finally, one decides which of the premises is the tendency and which premises are the counter-tendencies. If the result explains the movement *in its characteristic features rather than in all its aspects*, the test is successful. The aim is a theory with explanatory power, logically consistent and evidentially correct. There will be other factors affecting that particular tendential movement. But they can be ignored if the test is successful in the above-mentioned sense. This allows us to forecast the repetition of the movement in its characteristic features *as long as those premises are unchanged*. This answers the objection that it is impossible to know that an event will recur in the future simply because it has taken place in the past. This position makes forecasts impossible.[105]

7.4. *Verification*

Just as induction and deduction differ in the two approaches, so does the verification of what has been induced and deduced. Elements of knowledge should be tested in terms both of theory and empirically.

Consider first *empirical (evidential) verification*. It refers to the empirical consistency of factual data with the knowledge (for example, theory) being

---

[104] This holds also for induction. In formal logic, 'induction is rigorously impossible' (Lefebvre 1982, p. 136).

[105] Our daily routine is based on the assumption that certain premises will not change. If I plan to go to my work tomorrow, I do it on the assumption that I will not have been fired, that the means of transportation taking me there will work, that the sun will have risen, etc. To hold that, for example, we cannot assume that rate of profit will fall in the future on the basis that it has fallen in the past is equivalent to me staying home rather than going to my work simply because I cannot rigorously assume that I have not been fired.

tested. Empiricism holds that theories should be tested on the basis of neutral data. This view clashes with the thesis held in this work that all elements of knowledge are socially, class-determined and have thus a class-content. Neutral data, in the sense of being worked-out outside theories and thus with no social content, do not exist. This implies that a theory can be empirically tested only on the basis of the data it itself produces and that data collected and manipulated within a different theoretical framework (different in the sense of a different class-content) are, by definition, inconsistent with that theory. But this conclusion would seem to clash with the fact that different theories can use the same quantitative methods and collect the same quantitative data not only to substantiate their own validity but also to invalidate alternative theories. This dilemma can be solved on the basis of what was said above on the relation between formal and dialectical logic.

Quantitative methods (such as mathematics and statistics) are specific forms of formal logic. Therefore, they can measure quantitative change, but can neither measure qualitative change (since it is impossible to measure quantitatively a change in the class-content of knowledge) nor explain quantitative and qualitative change. Taken in themselves or within the context of formal logic, *they imply a non-contradictory reality void of a qualitative dimension (in terms of social content) and thus not subject to qualitative change.* This is their social content. *However,* as argued above, *they can be used as subsidiary tools* within dialectical logic, and thus can be used *within dialectical, class-verification.* In fact, quantitative methods and data can be subsumed under dialectical verification *to analyse only the quantitative change of realised reality,* to stop, as it were, for a moment, reality's movement to gain a better insight into its inner working. This is quite different from banishing from verification society's contradictory movement and change, as formal logic does and as exclusive focus on quantitative methods and data implies. It is the disregard of this fundamental difference that creates the illusion of the class-neutrality of quantitative methods.

The question is not one of a different use of the same, socially neutral quantitative methods. There is no third, neutral, rationality from which neutral elements of knowledge (including quantitative methods and data) can be derived. Rather, like all elements of knowledge, *quantitative methods and data acquire their class-content according to the wider body of knowledge within which they are devised and developed,* according to whether they are elements of formal or of dialectical logic (verification). Within one context, they emerge as aspects of a static reality, in the sense that only quantitative changes are allowed. Within another context, they are aspects of a dynamic, contradictory reality in which changes in the social content of phenomena are focused upon. Within one context, they are constituted as elements of capital's rationality, within another of labour's rationality. Different theories can produce the same quantitative results but their qualitative, social content is different according to the class-content of the framework within which they originate and are used. This is why the same quantitative results can be used both to verify the theories within which they emerge (so that only the data worked out within a theory can be used to verify that theory) and to debunk theories with different social contents (because those data, even though quantitatively the same, have acquired a social content different from that of the theory to be debunked). To refuse this view means to deny the class-character of social reality, to avoid choosing sides.

Consider next *theoretical (consistency) verification*. If the rules of formal logic (rather than formal logic itself, that is, the social content deriving from exclusively focusing on realised reality) are used to analyse the realised aspects of reality as a technique subsumed within a dynamic view encompassing the existence of both potentials and realisations, the theoretical verification of an element of knowledge is both in terms of the rules of formal logic and of dialectical logic, in terms of that knowledge's social content. Neither the rules of formal-logical verification nor dialectical class-verification is sufficient: both are necessary. From the point of view of labour, knowledge should be both internally consistent in terms of the rules of formal logic and consistent with labour's rationality. It follows that, *whenever the rules of formal logic cannot decide among contradictory (elements of) theories (all of them internally logically consistent), it is the social, class-content that decides.* Let us take three examples.

First, different initial premises lead to different results. If both are valid in terms of formal-logical deduction, the premises and results should be chosen that fit into labour's rationality. A pertinent case is the substitution of the premise from which some results have been deduced with another premise with a different social content. For example, we shall see in Chapter 2 that Okishio's critique of Marx's law of the tendential fall of the profit-rate is invalid because that critique is based on a notion of labour as a cost, while, for Marx, labour is indeed a cost for the individual capitalists but is also, and above all, the only value-creating activity. A capitalist's replacement of labour by machines is indeed cost-reducing for that capitalist, but it decreases at the same time the (surplus-) value produced, thus decreasing the average rate of profit. In the former case (Okishio), technological innovations lead to economic growth, in the latter case (Marx) to economic crises. In the latter case (tendential fall in the average rate of profit and thus tendency towards crises and supersession), labour's struggle is the conscious manifestation of the system's objective tendency towards its supersession. In the former case (tendency towards growth), that struggle lacks an objective basis and thus becomes voluntaristic wishful thinking. Thus, the notion of labour as a cost reflects the interests of capital, that of labour as the only value-creating activity reflects the interest of labour. In spite of the fact that both views are internally consistent in terms of formal logic, it is the notion of labour as the only value-creating activity that should be chosen by labour because it is this view that reflects the interests of labour, the liberation from capital's yoke.

Second, the same premise(s) can lead to a result that is consistent in terms of the rules of formal logic but contradictory in terms of class-content with the more general theory of which it is an element. In this case, it is the social content of the more general framework that determines the social content of those elements of knowledge that are encompassed within it (and that would be contradictory to it within a different class-context). For example, the initial premises that all Caucasians are equal and that Caucasians are superior to other races can lead to a view stressing solidarity among the member of a racist group, possibly in order to dominate and oppress other racial groups. The view stressing solidarity within that racist group cannot be considered to be an expression of labour's rationality, because its social content is given by the broader (racist) theory within which that view is held. It is the solidarity functional for the abolition of exploitation, rather than for its reproduction in new forms, that is an expression of labour's rationality. More generally, given a theory, the social content of the new elements of knowledge should be consistent with the social content of the more general theoretical framework. A test of theoretical consistency of a new element of knowledge within a broader theoretical frame fails if the former carries a social content different from that of the latter.

Third, some premise(s) can lead to a result that is amenable to be interpreted in two contradictory ways. This is the case of the premise that only labour creates value, from which it can be deduced that technological innovations can either increase the average rate of profit or decrease it (see the first case). In terms of the rules of formal logic, there is no reason to adjudicate the role of the tendency to the decrease in the average rate of profit and of the counter-tendency to its increase or vice versa. But, in terms of the result's class-nature, it is the fall in the average rate of profit that should be seen as the tendency for the reason submitted in the first case.

More generally, at each stage of the process of induction and deduction, it is possible that elements of knowledge with a certain social content are allowed into a more general theoretical perspective with a different social content. It is through this contradictory process that the outcome, the new element of knowledge, derives its contradictory social content.

Chapter Two
Debates

1. Recasting the issues

To understand the crisis from the perspective of Marx's labour-theory of value requires that his theory be shown to be valid and internally consistent. But, since its appearance (and especially after the appearance of the third volume of *Capital*), Marx's theory has been the object of sustained attacks aimed at showing its logical inconsistency. The critique has centred upon four issues: abstract labour as the only source of value, the materiality of abstract labour, the law of the falling rate of profit, and the so-called 'transformation-problem'. These are crucial areas of Marxist theory. If the critiques are proven to be correct, there would be no sound platform on which to build a truly radically alternative view of capitalism and thus of its tendency towards crises and its own supersession. This is the vital question underlying the issues discussed in the following four sections.

The debate on the four aforementioned issues has been lively. However, there is a crucial dimension which has been disregarded by both sides. The focus has been mainly on the *quantitative* and *formal-logical* aspect of the issues. But, as argued in Chapter 1, formal logic cannot explain *qualitative, radical* change. And this is the limit of the debate. Looking back, this limit has been a necessary evil. Marx's critics have used the rules of formal logic and mathematical tools to support their arguments. It has then been necessary to use the same rules and tools to rebut the critique. But this is no longer sufficient. To provide a complete proof that there is no inconsistency in Marx, one has to use Marx's own method, the dialectical method (of which the tools of formal logic are an aspect) and thus the class-determined perspective, as highlighted in Chapter 1.

This chapter will argue that Marx's theory is based on a view of reality whose essential co-ordinates are time (temporalism) and non-equilibrium. It requires the use of the dialectical method of social enquiry, which is sufficient to rebut the critiques which are based on an opposite view of reality, one in which time is banned (simultaneism) and the economy is in, or tends towards, equilibrium. This latter argument rests exclusively on formal logic. The two-fold aim of what follows is not only to show Marx's internal consistency (by adopting the temporalist, non-equilibrium approach) but also to argue that, in the debate between the two camps, the dialectical view of reality has been lost. In other words, both approaches suffer from a common constraint, the exclusive reliance on (the rules of) formal logic.

In terms of formal logic, there is general agreement that an interpretation that is logically consistent in its own terms (logically valid, for short) should be preferred to one that is not. There is no agreement, however, on which interpretation to choose from in cases where two or more interpretations derived from opposite postulates are equally logically valid. In this case, the debate has not produced a commonly agreed selection-criterion. Purely in terms of formal logic, no reason has been advanced as to why one approach (the temporalist, non-equilibrium approach or the simultaneist, equilibrium-approach) should be chosen rather than another if both lead to opposite and yet internally consistent interpretations. The cause of this indeterminacy is to be found in formal logic, which is implicitly based on methodological indi-vidualism (which implies that everybody is free to choose whatever theory she likes), while dialectical logic perceives the class-determination and thus the class-content of postulates and theories. From this perspective, it is the class-content that functions as the criterion on the basis of which to choose.

In other words, *if* (and this is the essential condition) participation in the debates is meant to be an aspect of the development of a theory represent-ing and defending the cause of labour, the selection-criterion (as argued in Chapter 1) should be whether the different postulates and the interpretations deriving from them are *an instance of a wider theory of radical social change*. In short, the criterion should be an interpretation's *class-content*. If the final aim of the debate is to contribute to labour's liberation from capital, this challenge cannot be avoided. If that is not the aim, the debate is not worth being pursued and should be left to idle academic disputations. The debate, then, should change focus, from exclusive reliance on formal logic to reliance on dialectical logic (of which the tools of formal logic are one aspect). It is time to move on. The debate has to shift grounds, from a restricted focus to a wider view, from formal logic to dialectical logic, from disregard of, to emphasis on, the different interpretations' class-content. Let us then consider the four aforementioned areas of debate.

2. Abstract labour as the only source of (surplus-) value

That abstract labour is the only source of value and surplus-value is *the* fundamental assumption of Marx's economic theory. First, why should labourers create (surplus-) value? The objection most often heard is that there is no reason to exclude the means of production and the capitalists from being the producers of (surplus-) value.

Concerning the means of production, the argument can be split into two variants. The more extravagant one holds that the means of production can produce (surplus-) value in the absence of labourers. For example, Dmitriev claims that

> It is theoretically possible to imagine a case in which all products are produced exclusively by the work of machines, so that no unit of *living labour* (whether human or of any other kind) participates in production, and nevertheless an industrial profit may occur in this case under certain conditions; this is a profit which will not differ essentially in any way from the profit obtained by present-day capitalists using hired workers in production.[1]

Basically, the argument is that, in a fully automated system, a certain input of machines can create a greater output of machines (or of other commodities). In this case, profit and the rate of profit would be determined exclusively by the technology used (productivity) and not by (abstract) labour. If 10 machines

---

[1] Dmitriev 1974, p. 63.

produce 12 machines, the profit is 2 machines and the rate of profit is $2/10 =$ 20%. This approach is stillborn because of the logical inconsistency deriving from the impossibility to aggregate different use-values (e.g. machines) into a homogeneous quantity. Money could not perform this aggregating function because it would represent different use-values rather than something they all have in common and that makes comparison possible. The discussion could stop here. But let us proceed. Here, value stands for the monetary expression of (quantities of) use-values produced by machines. This has nothing to do with Marx's notion of value, which is the monetary expression of *abstract* labour expended by labourers. The argument that value can also be created by machines and that this disproves Marx's value-theory could not be more wide of the mark. This view is logically inconsistent both in its own terms (due to the problem of aggregation) and as a critique of Marx's labour-theory of value.

An apparently more plausible argument could be the following: given that (obviously) both labour and machines are needed to produce machines, it seems reasonable to postulate that value is created by both labour and machines. But, *first*, one would have to explain why, as just shown, if machines without living labour cannot produce value (in Marx's sense), they can produce value (or a part of it) in combination with living labour. *Second*, even if machines could create 'value', this value would be *use*-value rather then value as the outcome of humans' abstract labour. This implies the problem of aggregation mentioned above. *Third*, if machines can create 'value', so can an infinity of other factors (animals, the forces of nature, sunspots, etc.) and the determination of value becomes impossible. This implies also the impossibility of a theory of distribution, of prices, relating production to distribution. One would then have to fall into the subjective theory of prices (based on demand and supply) with the theoretical consequences highlighted in Section 6 below. *Fourth*, the same objections against machines creating the value of the product apply to the machines transferring their value to that of the product. In fact, they would transfer their use-value and this would immediately crash against the problem of the aggregation of different use-values. Thus, the means of production neither create nor transfer their value to the product.

Fifth, there are consequences in terms of the class-content of the theory that are of the utmost importance for labour. In this connection, it might be useful to recall that, in Marx, machines do not create value. Rather, *concrete* labour transfers the *value* of the machines (and, more generally, of the means of pro-duction) to the product. Why? If labour is always both abstract and concrete at the same time, thus if the commodity is (has) always both value and use-value at the same time, *value is incorporated in the use-value* of the commodities. Then, if the means of production are consumed and thus lose progressively their use-value through concrete labour, they lose at the same time also the value incorporated in their use-value. And, if the use-value of the means of production is transformed into the use-value of the product, the value of the means of production is not lost but is transferred by and through concrete labour to the product.

The difference between the thesis that machines create (or transfer) their value to the product and Marx's thesis that concrete labour transfers the value of the means of production to the product becomes clear if we consider Marx's critique of Senior's last hour. Suppose a working day of 8 hours and that the value produced is 80c+20v+20s = 120V, where c is constant capital, v is vari-able capital and s is surplus-value. Then, the rate of profit is 20s/100(c+v) = 20% and the rate of surplus-value is 20s/20v = 100%. For Marx, each moment of the 8 hours of *concrete* labour *transforms the use-value* of the means of pro-duction and *transfers the value* of the means of production (80c) to the product. At the same time, each moment of the 8 hours of *abstract* labour creates new value, which, in this example, is subdivided in equal parts between capital and labour: the first 4 hours for the labourers (20v) and the last 4 hours for the cap-italists (20s). The rate of surplus-value is 100%. If the working day decreases to 6 hours and if wages do not fall (v = 4), the surplus labour-time falls to 2 hours and the rate of surplus-value falls to 2/4 = 50% from 100%. Consider now Senior's argument. In the first 4 hours, labour creates the value of the machines and, in the two remaining hours, it creates the value of the means of consumption. If the working day is reduced from 8 to 6 hours, the surplus-value falls to zero instead of 2 as in Marx (given that 2 hours are needed to produce the wage-goods) and the rate of surplus-value falls to zero instead of 50% as in Marx.[2] The ideological function of rejecting the distinction between concrete and abstract labour, that is, of considering an undifferentiated notion of labour, becomes then clear: it hides the true rates of exploitation and their

---

[2] For the purposes of this discussion, 1 hour of labour is set equal to 1 unit of value.

horrible effects on the working class. As Marx exclaimed, 'Dante would have found the worst horrors of his inferno surpassed in this manufacture.'[3]

But there is another fundamental reason for rejecting the notion that machines create value. In order to comprehend it more clearly, let us anticipate some elements of Marx's theory of crises to be expounded later on in this chapter and the following chapters. For Marx, the means of production do not create value. However, they increase human productivity and thus the output per unit of capital invested, while decreasing the quantity of living labour needed for the production of a certain output. Given that only labour creates value, the substitution of the means of production for living labour decreases the quantity of value created per unit of capital invested. Since value, in the approach criticised here, would be produced by both machines and labour, the same quantity of value would be produced by a unit of capital invested, irrespective of the relative percentage-weight of machines and labour. For this approach, 90% machines and 10% labour would create just as much value as 10% machines and 90% labour (so that 90% machines would create more value than 10% machines). In Marx's theory, on the contrary, 90% machines and 10% labour create much less value than in the opposite case. It follows that, in the former case, lower profit-rates and thus crises are not originated by a decreased production of (surplus-) value due to less living labour employed, whereas for Marx this is indeed the case. In the former approach, labour-shedding and productivity-increasing technological innovations leave the production of value unchanged, so that the greater the capital invested the greater the production of value. In the latter approach (Marx), the greater the capital invested by introducing labour-shedding and productivity-increasing means of production, the greater the fall in employment, the less the value produced and incorporated in a greater quantity of output. In the former approach, technological innovations lead to economic growth. In the latter, they lead tendentially to crises. Given that labour-shedding and productivity-increasing technological innovations are the motor of capitalism's dynamic, for the former approach capitalism tends towards growth and reproduction while, for the latter (Marx), it tends towards crises and its own supersession.

If one holds that the economy tends towards growth and thus towards its own reproduction and that crises are only temporary interruptions of this

---

[3] Marx 1967a, p. 246.

growth (the countertendencies), one deprives the working class of the objective basis of its struggle. This stand makes the struggle of the working class not only a pure act of voluntarism – because it is contrary to the objective movement of the economy – but also irrational because it aims at doing away with a rational system, a system that tends towards growth and equilibrium. This is capital's view. On the other hand, the thesis that the system tends towards crises and thus its own supersession not only grounds labour's struggle on sound, objective foundations, because this struggle is in accordance with the real, objective tendential movement (growth is then seen as the countertendency), but is also rational because it aims at doing away with an irrational, exploitative, and destructive system. *Only a view stressing the capitalist economy's objective tendency towards its own supersession can provide an adequate basis for labour's cause.* The thesis that machines create value is then contrary to labour's interests. Admittedly, this is a class-determined stance. But a view of society tending towards equilibrated growth and reproduction or a view incapable of discerning the tendency from its counter-tendency (as in the case of many Marxists, see below), is equally class-determined and thus carries a definite class-content, a content inimical to labour, whether the individual theorists are aware of it or not.

The second candidate for the role as producer of value besides the labourers is the capitalists. Capital and labour would receive their share of their joint product. Income-differentials between capital and labour would be explained in terms of the 'capitalists' higher skills', 'greater responsibility', 'reward for risk-taking', and so forth (something, by the way, that makes it hard to explain why some managers' income is thousands of times higher than that of an unskilled or even a skilled labourer). As for the capitalists' responsibility, the fate of the enterprise is just as dependent on the capitalists' as on the labourers' responsibility. With regard to rewards for risk-taking, there is no empirical work whatsoever establishing a correlation between these two factors. And, as for the capitalists' higher skills, it cannot be denied that the capitalists (and thus the top managers and the whole bureaucratic structure that serves the interests of the capitalists) wield power over the labourers and that they see to it (either by force or by persuasion) that the labourers obey. The former, if they must force the latter to labour, cannot themselves labour. There is no way I can force somebody to labour and *at the same time* labour myself. The capitalist as such must perform the function of capital, which Marx calls the function of control and surveillance. Thus, inasmuch as they perform the function of capital, the capitalists cannot produce value. As a variation on the theme, managerial theories hold that value (understood by these theories as the monetary expression of use-value) is produced by both the capitalists as the organisers of the production-process and by the labourers. Marx agrees but adds that, when performing this function, the capitalists are part of the collective labourer because they organise the labour-process. But the capitalists also perform another function, the function of capital, the extraction and appropriation of surplus-value. When performing this function, they do not produce but rather expropriate and appropriate surplus-value. When they perform one function, they cannot perform the other.[4]

3. The materiality of abstract labour

For Marx, abstract labour is the 'expenditure of human labour-power in the abstract'.[5] It is the substance of value and is the expenditure of human energy irrespective of, abstracting from, the concrete, specific forms it takes (concrete labours). Concrete labour 'creates their distinctive character and makes them into concrete use-values to be distinguished from others'.[6] Since labour is always and at the same time both concrete and abstract, value is contained in the commodity as use-value before it realises itself as exchange-value, that is, before the commodity is sold. At present, the proponent of the opposite view is Chris Arthur, the major exponent of the value-form approach.[7] Arthur rejects this notion of abstract labour and thus Marx's labour-theory of value. 'My position is quite different from that of the orthodox tradition, which sees labour creating something positive, namely value, then expropriated.'[8] The author submits two critiques.

3.1. *Arthur's first critique*

The first objection is that concrete labour cannot be reduced to abstract labour. Arthur quotes the following passage from the *Grundrisse*:

---

[4] See Carchedi 1977. See also the next section for further details.

[5] Marx, 1967a, p. 200.

[6] Marx 1976b, p. 92.

[7] As Likitkijsomboon 1995 notes, there are different value-form theories. However, they all deny materiality to abstract labour (see below). In this sense, it is warranted to speak of a value-form approach.

[8] Arthur 2004b, p. 45.

> This economic relation...[of production – G.C.] develops more purely and
> adequately in proportion as labour loses all the characteristics of art; as its
> particular skill becomes something more and more abstract and irrelevant,
> and as it becomes more and more a *purely abstract activity*,...a merely *physical*
> activity, activity pure and simple, regardless of its form.[9]

This is a misreading of Marx. Marx's argument is clear: inasmuch as capitalism develops 'as a particular mode of production', labour 'becomes more and
more a purely abstract activity...a merely physical activity, activity pure and
simple, regardless of its form'.[10] In other words, labour as a purely physical
activity regardless of its specific forms, or abstract labour, emerges with the
onset of capitalism and asserts itself as capitalism becomes the dominant
mode of production. Arthur misreads this quotation *as if Marx were dealing
with the process of the deskilling of concrete labours and as if this were to culminate in
abstract labour.* But this is simply mistaken. Abstract labour emerges because
general exchangeability requires a rod with which to measure exchange-
ratios. For these ratios, the specific features of commodities and thus the
skills needed to produce them are irrelevant.[11] If Arthur's interpretation were
correct, Marx would have made a 'conceptual mistake' because deskilling,
no matter how extreme, cannot cancel all concrete qualities so that de-skilled
labour 'can never be abstract as such'.[12] But it is Arthur who makes a conceptual mistake by attributing to Marx the view that concrete labour can be
reduced to abstract labour. Marx could not be clearer: 'As use-values, commodities are, above all, of different qualities but as exchange-values they
are merely different quantities, and consequently do not contain an atom
of use-value.'[13] The rejection of Marx's notion of abstract labour on these
grounds is thus unwarranted.

3.2. *Arthur's second critique*

Let us next consider Arthur's second critique, that abstract labour lacks direct
empirical evidence:

---

[9] Arthur 2004b, p. 43.
[10] Marx 1967a, pp. 37–8.
[11] I disregard, of course, the greater value produced by skilled labour-power.
[12] Arthur 2004b, p. 44.
[13] Marx 1967a, pp. 37–8.

> The natural body of the commodity under this description [that is, as a use-value – G.C.] is clearly a substance present to inspection. To speak of 'value' as a substance, by contrast, could be taken as highly objectionable. From the time of Samuel Bailey's attack on Ricardo, such a view has been rejected (other than by Marx) in favour of an account in which there is no value substance, and insofar as it appears as a property of commodities, something they 'have', this has been analysed as a purely relational property identical with 'value in exchange' and accordingly labile.[14]

The argument seems to be: use-values can be seen to exist in their materiality before exchange but the same cannot be said of value. If value were (had) a material substance before exchange, it would have to be empirically observable during or at the end of the production-period. Since this is not the case, Arthur holds, one can justifiably call into question the materiality of abstract labour and thus the material existence of value before exchange, before it appears as exchange-value in its money-form.

At least three counter-arguments can be mentioned. First, material existence does not require observability (think of electricity). Arthur would have to explain why this is a requisite in this particular case. Second, if concrete and abstract labour are two aspects of the *same* human activity, that is, of labour (a proposition no value-form theorist calls into question, to the best of my knowledge) and if concrete labour is a material substance existing before exchange, why is it not the same for abstract labour? Third, aside from these two objections, it can be shown that *abstract labour* and thus the substance value, *can be observed to be a material substance expended during production and thus existing materially before exchange*.[15] If this is the case, what can be observed at the moment of exchange is the social form of existence of that pre-exchange material substance, namely abstract labour.

The following argument cannot be explicitly found in Marx. However, it is inherent in and consistent with his work as the following quotation shows:

---

[14] Arthur 2004b, pp. 154–6.

[15] There are many similarities between Arthur and the precursors of the value-form approach. For example, 'Rubin's approach shows a certain "discomfort" with the materiality of the production process of human life'. This leads him 'to an inverted conception of the relationship between production and exchange.' Kicillof and Starosta 2007a, p. 16. This inverted relation is a feature of Arthur's approach, and, more generally, of other value-form theorists, to be discussed below.

What Lucretius says is self-evident; 'nil posse creari de nihilo,' out of nothing, nothing can be created. Creation of value is transformation of labour-power into labour. Labour-power itself is energy transferred to a human organism by means of nourishing matter.[16]

This is a description of human metabolism, a notion well known to Marx and Engels:

The concept of metabolism was already widespread within biology, chemistry and physiology at the time they [that is, Marx and Engels – G.C.] were writing and was used by many other thinkers with whom they were familiar, including Liebig, whose influence on Marx and Engels's work was much more profound.[17]

The human metabolism shows that people, irrespective of their differences, produce the *same* type of energy and thus consume the *same* type of energy, no matter which specific activities they engage in. More specifically, the human metabolism is a two-stage process. In the anabolic phase, human energy is produced in the form of calories[18] and stored. There are, of course, differences between the organs and functions of different individuals, but these differences do not affect the *general, common* way in which we all produce energy in the aforementioned form. This stored-up energy is nothing else than our labour-power, the capacity to transform both the reality external to us and the knowledge of this outer world. This phase is followed by the catabolic phase, the use of the stored energy. This use or expenditure cannot but be the *consumption of the same type of energy* (calories). Both the storage and the expenditure of human energy, of calories, is a material process: the storage is the transformation of 'nourishing matter' into calories and thus in labour-power and the expenditure is the 'transformation of labour-power into labour'. Being a material process, it is also a real process.

The expenditure of human energy is measured in medicine by referring to the basic metabolic rate (that is, the amount of energy or calories the body of an average individual sitting and at rest burns to maintain itself in its resting

[16] Marx 1967a, p. 215.
[17] Burkett and Foster 2008, p. 152. After reading this work, I realise that, in Carchedi forthcoming, I state erroneously that the notion of metabolism was not known to Marx.
[18] Along with ATP (Adenosine 5'-triphosphate) as well.

state). For example, the direct calorimetry-method involves placing a person in an insulated chamber. As the person's body heat is released, it raises a layer of water surrounding the chamber, and this allows scientists to measure the temperature. A kilocalorie (Kcal) is the amount of heat it takes to raise the temperature of one litre of water by 1 degree celsius. In this manner, one can calculate the number of calories a person expends. Various types of activities use different quantities of energy as shown by tables of metabolic rates. This is commonly done by sports-institutions. For example, in 10 minutes, 227 Kcal are needed to run at 8 kilometres per hour, 225 of the *same* Kcal to play squash, 116 of the *same* Kcal to windsurf, etc. *Human energy in the abstract does exist, is material and its expenditure can be measured.*

It is because of the aforementioned reasons that abstract labour is a real process, in the sense of a 'physiological' process,[19] a 'material' process,[20] the expenditure of the same type of human energy, of human energy in the abstract. As Marx says: 'all labour is an expenditure of human labour-power, in the physiological sense, and it is in this quality of being equal, or abstract, human labour that it forms the value of commodities'.[21] Abstract labour is a '*purely abstract activity*, a purely mechanical activity…a merely *formal* activity, or, what is the same, a merely *material* [*stofflich*] activity, activity pure and simple'.[22] Or, labour-power is 'the energy transferred to a human organism by means of nourishing matter'.[23] The observation of the expenditure of calories during production is the observation of abstract labour. If one wanted to, one could measure a labourer's physical fatigue or the consumption of calories while at the same time observing her producing a specific use-value, that is, engaging in concrete labour. Denial of the existence of the material substance of value is simply incompatible with modern medical science. Therefore, it lacks the scientificity needed by labour for its struggle against capital. Some might agree, but object that what we see is abstract human labour, the substance of value, and not value itself. However, if the substance of value can be observed to exist *materially* and therefore can be measurable before exchange, it can safely be concluded that value also exists *materially* and is measurable before exchange, whether value is observable or not.

---

[19] Marx 1976a, p. 137.
[20] Marx 1973a, p. 297.
[21] Marx 1976a, p. 137.
[22] Marx 1973a, p. 297; emphasis in the original.
[23] Marx 1967a, p. 215.

Milios asserts that 'Value is determined by abstract labor. But abstract labor is not an empirical magnitude that can be measured with a stopwatch. It is an "abstraction" constituted (that is, acquiring tangible existence) in the process of exchange (which does not take place just in the mind of the theoretician).'[24] The above shows that this assertion is unfounded. Marx's assertion that 'Social labour-time exists in these commodities in a latent state, so to speak, and becomes evident only in the course of their exchange',[25] far from rejecting the material and quantifiable nature of abstract labour, supports this thesis because 'latent' in Marx means potential, as argued in Chapter 1. By holding that the difference between values and prices (of production) 'is a difference between two incommensurate and hence not comparable "entities" which are, however, integrated in a notional link connecting causal determinations (values) and their forms of appearance (prices)' and by stressing that 'at certain points in volume 3 of *Capital* (especially when dealing with the "transformation of values into prices of production"), Marx distances himself from the implications of his own theory (incommensurability between value and price), making quantitative comparisons between values and production prices',[26] Milios discovers yet another theoretical ambivalence in Marx. But this supposed ambivalence derives from the unfounded principle that values and prices are quantitatively not comparable. If values are potential prices, that is, if prices are values after redistribution, the ambivalence fades away (see Section 5 of this chapter). The thesis defended by Milios that 'the transition from values to production prices is conceptual, not quantitative,' is yet another way to solve a non-existent problem.

Whether value-form theorists are aware of it or not, the denial of the material existence of abstract labour, or, more precisely, of the material existence of the abstract labour embodied in a commodity before that commodity's exchange and therefore also after exchange, clashes with the reality of the human metabolism. If the original aim of the value-form approach was (under the neo-Ricardian attack) to avoid the transformation-'problem' by denying the existence of value before its exchange, the strategy has misfired. The value-form approach, to be credible, must show that the human metabolism does not exist or that it can be justifiably assumed not to exist. Marx's

[24] Milios 2009, pp. 264–5.
[25] Quoted in Milios 2009, p. 264.
[26] Milios 2009, p. 267.

premise, upon which *Capital* rests, that abstract labour is the expenditure of human energy irrespective of the specific (concrete) activities carried out, stands firmly with both feet on sound scientific, theoretical and empirically observable ground.

At this juncture, three crucial points should be stressed. First, the argument concerning the real, material existence of abstract labour as the expenditure of homogeneous, undifferentiated human energy as measured for example by Kcal is *not* meant to reformulate Marx's analysis of value simply in terms of the expenditure of human energy in the abstract. There is no question here of energy-reductionism. But it should be stressed that abstract labour does imply the expenditure of human energy in the abstract and that, therefore, it is both material and measurable.[27] However, abstract labour, while having a metabolic dimension (the expenditure of human energy in the abstract), is not reducible to that dimension only. *Abstract labour is the social dimension of that metabolic process and therefore value is the social evaluation of the expenditure of human energy.* For example, the same amount of calories can be expended in an hour by a skilled as well as by an unskilled labourer. Yet the value created by the former is greater than that created by the latter because society's previous labour and thus society's previous expenditure of human energy needed to form the former's labour-power has been greater than that needed to form the latter's. This does not mean that if the creation of a skilled labourer's labour-power has cost twice as much as that of an unskilled labourer, the former labourer creates necessarily in an hour double as much value as the latter. It all depends on the social valuation of different types of labour-power at the moment the labourer expends her labour-power. For example, a certain skilled labourer's labour-power might be devalued because, due to technological improvements, that labour-power might now cost less to be produced than it had cost previously; or a certain type of skilled labour might have become useless or less desired; or the value of the unskilled labourer's labour-power might have risen, etc. The relation between the value of (different levels of) skilled labour-power and unskilled labour-power depends on their social valuation. In an hour, a skilled labourer produces a (socially determined) multiple of the value created by an unskilled labourer. But,

---

[27] For a convincing critique of an influential energy-reductionist author, Podolinsky, see Burkett and Foster 2008.

given a certain social valuation of a skilled labour, two hours of expenditure of human energy in the abstract by that skilled labourer produce double as much value as one hour. The same holds for unskilled labour.

Thus, the aim of the argument submitted here is not to reduce abstract labour (and thus value) to an ahistorical metabolic process. Rather, the aim is to rebut the critique concerning Marx's notion of abstract labour and to argue that this metabolic dimension is perfectly consonant with the architecture of Marx's value-analysis, in that it provides the material and thus the objective substratum of a social process. It follows that, *if human energy in the abstract is both material and quantifiable before exchange, so must be its social evaluation and thus abstract labour and thus value*. Without this material and objective dimension, the value of commodities becomes arbitrary, it lacks an objective basis for its quantitative determination. Value-form theory, in whatever variation, cannot explain why more intensive labour creates a measurable multiple of less intensive labour or why skilled labour creates a measurable multiple of unskilled labour. As Burkett and Foster put it, Marx and Engels's approach 'was both historical and metabolic. While incorporating energetic factors, it also recognised the irreducibly material (including biochemical) and irreducibly social character of human production'.[28]

Second, the physiological and material expenditure of undifferentiated human energy does not imply that this material expenditure excludes the production of knowledge and thus human consciousness. The expenditure of material, undifferentiated human energy encompasses the *working of the whole human body,* that is, it comprises the physiological expenditure due to the working of the human brain as well. The material expenditure of human energy is not equivalent to 'manual' labour or to any other such concept that excludes 'brain work'. I know of no passage where Marx holds a notion of a machine-like type of material expenditure of undifferentiated human energy as if it excluded the working of the brain and thus the production of knowledge. And this is certainly not the thesis of this work. Abstract labour can be expended both in 'material' labour (production of 'material' objects) and in mental labour (production of knowledge).[29]

---

[28] Burkett and Foster 2008, p. 154.
[29] We shall see in Chapter 4 below that it is incorrect to speak of material labour as opposed to mental labour. That is why the term material has been placed within quotation marks. The correct term is objective labour.

Third, the expenditure of undifferentiated human energy is common not only to all people but also to all people in all societies. In this sense, it is trans-epochal. Nevertheless, its discovery as a trans-epochal phenomenon is socially determined and its practical significance (as abstract labour and thus as the substance of value) is socially specific. It is perhaps not by chance that studies on the human metabolism started in the seventeenth century with Sanctorious Sanctorious (1561–1636), just as it might not be by chance that Sanctorious wanted to apply the principles of mechanics to the problems of health and sickness. In his book *Ars de statica medecina* (1614), which was translated into English during the eighteenth century, he reports experiments in which he weighed himself in a chair suspended from a steelyard-balance, before and after eating, sleeping, working, making love, fasting, deprived from drinking, and excreting. He found that by far the greatest part of the food he took in was lost from the body through *perspiratio insensibilis* (perspiration which, contrary to sweat, cannot be perceived by our senses).[30] The reason why abstract labour is socially relevant as the substance of value only under capitalism is that, in a society in which the different products of labour (use-values) must be exchanged, there must also be a feature common to all different concrete labours. This is abstract labour. Far from being a 'metaphor', the existence of abstract labour in all modes of production is a socially determined *real abstraction*, in the sense that it is a notion abstracted from a real process, the undifferentiated expenditure of human energy in the *capitalist* production-process, and then applied to all societies. An analogy can be drawn with the way Marx conceptualises the laws of motion. They are 'the same under all modes of production'[31] and thus 'cannot be done away with. What can change in historically different circumstances is only the *form* in which these laws assert themselves'.[32] Similarly, it can be said that the expenditure of undifferentiated human energy is 'the same under all modes of production' and 'cannot be done away with', yet it is its historical and social specificity that counts.

Thus, there can be no question that value does have a material substance before exchange abstract labour. Yet Arthur holds that Marx held contradictory views. Arthur mentions the following quotation from Marx: 'not an atom

---

[30] See Guthrie 1967, p. 190.
[31] Marx 1967b, p. 790.
[32] Marx 1969a, p. 419; emphasis in the original.

of matter enters into the objectivity of commodities as values'. Arthur reads this quotation as if Marx contradicted himself, as if, for Marx, abstract labour were not the conceptualisation of the material substance of a social process. But this is not the case. What Marx says is that not an atom of the matter *of use-values* enters into the objectivity of commodities as *values*. In fact, the text continues 'in this it [the objectivity of commodities as values – G.C.] is the direct opposite of the coarsely sensuous objectivity of commodities as physical objects [that is, as use-values – G.C.].' And further: 'we may twist and turn a single commodity [as a use-value – G.C.] as we wish; it remains impossible to grasp it as a thing possessing value'. And finally, 'as exchange-values [commodities – G.C.] are merely different quantities, and consequently do not contain *an atom of use-value*'.[33]

Let us read Marx's text further:

> If, however, we bear in mind that the value of the commodities has a *purely social reality*, and that they acquire this reality only insofar as they are expressions or embodiments of one identical social substance, viz., human labour, it follows as a matter of course, that value can only manifest itself in the social relation of commodity to commodity.[34]

This passage has been read as if Marx, by stressing the purely social character of value, denied the materiality of abstract labour and thus of value. The critics think they have found yet another logical inconsistency in Marx. In reality, what Marx means and cannot but mean is that the materiality of abstract labour is purely social because it acquires social significance only under capitalism. Outside of capitalism, abstract labour is not value. *It is the social setting that confers the quality of being (creating) value to abstract labour. But this does not deny the materiality of abstract labour and the possibility of it being quantified.* Value is the specific social dimension of a material and quantifiable reality. It is neither only physical, irrespective of the social relations within which it is produced, nor only social, irrespective of its materiality: it is *both*.[35]

---

[33] Marx 1967a, pp. 37–8; emphasis added.
[34] Marx 1967a, p. 47; emphasis added.
[35] For similar conclusions see Kicillof and Starosta 2007b, p. 16. The question as to whether value is a quantity *or* a historically specific social relation (as submitted by Milios 2009, p. 260) is thus misleading and creates a false alternative.

3.3. *Two more value-form approaches to abstract labour*

There are other angles than Arthur's own from which the value-form approach denies materiality to abstract labour. Here, I shall focus on two other value-form theorists.

Patrick Murray's position is, in many ways, close to mine. I share with this author a range of concepts relating more-or-less directly to the question of the (im)materiality of abstract labour, such as the rejection of the thesis of the neutrality of the forces of production,[36] along with the view that, for Marx, value was only a natural substance,[37] and what Murray calls the 'Rubin dilemma', that is, 'that it is not possible to reconcile a physiological concept of abstract labour with the historical character of the value it creates'.[38] I also agree with Murray that 'Marx's theory of value is nothing but his theory of the distinctive social form of wealth and labour in capitalism';[39] that Marx's notion of value is purely social (but, for me, in the sense specified above); that *Capital* begins with 'commodity *capital* and *surplus-value* producing capital';[40] that the commodity is the right starting point for Marx's *Capital*[41]; and that value is not fully actualised in production but rather requires that the commodity be sold (but, in the sense of my own perspective, whereby the value contained is a quantity that must realise itself through exchange, as a modified quantity).

Moreover, Murray distinguishes among (a) the general concept of labour, which concerns 'the essential features of any actual act of human labour';[42] (b) the general concept of abstract labour, which is the 'pure expenditure of human energies';[43] and (c) the concept of 'practically abstract' labour, that is a historically specific abstract labour, the only type of value-producing labour under capitalism.[44] Categories (b) and (c) correspond broadly to my categories of trans-historical abstract labour (both objective and mental) and of capitalist abstract labour respectively. However, there is a fundamental difference.

---

[36] Murray 2000, p. 28.

[37] Murray 2000, p. 59.

[38] Murray 2000, p. 53.

[39] Murray 2000, p. 29.

[40] Murray 2000, p. 42; emphasis in the original.

[41] Murray 2000, p. 62. As Likitkijsomboon 1995, p. 82 points out, one must start from the commodity in order to understand money.

[42] Murray 2000, p. 48.

[43] Ibid.

[44] Ibid.

For Murray, general abstract labour is 'nothing actual'.[45] 'To treat commodities as if they "embodied" abstract labour is to reify a distinction of reason; it is to treat an analytical abstraction as if it picked out some actual, natural or natural-like property of a product.'[46] Murray's 'general abstract labour', then, lacks materiality and is not contained in the commodity before exchange. What, then, exactly is abstract labour for this author?

As Murray puts it in a private communication, 'My abstract labor does lack materiality...value is an objective property of the commodity...but this objectivity is a purely social reality and immaterial'. However, 'there must be potential value or else there would be nothing to be validated or realized in exchange.' This potential value is concrete value that must be validated as abstract labour through exchange: 'to have value-producing labor, the social validation of concrete labor must involve a social practice (exchange in the market) that actually treats concrete labor as abstract'. In short, by being exchanged on the market, concrete labour becomes abstract.

This position is far from Marx, from his view of 'the two-fold nature of the process of production itself – which, on the one hand, is a social process for producing use-values, on the other, a process for creating surplus-value'.[47] Use-values acquire a social nature in production before this social nature manifests itself in exchange. The social nature of the production of use-values is that they are produced (1) by the non-owners of the means of production who, under developed capitalism, are not the individual but the collective labourer, that is, the whole of the labourers producing a use-value through the articulation of the different tasks needed for the production of that use-value; (2) for the capitalist who, under developed capitalism, is the appropriator(s) of surplus-value extracted by a complex bureaucracy of many individuals each performing a different aspect of the work of exploitation – what Marx calls the work of control and surveillance. Of course, those use-values must be sold but this only realises what is potentially present in them, their use for the purchasers: 'The use-value of a commodity does not serve its end, does not begin to function until the commodity enters the sphere of consumption. So long as it is in the hands of the producer, it exists only in potential form.'[48] In

---

45 Murray 2000, p. 48.
46 Murray 2000, p. 58.
47 Marx 1967a, pp. 331–2.
48 Marx 1967b, p. 279.

short, for Marx, *both* use-values and value exist before, but must be validated (realised) through, exchange. For Murray, and more generally for the value-form approach, use-values are validated as value through exchange.

Lack of conformity with Marx is, in and of itself, no reason for rejection. There are, however, three reasons why Murray's approach is untenable. The first is that it is impossible to *treat* concrete labour as if it were abstract labour. Concrete labours are, by definition, different and they cannot be treated as equal (exchanged) unless there is something that homogenises them *before* they can be exchanged. This is abstract labour. In other words, labour must already be abstract for it to be treated as abstract. Like the neo-Ricardian approach to be discussed in Section 5 below, this approach crashes up against the incommensurability problem. It is precisely because of this problem that Marx introduced abstract labour at the level of production. Second, for Murray, use-values are validated as values through and at the moment of exchange so that concrete labours are transformed into abstract labour, value, also through and at the moment of exchange. However, *at the moment of exchange, the use-value of the commodity sold is null*, the commodity sold has no use-value for the seller for the simple reason that the seller cannot use it any longer. Exchange would conjure up value out of nothing.[49] Third, if concrete labour is created in production and thus is both material and embodied in the product before exchange (a non-contentious point) and if abstract labour is socially validated concrete labour in exchange, then the substance of abstract labour, use-values, is both material and embodied in the commodity *before exchange*, contrary to Murray's stated position.

The second value-form author to be briefly discussed here is Michael Heinrich. This author builds his argument without any reference to Hegelian dialectics. Heinrich is to be commended because of his rejection of an equilibrium-approach[50] and because of his insistence that production and realisation form a unity, a whole. But Heinrich, too, is critical of Marx. His

---

[49] The commodity might have a subjective value for the seller but this is irrelevant unless one steps over to a subjectivist theory of prices, that is, unless one leaves Marx definitely. The price for this move is given by the internal contradictions pointed out in Section 6 below.

[50] 'Marx tries to show that...in capitalist economies we find an inherent *instability*, which does not come from the outside but is in the basic structures of capitalism itself'. Heinrich 2004a, p. 89.

starting point is that the notions of value, value-form and money are ambivalent.[51] More specifically, one can find in *Capital* elements of two distinct approaches to value. The *substantialist* theory of value focuses on the value of 'the *single* commodity' and the labour contained in it. This value is socially determined only inasmuch as it is socially-necessary labour. But, in the substantialist approach, value seems to have nothing to do with other commodities, it exists as a kind of independent substance inside the single commodity. Combined with this substantialist view on value, there is thus a *naturalist* view of abstract labour, a notion of abstract labour in the physiological sense. Heinrich submits that this substantialist/naturalist approach does not break with classical political economy. Such a break requires a non-substantialist theory of value and an anti-naturalist determination of abstract labour. From this perspective, value depends not only on a social substance, it depends also on a substance that cannot exist in a single commodity and that is not determined by production alone. It follows that value can only exist if there is an independent and general form of value – money.

These are the main contours of Heinrich's argument. Problems arise within it because commodities are not produced in isolation. Therefore, capitalist abstract labour and value exist in a single commodity (before exchange). A single commodity is a fraction of the whole. If the whole has a certain characteristic, so does a part of it, given that both are the product of the same undifferentiated human labour under the same capitalist production-relations. Money is the necessary form of existence of capitalist abstract labour and value.

What is missing not only in Heinrich but in all participants in the value-debate (both on the value-form side and elsewhere) is Marx's *dialectical* view of social reality, the view of social reality as a temporal flow of contradictory phenomena changing from being determining to being determined and vice versa and continuously emerging from a potential state to become realised and going back to a potential state. What is missing is the view of social phenomena as both realised and potential, as both determinant and determined, and as subject to constant movement and change. The consequences arising from the lack of these distinctions is exemplified by the statement that value

---

[51] Heinrich 2004b.

cannot exist in a single thing and is not determined by production alone. While it is true that production and distribution (circulation) form a whole, it is production that is determinant vis-à-vis distribution, because only what is produced can determine what is distributed and because the social character of production determines the social character of distribution (see Chapter 1). It is in this sense that production and distribution form a unity, a contradictory unity in determination. It follows that individual value does exist in a single commodity but only in a *potential* state, as a potentially realisable value before realisation and thus before its value contained is redistributed through and at the moment of sale (this is the transformation-procedure, or the price-forming process to be discussed in Section 5 below). The phantom-like actualisation of value as presented in the value-form approach is nothing more than its redistribution through exchange. It is the quantitatively realised value by each commodity that is determined by both production and distribution in their contradictory relation. As for money, Heinrich holds that '[i]n the traditional Marxist view, the main thing was to show that the value of a commodity is dependent on the amount of labor embodied. Money only counts as means of circulation'.[52] This 'traditional Marxist view' is a straw man. No serious Marxist would determine the value of a commodity only in terms of the value contained within it. This is certainly not Marx's theory, which is based on the dialectical relation between production and distribution. On the other hand, Marxian value-theory is not a 'monetary theory of value', if this is meant to be a denial of the physiological, material nature of abstract labour and of the fundamental principle (a common-sense principle) that only what exists potentially can become realised.

I agree with Heinrich that Marx's work is incomplete, that it is the result of a long process of self-clarification and that it can be interpreted in different ways. This, however, does not imply necessarily that it is internally contradictory or ambivalent, especially on questions of such fundamental importance as those discussed here. And, in any case, the point is whether an interpretation is available that unifies apparently contradictory statements into a coherent whole. This is indeed the case with the notion of abstract labour submitted here. There is thus no reason to introduce other notions of abstract labour if these notions create logical contradictions in Marx's theory.

---

[52] Heinrich 2004b.

3.4. *The inconsistencies of the value-form*

A few inconsistencies have already been pointed out in the three value-form theorists just discussed. Let us now provide a more complete and systematic assessment by considering once again Arthur's work.

3.4.1. *Abstract labour*

As was seen above, for Arthur, abstract labour (in Marx's sense) does not produce value since there is no value in production yet. However, capital does not produce value either. Capital's work of exploitation cannot be abstract: 'I never argued it is abstract.'[53] In a previous critique, I wrongly stated that, for Arthur, capital produces value.[54] It should be said, however, that my mistake was not without justification. As Arthur concedes,

> It seems that the point causing difficulty here is that I have not sufficiently made clear [that] I attribute to capital as a social form the positing of the product of labour as value. A related point is that although I slip into the standard terminology by speaking of the 'creation' and 'production' of value, I reject any analogy here with material production.[55]

However, in his recent book, Arthur repeats, quite confusingly, that 'to be the source of new value is to be that out of which capital *creates* value'.[56] Notice also that the question as to whether capital creates value or not in production is eluded rather than answered by using the vague term 'posits', that is, capital affirms the existence of value in production.

For Arthur, if capital does not create value, it *posits* value in production. More specifically, concrete labour 'becomes socially posited as abstract in virtue of its participation in the capitalist process of valorisation',[57] because it is exploited by capital. And why is this so? 'The reason why [concrete – G.C.] labour is properly conceptualised as 'abstract' within the capital relation [of production – G.C.] is that industrial capital treats all labours as identical because it has an equal interest in exploiting them regardless of their concrete

---

[53] Arthur 2004a, p. 18.
[54] Carchedi 2003a.
[55] Arthur 2004a, p. 18.
[56] Arthur 2004b, p. 211; emphasis in the original.
[57] Arthur 2004b, p. 45.

specificity.'[58] Thus, by subjugating concrete labours to exploitation irrespective of their specificities, capital treats them as equal and thus posits them as 'abstract'.[59] This view is flawed on at least three accounts. First, as mentioned in discussing Murray, to treat concrete labour as if it were abstract does not mean that the former becomes the latter. Due to the incommensurability-problem, labour must already be abstract for it to be treated as such.

Second, suppose it were possible for capital to treat different use-values equally in the process of exploitation, thus erasing their specificities. In this case, given that concrete labours are such in virtue of those specificities, what would be left would not be abstract labour as a pure form devoid of content but rather nothing would remain. Abstract labour as pure form, exploitation without the object exploited, is a figment of the imagination, a metaphor lacking substantiation in reality.

Third, in spite of an equal interest in exploiting different use-values, it is *not* possible for capital to treat different use-values equally in the process of exploitation. It is certainly true that capital has an *equal interest* in exploiting all different concrete labours irrespective of their specificities. But this does not imply that it exploits them *equally*. There is no general, equal way to carry out what Marx calls in *Capital*, Volume III, the work of control and surveillance, a way to control and keep labourers under watch that is indifferent to the object of surveillance. Concrete labours are, by definition, different. If they are different, *each one of them is exploited in its own specific, different way*. There are as many works of control and surveillance as there are concrete labours. The caretaker and the engineer working under capitalist production-relations are both exploited. But the way the former is exploited differs from how the latter is exploited. Arthur might assert that, if all concrete labours are exploited by capital, they acquire a common characteristic which 'abstractly negates all difference of use-value between commodities and thereby declares them all identical as values'.[60] But capital's practice shows that the opposite is true, that the work of control and surveillance can only be concrete and differentiated, in spite of capital's equal interest in exploitation, that it is not possible

---

[58] Arthur 2004b, p. 42. See also Arthur 2001, p. 23.

[59] While, for Murray, concrete labours are homogenised because they all produce use-values for exchange, for Arthur, the homogenising factor is that they are all equally subjected to exploitation.

[60] Arthur 2004b, p. 41.

for capital to treat different use-values equally in the process of exploitation, and that, therefore, capital's exploitation cannot 'declare' use-values as equal, as abstract labour. Capital's actual practice, the reality of capitalist exploitation, can only re-affirm the differences between the objects of its exploitation. On this account as well, Arthur's approach cannot theorise abstract labour in production. 'Carchedi's proof that the labour of supervision is concrete only'[61] far from being 'irrelevant' is precisely the crux of the matter.

But 'abstract labour is constituted in the capitalist relation as well as in commodity exchange'.[62] In Arthur's words, it is 'the exchange abstraction itself [that – G.C.] posits value'[63] or, even more clearly, *'only the very fact of being exchanged unites the commodities generally'*.[64] Two objections can be raised here as well.

First, on the one hand, concrete labour 'becomes socially posited as abstract in virtue of its participation in the capitalist process of valorisation'.[65] On the other, it is 'the nature of commodity exchange which abstracts from...the entire substance of use-value'.[66] If these two notions are unrelated, Arthur has a problem. If they are related, *how* are they related? Arthur does not pose this question, let alone answer it.[67] The problem is magnified by the introduction of money. Arthur holds that money 'does not merely solve the *quantitative* problem of providing a measure common to values, it solves the *qualitative* problem of establishing the very commensurability of commodities through relating them to each other as values'.[68] Which aspect of the quantitative commensurability of use-values is expressed by money? The fact that they are all 'equally' subjected to exploitation or that they are all produced for exchange?

---

[61] Arthur 2004a, p. 18.
[62] Arthur 2004a, p. 14.
[63] Arthur 2004b, p. 95.
[64] Arthur 2004b, p. 158; emphasis in the original.
[65] Arthur 2004b, p. 45.
[66] Arthur 2004b, p. 153.
[67] 'Arthur thinks that he can, and must, determine what the value-form is in terms of the sphere of exchange independently of production' (Murray 2005, p. 70). But, for Arthur, 'abstract labor is constituted in the capitalist relation as well as in commodity exchange'. The point is that abstract labour in production and abstract labour in exchange are unrelated.
[68] Arthur 2004b, p. 99.

Second, this position forecloses a price-theory. As Arthur explains, 'There is no such thing as "intrinsic value", only conjunctural correlations of different amounts of use-values'.[69] But, then, *any* exchange-ratio goes, including the exchange of a transatlantic ship for a pencil. Exchange-ratios are simply 'shaped by external conditions'[70] and no explanation is offered of their level or of the relative stability of prices. More than a theory of exchange-ratios, this is an open admission of the inability to provide such a theory. Even a price-theory based on the interplay of supply and demand, in spite of its numerous contradictions (see Section 6 below), is superior to this 'determination' of exchange-ratios.

3.4.2. *Concrete labour*

The difference between Arthur and Marx does not concern the notion of concrete labour. Rather, divergent views emerge concerning the assessment of its role in the production-process, especially in the complex and fragmented production-process. For Marx, 'As the commodity is immediate unity of use-value and exchange-value, so the process of production, which is the *process of the production of commodity,* is the immediate unity of process of labour and process of valorisation.'[71] Then, the labour-process is the transformation by the labourers of use-values into new use-values through their concrete labour, through the specific form of their activity; and the (surplus-) value-producing process (the valorisation-process) is the process through which the capitalists force the labourers to labour for a time longer than that needed for the reproduction of their labour-power. As the capitalist production-process increases in complexity and is segmented due to the technical division of labour, the individual labourer develops into the collective labourer and a 'directing authority' is needed 'in order to secure the harmonious working of the individual activities...A single violin player is his own conductor; an orchestra requires a separate one.'[72] And, Marx adds, 'If, then, the control of the capitalist is *in substance two-fold* by reason of the two-fold nature of the process of production itself – which, on the one hand, is a social process for

---

[69] Arthur 2004b, p. 93.
[70] Arthur 2004b, p. 156.
[71] Marx 1976b, p. 81.
[72] Marx 1967a, pp. 330–1.

producing use-values, on the other, a process for creating surplus-value – *in form* that control is despotic.'[73]

In other words, on the one hand, the labour-process must be co-ordinated. The function of co-ordination and unity of the labour-process *is part of the function of labour even though carried out in a despotic form*. On the other hand, the function of capital, the work of control and surveillance, is performed not any longer (only) by the capitalist but by a bureaucratic structure, going from the top managers to the first line-supervisors, that performs that function on behalf of and for the benefit of the capitalist as the appropriator of surplus-value. 'An industrial army of workmen, under the command of a capitalist, requires, like a real army, officers (managers), and sergeants (foremen, over-lookers), who, while the work is being done, command in the name of the capitalist. The work of supervision becomes their established and exclusive function.'[74] Put simply, the same person who is a co-ordinator of the labour-process may be a worker (it does not matter that she co-ordinates the pro-duction of use-values in a despotic way, as long as her task is part of the production of those use-values) and also an agent of capital if she carries out the work of control and surveillance (without being necessarily a capital-ist). 'The genuine, specific function of capital ... is the [extraction and – G.C.] appropriation of unpaid labour.'[75]

It is here that the difference between Marx and Arthur emerges. While the notion of use-value is the same in Marx as in Arthur, the question as to who creates use-values is answered in two radically different ways. For Marx, the work of co-ordination of the labour-process is part of the labour-process itself, that is, is part of the function of labour, of the collective transformation of use-values. Therefore, for Marx, neither the capitalist (as the *ap*propriator of surplus-value) nor the agents of capital (the *ex*propriators of surplus-value) perform the function of labour. Capital does not produce the commodity: labour does. For Arthur, on the other hand,

> Since all [labourers – G.C.] contribute piecemeal to the process of production, the whole is not constituted as their productive power but as that of the

---

[73] Marx 1967a, pp. 331–2; emphasis added.
[74] Ibid.
[75] Marx 1976b, p. 80. These themes are only hinted at here. They are developed in Carchedi 1977, 1983, 1987, 1991.

capital hiring them. This means not only that each individual does not produce a commodity but that since the collective labourer is set up under the direction of capital it is hard to say that the collective does either. It seems more reasonable to say that capital produces the commodity than that labour does.[76]

Or, the commodities 'are taken as products of capital'.[77] Arthur quotes Marx to the effect that 'Capital...necessarily produces commodities, produces its product as commodities, or it produces nothing'.[78] Taken out of context, it would seem that, for Marx, it is capital, rather than labour, that produces the commodity. But a cursory glance at Marx's text shows very clearly that here 'capital' is used by Marx as a shortcut for 'capitalist mode of production'. This quotation is preceded by the sentence 'it is only on the basis of *capitalist production* that the commodity first becomes the *general* form of the product'[79] and is followed by the sentence: 'Therefore...that the value of the commodity is determined by the socially necessary labour time contained in it, first come to be realised with the development *of capitalist production, that is, of capital.*'[80] Thus, it is the capitalist mode of production and not capital (as opposed to labour) that produces commodities. But, be that as it may, the point is not whether Arthur is in conformity with Marx. The point is whether Arthur's alternative approach is free from inconsistencies.

Since, as seen above, capital does not produce the value of the commodity (it posits, it affirms the existence of, that value by equally exploiting concrete labours), the statement that capital produces the commodity can only be understood as capital producing the *use-value* of the commodity, its empirically observable form. Arthur can hold this position because he departs from Marx's analysis of the production-process on a significant point, the work of co-ordination and unity of the labour-process. More specifically, Arthur (a) ignores the fundamental distinction between the function of capital and the function of labour; (b) fails to see that the capitalists (and other agents of capital) can perform this double function, that is, that as co-ordinators of the labour-process they are part of labour and as supervisors and controllers of

---

[76] Arthur 2004b, pp. 47–8.
[77] Arthur 2004b, p. 41; see also pp. 47–8.
[78] Arthur 2004b p. 28.
[79] Ibid. Emphasis added.
[80] Ibid. Emphasis added.

the same process they are part of capital (even if these two functions might be combined in the same person); and (c) therefore mistakes the despotic form of that aspect of the function of labour (co-ordination and unity of the labour-process) for an aspect of the function of capital. What conclusions follow from this stance?

First, if the individual labourers participate in the labour-process, even though piecemeal, it would seem reasonable to conclude that the commodity is the product of the joint effort of capital (because it co-ordinates and unifies labour, which, for Arthur, is the function of capital) and of labour. But this would contradict the assertion that 'It seems more reasonable to say that capital produces the commodity than that labour does'. Second, Arthur, on the one hand, holds that labour does not produce the commodity,[81] while holding, on the other, that 'workers can produce more than they consume and, hence, there is a surplus product'.[82] This is an inconsistency here. Third, if the labourers do not produce the commodity, *they labour but do not produce*. The capitalists do produce the commodity by co-ordinating the labour-process. However, '*qua* capitalists they do not labour'.[83] They produce but do not labour. It follows that *commodities* are produced (by capital) but that they *are the result of nobody's labour*.

3.4.3. *Exploitation in production*

Let us finally consider Arthur's notion of exploitation. The author distinguishes between exploitation in production and exploitation in distribution. In Arthur's conception, labourers are exploited in production, in the sense that they are forced to labour through the expropriation of their productive powers. The relation between the expropriation of productive power and the extraction of labour is unclear. I think it can be stated as follows. First of all, since, for Arthur, 'the whole [that is, the commodity as a whole – G.C.] is not constituted as their [the labourers' – G.C] productive power but as that of the capital hiring them',[84] the labourers' productive power would seem to be the capacity to produce not single parts of the commodity but the whole of the commodity. If so, then labour is expropriated of its productive power

---

[81] Arthur 2004b, pp. 47–8.
[82] Arthur 2004b, p. 202.
[83] Arthur 2004a, p. 18.
[84] Arthur 2004b, p. 47.

in the sense that the work of co-ordination and unity of the labour-process has become a part of the function of capital (rather then being, as in Marx, a part of the function of labour) and thus performed by capital. It is through the work of co-ordination and unity that (surplus-) labour can be extracted from the labourers. The above remarks have shown the inconsistency of this approach.

Aside from this, there are two dimensions in Arthur's notion of exploitation in production, the qualitative and the quantitative. Qualitatively, '[t]here is a close connection...between abstract labour and alienated labour'.[85] Quantitatively, since the labourers labour the whole of the working day for capital, exploitation 'comprises the whole of the working day, not just the so-called "surplus labour time"'.[86] This implies that the distinction between necessary labour and surplus-labour is obliterated and that it is impossible to distinguish between them *ex ante*.[87] However, the quantity of value can be measured, irrespective of what goes to capital and what goes to labour: 'the magnitude of value is determined by the socially-necessary exploitation-time',[88] in other words, by the socially necessary work of control and surveillance. Two objections can be made against the notion of socially-necessary exploitation-time (SNET for short).

First, it has been shown that if concrete labours are different, so must be the work needed to control them. It is thus impossible to compare quantitatively different works of control and surveillance and thus to find a SNET. Second, even if the SNET were a viable concept for the measurement of the value created, the notion of SNET as a measure of value clashes head-on with the contrary notion that value can be measured by the socially-necessary labour-time (SNLT for short): 'only because capitals are inherently time-oriented in virtue of their form is the measure of such amounts of labour [the amounts of labour extractable – G.C.] socially necessary labour time'.[89] This point seems to have escaped Murray for whom 'Arthur...attributes the quantitative determina-

---

[85] Arthur 2004b, pp. 47 and 56.
[86] Arthur 2004b, p. 55.
[87] As Bell remarks, 'In order to avoid attributing the creation of surplus-value to labour, [Arthur – G.C.] invents a novel definition of exploitation that excludes the concept of surplus labour time' (Bell 2005).
[88] Arthur 2004b, p. 55.
[89] Arthur 2004b, p. 205.

tion of value...to (socially necessary) abstract labour'.[90] Bidet seems to think that, for Arthur, value is determined by the SNLT (socially-necessary labour-time) which, in its turn, is determined by class-struggle.[91] Neither author sees the contradiction between SNLT and SNET. Murray accepts Arthur's words at face value: 'Arthur's first notion...just renames alienation, while the second doubles back to the traditional conception'.[92] Murray thus misses the point that Arthur's notion of exploitation in distribution is incongruous with his view of the production of both use-values and value. The same point escapes also Hunt.[93] The question remains: which one determines the magnitude of value, the SNLT or the SNET?

3.4.4. *Exploitation in distribution*

The second notion of exploitation is in distribution. This 'arises from the discrepancy between the new wealth created and the *return* to those exploited in production'.[94] For Arthur, those exploited in production are the labourers. But the labourers neither create the use-value of the commodity (capital does, by co-ordinating and unifying their activities) nor the value of the commodity (their labour is the source of value, but does not create value because-value is posited by capital through their exploitation). But, if the labourers create neither value nor use-value, no wealth can be *returned* to them. If commodities as use-values are received by labour, it is labour that receives a part of the use-values created by capital, that is, it is labour that exploits in distribution. If commodities as value are received by labour, it is again labour that exploits capital because it is capital that posits the concrete labour which has gone into those commodities as abstract labour through the work of control and surveillance. In short, given Arthur's theory of the production of value and use-values, exploitation in distribution leads to the notion that *capital is exploited by labour*.

---

[90] Murray 2005, p. 73.
[91] Bidet 2005.
[92] Murray 2005, p. 81.
[93] Hunt 2005, p. 163.
[94] Arthur 2001, p. 33; emphasis added.

3.4.5. *Conclusions*

To conclude, Arthur's position can be summarised as follows. The commodity as a use-value, in its empirical concreteness, is the result neither of the individual labourers' labour nor of the collective labourer's labour. Rather, it is the capitalists who, by co-ordinating and organising the labour-process (seen as a function of capital), are the creators and the producers of the commodity as a use-value. As for value and surplus-value, labour does not produce them either. Rather it is capital, which, even though not producing them, 'posits' the labourers' concrete labour as abstract, as value, because it equally exploits it irrespective of the specificity of the concrete labours. Finally, exploitation in production is similar to alienation and can be measured by measuring the socially-necessary exploitation-time. Exploitation in distribution is the return of the wealth to the exploited. The discussion above has highlighted the many internal inconsistencies of this approach and has also argued that Arthur's theory shares with the other value-form theories the implicit and unconscious assumption that the human metabolism does not exist.

But this aside, for Marx, the labourers are the protagonists because their labour, under coercion, produces both the use-value of the commodities and the (surplus-) value contained in them. In Arthur's approach, on the other hand, the labourers have become the 'servants of a production process originated and directed by capital',[95] so that labour is 'reduced to a resource for capital accumulation'.[96] Capital is the subject of valorisation even if valorisation depends on labour being exploited. I cannot but repeat my conclusions in my 2003 critique of Arthur. In spite of its laudable intentions, the 'new dialectics' renders a better service to capital than capital's own ideologues. It gives away the most precious legacy Marx left us, the ability to see reality from the perspective of labour as the protagonist, as the producer of wealth and value, a perspective which, contrary to what is held by the new dialectics and the concomitant value-form approach, is grounded in a logically coherent, and as yet unsurpassed, economic theory of capitalism.

Moreover, aside from Arthur, all the value-form theorists share a characteristic feature, the belief that value and surplus-value come into existence only

---

[95] Arthur 2004b, p. 47.
[96] Arthur 2004b, p. 51.

at the moment of realisation. Consequently, production and the realisation of value and surplus-value are collapsed into each other and *time is wiped out*. This is the notion upon which the value-form's critique of Marx is built. In short, to be able to criticise Marx (and, as we shall see below, to avoid the so-called transformation-problem) this approach chooses a view in which production and realisation are simultaneous.[97] The theoretical consequences will become clear in the next sections. Here, suffice it to mention that a reality in which time does not exist is a static reality and that all theorisations of reality in which change is banned cannot but be functional to the interests of capital rather than of labour.

4. The tendential fall in the average profit-rate (ARP)

In Marx's theory, new means of production, that is, innovations, increase labour's productivity, defined as units of output (use-values) per unit of capital invested, in a given period of time: 'the increasing productivity of labour is expressed…in the increasing amount of raw material converted in, say, one hour into products, or processed into commodities'.[98] But, at the same time, they usually replace people with means of production. The economy's organic composition of capital, that is, the proportion of constant capital (invested in means of production) to variable capital (invested in labour-power), and thus of machines to labourers, rises. If less labour-power is employed, less (surplus-) value is created by the innovating capitals. But this smaller quantity of (surplus-) value is embodied in a greater quantity of use-values, units of output. The economy, as a whole, produces more use-values but less (surplus-) value. The average rate of profit falls. The latter, as we shall see, is a tendential movement interrupted by periods of rising average profitability. This is the contradictory outcome of technological

---

[97] It could be argued that production and realisation are simultaneous in the production of knowledge. But this refers to the mental producer herself and to the incorporation of the knowledge produced by her into her labour-power. However, within the capitalist production-process, mental producers are employed by the capitalists not to incorporate the new knowledge they produce into their own labour-power but to alienate that knowledge to the capitalists who will then sell that knowledge (see Chapter 4, especially Section 6). There is thus a time-lag. When knowledge is produced by the mental labourers for the capitalists, the production of value and surplus-value and their realisation are *not* simultaneous.

[98] Marx 1967c, p. 108.

innovations and, at the same time, the ultimate cause of economic crises. Chapter 3 will develop a theory of crises built on this fundamental aspect of the capitalist economy. Before this task can be attempted, however, the thesis of the tendential fall in the average rate of profit has to be evaluated in the light of recent critiques.

4.1. *The multiplicity of the average profit-rates*

The calculation of the average profit-rate, to be theoretically significant, must be a mathematical rendition of a real economic process. It is usually thought that this real process is the movement of capitals from low-profitability to high-profitability braches and the concomitant tendential equalisation of the different profit-rates. This approach is vulnerable to the objection that, with the rise of monopolies and thus with the barriers to entry they pose, the real grounds for the calculation of the average profit-rate are lacking. There would be a multiplicity of profit-rates, an average for the free-competition sector with no barriers to capital-entry, and one or more profit-rates for each monopoly. The law of the tendential average profit-rate would not hold any more for the economy as a whole. However, the significance of this calculation is that it indicates whether the total surplus-value produced rises or falls relative to the total capital available for investment because this is the indicator of the economy's state of health. From this perspective, it would make no difference how many rates of profit there are in reality. But, actually, there is a tendency towards only one average rate of profit even in the absence of capital movement. The cause of this tendential equalisation is technological competition.

Each time a firm in the free-competition sector introduces a new technology, it increases its productivity (output per unit of capital invested) while reducing the surplus-value created (due to the replacement of labour-power by means of production). Its greater profit-rate is made possible by the appropriation of surplus-value from the rest of the economy due to the price-system. If that firm's greater output can be sold at a price such that extra surplus-value is appropriated, the economy's purchasing power is shifted to that firm not only from that capital's competitors but also from the rest of the economy. The purchasers will spend more for the innovator's product and less for the rest of the economy's output. If this different allocation of purchasing power affects also the demand for the monopoly's output and thus its profitability, the innovator appropriates surplus-value both from the free-competition sector and from the monopoly-sector. In their turn, the innovators' extra profits are eroded as soon as the new techniques are introduced by the technological laggards. Technological competition tends to equalise the profit-rates of both sectors. In any case, less surplus-value is produced percentage-wise by the innovator and the rate of profit for the economy as a whole falls. The calculation of the average profit-rate is thus theoretically warranted and indeed necessary to understand the movement of the economy, be it monopolistic or not.

4.2. *The logical-inconsistency critique*

This stance has been criticised on two accounts. First, the debate has focused on the Okishio-theorem.[99] Okishio argues that capitalists introduce new techniques not when they raise the productivity of labour but when they decrease the costs of production.[100] If real wages are held constant, the average rate of profit must necessarily rise, contrary to Marx.[101] More specifically, Okishio's cost-criterion states that, if the *physical* inputs are multiplied by their monetary prices, holding wages constant, lower costs due to increased productivity *must* increase *monetary* profits.[102] This is contrary to Marx. Let us see why.

In line with the examples usually provided by Marx's critics, let us assume an economy producing only one commodity, such as corn. For the sake of argument let us disregard that there is, at the very least, also another commodity, labour-power. Corn is the input and the output as well as the only means of production and of consumption. Let u be a unit of use-values (physical commodities and labour which is seen here as concrete labour); m a unit

---

[99] Okishio 1961. For a variety of assessments, see Cullenberg 1994; Fine and Harris 1976; Foley 1999, 2000; Freeman 1999; Kliman 1996, 1999, 2007; Kliman and Freeman 2000; Laibman 1999a, 1999b, 2000a, 2000b, 2001; Reuten 2004; Shaikh 1978a; 1978b.

[100] Okishio 1961, p. 86.

[101] For some, like Brenner (2002, p. 12), this is self-evident, even if they have little knowledge of the matter. The Okishio-theorem has been subjected to a number of critiques (Laibman, 1982, p. 100; Foley, 1986, p. 139; Alberro and Persky 1981; Shaikh 1978a and 1978b) whose common feature is that of being based on a modification of Okishio's initial assumptions.

[102] Okishio's formula is $\Sigma a_{kj}q_j + \tau_k$ where a_{kj} denotes the amount of the jth commodity directly necessary to produce a unit of the kth commodity, q_j denotes the ratio of the price of the jth commodity (p_j) to the wage-rate (w), and τ_k denotes the amount of labour directly necessary to produce a unit of the kth commodity.

of money; M the total quantity of money in circulation (holding the velocity of circulation constant); Πm the average rate of profit in money-terms; Πu the average rate of profit in physical terms; p the price per unit of output; c, v, s constant capital, variable capital and surplus (-value); and to–t1 and t1–t2 two successive production- and distribution-periods, where the end of the first period coincides temporally with the beginning of the next one (but the addition of an intermediate period would not change matters). M, p and output refer to the end of each period.

Take the period to–t1 first. Suppose that, at to (the initial point of to–t1), 80u=80m (as means of production) plus 20u=20m (as wages) are invested. At t1 (the end point of to–t1), an output equal to 120u is produced. Profits in physical terms are 20u, and Πu=20%. Suppose that at t1, M=120. Then the unit-price is 120m/120u=1; profits are 20m; and Πm=20%. Πm=Πu because the price of the inputs purchased at to has been arbitrarily set equal to 1, which is also the price of the outputs at t1 by assuming M=120m. Notice that, here too, the incommensurability-problem makes it necessary to assume one and only one commodity, such as corn. As soon as the example, or theory, is extended to more than one commodity, the whole construction becomes useless because undermined by the impossibility to compare different use-values. Okishio's approach and thus critique of Marx is built upon quicksand. The discussion could end here. It is however instructive to proceed and analyse Okishio's arguments.

Suppose that at t1, as the beginning of t1–t2, productivity increases. More means of production and less labour-power are used. The output per unit of capital invested rises, that is, *unit-costs in physical terms decrease*, consonant with Okishio. Suppose that instead of 80u+20u (as at to, the initial point of to–t1) 90u+10u are employed. The assumption is that each worker receives the same quantity of corn as before. Thus, 10u indicate a labour-force that has been halved relative to 20u. Due to higher productivity, the output rises to, say, 200u. Profits in physical terms are 200u-100u=100u and Πu=100%. However, if at t2, M=180, p=180/200=0.9, profits in money-terms are 180–100=80 and Πm=80/100=80% < 100%. If M=30, p=30/200=0.15m, the output is sold at 15×200=30m and capital suffers a loss of 100–30=70m. Contrary to Okishio, prices have fallen, but Πm has fallen too (rather than rising) while Πu has risen. *Lower costs do not necessarily result into higher money-profits and Πm does not necessarily track Πu.* Whether the Okishio-theorem holds or not depends on how M changes between t₁ and t₂. This is squarely contrary to Okishio's claim that a price-fall (cost-reduction) leads necessarily to an increase in profits (wages being constant). In its original formulation, which is the one invoked by Marx's critics, the theorem is invalid. Notice that these results depend crucially on a distinction between the initial and the final moment of the production-period, that is, on a temporal perspective.

Nevertheless, Okishio's theorem can be rescued if two additional assumptions are added. These are not contrary but complement the original ones and therefore do not introduce an element of internal inconsistency. One is to let the quantity of money vary with the variations in the physical output. The price paid for internal consistency is the extremely limited application that makes the theorem practically useless. For Marx, value is the monetary expression of abstract labour, that is, of exchange-value, not of concrete labour, that is, use-values: 'Money is labour time in the form of a general object, or the objectification of general labour time, labour time as a general commodity.'[103] Thus, the quantity of money must rise or fall if value, rather than use-values, rises or falls. Now, in discussing the dynamics of the average rate of profit, Marx assumes 'the value of money...as constant throughout'.[104] This would seem to limit the scope of the approach, just as in Okishio's hypothesised case. But this is not so. Whether the quantity of money rises or falls, inasmuch as labour is shed due to new technologies, the average rate of profit falls in value-terms and, sooner or later, it falls also in money-terms. Greater money-rates of profit in the presence of decreasing value-rates of profit denotes only an inflationary process. More specifically, as we shall see in Chapter 3, Marx has a theory of crises, while Okishio does not.

The other assumption would be to value the inputs at the price they would have when the output is sold (at t₂) rather than at the price actually paid for them when they are bought (at t₁) and enter the production-process.[105] The prices of the inputs and of the outputs are made to coincide because they are computed *simultaneously* at the end of the period (at t₂). Given that, at the end of the period, the price has fallen (as a consequence of the increased

---

[103] Marx 1973, p. 168.
[104] Quoted in Ramos 2004, p. 71.
[105] Kliman 1996, p. 212; Carchedi, forthcoming, *Capital and Class*.

productivity), the inputs are devalued retroactively not as a consequence of a real process but simply to make accounts square. In the example above, from a temporal perspective, if M=30, the capitalist suffers a loss of 70m. But, if the inputs (90u+10u) are valued not at the price they have actually cost at t1 (100u×1=100m) but at the price they would cost if they were bought at t2 (100u×0.15=15m), then Πm=15/15=100%. Prices fall and Πm rises to the level of Πu, conforming with Okishio.

But the accounts square simply because time has been cancelled. Moreover, due to simultaneous valuation, Πm is unaffected by the level of prices (as long as input and output prices are determined simultaneously) so that *only physical quantities determine the profit-rate*. This is the *physicalist* approach. It follows that, to obtain the desired result, Okishio would have to explicitly pose as its premise the simultaneous valuation of inputs and outputs. But this premise is posed neither by Okishio nor by those who defend its validity.[106] Nevertheless, let us grant that this assumption is made. In this case, Okishio is internally consistent. It can hardly be seriously held that an approach that jettisons value and time, even if internally consistent, can be seen as an internal critique, a refutation, of Marx's law. Yet this is what the critique boils down to.[107] Okishio's theorem is then not an internal critique of Marx but an alternative theory to Marx's. But, is it a *valid* alternative, a theory functional for the liberation of labour?

In Okishio, the quantities of the inputs multiplied by their prices are a cost and the labour necessary to produce a certain commodity is also a cost.[108] Thus, *Okishio's perspective is that of the capitalists, for whom both the labour contained in the commodities' inputs and the new labour added are exclusively a cost.* Clearly, if costs are reduced and wages are unchanged, profits must rise. Okishio's critique, by seeing labour as a cost (the capitalists' point of view), disregards Marx's absolutely essential assumption that labour is the (only) creator of value (the labourers' point of view).[109] To show that Marx's law is logically inconsistent, Okishio would have had to use Marx's own assumption. Since

---

[106] But see Laibman, 2000a.

[107] See Kliman 1996, 1999; Freeman 1999; Laibman 1999a; Foley 1999, 2000; Kliman and Freeman 2000; Laibman 2000b, 2001; Kliman 2001; Mohun 2003; Kliman and Freeman 2006; Mohun and Veneziani 2007; Freeman and Kliman 2000, 2008. The last five entries are only indirectly related to the debate around the law. For a comprehensive review of the debates, see Kliman 2007.

[108] (τ_k) in the formula in note 102 above.

[109] See Section 2 of this chapter.

he does not do this, he cannot argue that the law is internally inconsistent. Okihio could assume explicitly labour as a cost and not as the value-creating factor. But then Okishio would become explicitly irrelevant for a critique of the law.[110] The social, class-content of the Okishio-theorem is incompatible with the interests of labour. It is because of both its internal inconsistency (incommensurability) and of its inconsistency in terms of class-content with Marx that it should be discarded.

But labour *is* indeed a cost. Do we not have a contradiction here? No. Labour is a cost from the perspective of the *individual* capitalists (when they purchase it as labour-power) but is also and above all (as abstract labour) the sole value-creating factor. Less living labour might mean lower costs, and thus higher profits, for the capitalists introducing labour-shedding and productivity-increasing technologies, but it means also less new value and surplus-value produced by them and thus, exclusively on this account, a lower average rate of profit. The technological innovators do indeed realise a higher rate of profit but, if they have produced less (surplus-) value, *ceteris paribus* their higher profit-rate can be realised only at the expense of, that is, by appropriating the surplus-value produced by, the other producers who have not yet introduced those labour-shedding and productivity-increasing technologies. This happens through the price-mechanism. Assuming an unchanged total purchasing power, the greater combined output must be sold for a lower unit-price. The innovators, by selling their greater output for the same unit-price as that of the technological laggards (whose output per unit of capital invested is lower), realise a greater surplus-value per unit of capital invested (a greater rate of profit) at the cost of the laggards.[111]

The two major conclusions reached above are (a) that Marx's law is internally consistent if labour is seen not only as a cost but also and above all

---

[110] Kliman mounts a sustained defence of Marx's law in Chapter 7 of 2007. However, Kliman does not explicitly criticise Okishio for having substituted labour as value-creator with labour as a cost. Moreover, his defence of Marx's law is incomplete because, while mention is made of the tendential nature of the law, no argument is submitted to support Marx's thesis that the fall rather than the rise is the tendency. See further below.

[111] See Carchedi, 1991, 2001. For Kliman (2007, pp. 21–3), a less-than-average-productivity firm (a firm employing more labour than socially necessary) does not create more value, while a firm that increases its productivity with the same amount of abstract labour produces not only more use-values but also more value. The former proposition makes value vanish into nothing; the latter makes it appear out of nothing. In reality, the extra value produced by the former is appropriated by the latter through the price-system.

as the only value-creating activity; (b) that Okishio's theorem is internally inconsistent due to the incommensurability-problem; and (c), given that, for Okishio, labour is seen only as a cost, Okishio is premised on an assumptions alien to Marx's law and thus cannot hold as a critique of Marx's law. But suppose, for the sake of argument, that Okishio's theorem were internally consistent. Would it then be a *valid* alternative to Marx's law?

Okishio's last-ditch effort would be to concede that costs are the monetary expression of abstract (instead of concrete) labour. This would resolve the incommensurability-problem, but it would mark the end of the physicalist approach. Would this modified approach be a valid alternative to Marx's law? The answer is negative. In this revised Okishian approach, value would be the monetary manifestation of the abstract labour contained in the physical output, but, in a different sense from Marx, abstract labour would be only a cost. Thus, if the physical output grows as a result of productivity-increasing technologies, and if the quantity of money also grows proportionally, the average rate of profit and thus the economy grow too. On the contrary, in Marx's approach, labour-shedding and productivity-increasing technologies lead tendentially to economic crises because abstract labour is the source of value, because the technological innovator decreases her own costs of production but also, at the same time, the surplus-value she produces. Given that these technologies are the motor of capitalism's dynamic, for Okishio capitalism tends towards growth and reproduction while, for Marx, it tends towards crises and its own supersession. In terms of formal logic, both approaches are internally consistent. Two opposite initial assumptions lead to two opposite conclusions. How, then, do we choose between these two opposite theories? As mentioned above, according to their class-content. Only Marx's theory identifies capitalism's tendency towards its own supersession and thus grounds labour's struggle in that objective tendency.

4.3. *The indeterminateness-critique*

The rejection of the Okishio-theorem, both as a critique of, and as an alternative to, Marx's law is necessary but not sufficient. Marx's law must also be shown to be immune from a second line of critique, indeterminateness. If this cannot be shown, the discussion above becomes irrelevant: what would be the relevance for the collective labourer of proving that the average rate of profit can fall if it cannot be proved that it *must* fall and that this fall is the *tendency* rather then the counter-tendency? The objective basis upon which to base labour's struggle would be negated.

Chapter 1 has distinguished among three types of tendencies. Here, we deal with the second one, whose specificity is the alternation of the tendency and of the counter-tendencies that is, the realisation at any given time of *either* the tendency *or* the counter-tendencies. We have seen that the average profit-rate tends to fall due to the reduction of the surplus-value created, itself a consequence of the introduction of labour-shedding and productivity-increasing new technologies. This fall is tendential because it is held back and delayed by a number of counter-tendencies. The alternative manifestation of the tendency and counter-tendencies is perceived by formal logic as an indeterminate movement. From a formal-logic perspective, there is no reason to think that the average rate of profit must fall, since it now falls and then rises. Nor can it be argued that the downward movement is the tendency and the upwards movement is the counter-tendency. These are the limits of formal logic.

As argued in Section 7 of Chapter 1, for formal logic, all contradictions are simply mistakes. This applies not only to the conclusions but also to the premises. The reason is that deduction, to reach non-contradictory conclusions, must start from premises that are not mutually contradictory. But, for Marx, the premise needed to explain the movement of the average rate of profit *is* contradictory because labour-shedding and productivity-increasing technologies expel labour, thus decreasing the value produced, but, for example, can also decrease the value of the means of production. Given the cheaper constant capital, proportionally more variable capital is invested and more (surplus-) value is produced per unit of capital invested, so that the average rate of profit can rise in the next period. Thus, if the premise is contradictory, the conclusion that the rate of profit can both increase and decrease is no logical mistake but, rather, follows logically from the initial premise, from a premise that accounts theoretically for a *real* contradiction. This does not mean that the *rules* of formal logic should be discarded. They allow us to distinguish correct from incorrect statements about social phenomena, but *only if non-contradictory premises are considered* (see Section 6 of Chapter 1). Formal logic cannot explain contradictory movement. Given that the average rate of profit has both an ascending and a descending phase, if the two trends are explored independently, each is seen as being caused by non-contradictory factors. For example, given only the premise of labour-shedding, the average rate of profit can only fall. Within this partial and static approach, the rules of formal logic apply. However, they are only an auxiliary device in the analysis of contradictory movements. To understand the contradictory movement of reality in its many-sidedness, a different logic is needed. Dialectical logic, on the other hand, explains dialectical contradictions, those between realised and potential aspects of reality and are thus inherent to its contradictory nature. These contradictions manifest themselves as tendential movements, movements in terms of tendencies and counter-tendencies.

It is empirically observable that the movement of the average rate of profit is cyclical, that is, from peak to trough and then again to peak. Let us call these two movements the downwards cyclical movement, or *downward-trend* and the upwards cyclical movement or *upward-trend*. We also observe that, within these two trends, the movement is only temporarily stopped or reversed. This is due to *negative factors* that exert a downward-pressure within the upward-trend and to *positive factors* that exert an upward-pressure within the down-ward-trend. In short, if the downward-trend is actualised, the upward-trend is potentially present within it and manifests itself as a temporary reversal of the trend. The same applies to the upward-trend. At any intermediate moment between the peak and the trough, some positive factors can stop or reverse the course of the trend, but only temporarily, as long as the average rate of profit has not reached the trough. At any moment within this movement, it is impossible to forecast whether the average rate of profit will actually fall or not *relative to its previous level*. However, as empirical observation shows, the downward-trend proceeds by its own course and reaches the trough in spite of all the positive factors which have temporarily obstructed it. These positive factors cannot prevent the average rate of profit from falling *relative to its previous peak*. How can this be explained? Why can the positive factors not prevent the average rate of profit from falling relative to its previous peak? These positive factors are the counter-tendencies, but it is premature to refer to them as counter-tendencies at this stage of the exposition because it has not been shown yet that the falling movement is the tendency.

Let us consider four positive factors. Take, first, the increase in the extraction of surplus-value. As labourers are replaced by means of production, less (surplus-) value is produced and the average rate of profit falls *ceteris paribus*. This can be countered through a greater extraction of surplus-value. First, the length of the working day may rise. However, Marx stresses that this compensating mechanism has 'certain insurmountable limits', given that labourers, 'even if they could live on air' cannot work longer than 24 hours a day.[112] To this it can be added that there is also another limit, that is, what is deemed to be socially unacceptable given the power-relations between capital and labour. If the length of the working day reaches the biologically or socially determined limit, the average rate of profit starts falling. Second, the same applies to increases in the intensity of labour. They too come up against biological and/or socially determined limits. Third, the costs of producing the wage-goods and thus value of labour-power might fall due to labour-shedding and productivity-increasing technologies. The average rate of profit rises on this account. But, here too, the value of labour-power can decrease up to a certain point, be it determined biologically or socially, whereas there are no bounds in productivity-increases in that branch. The interplay between innovations and increased exploitation explains both the indeterminateness within the downward-cycle and the determinateness of this cycle. These positive factors can hold back the fall in the average profit-rate only temporarily. If the fall is the tendency (something which will be argued below), then they are counter-tendencies.

A second positive factor is the cheapening of the elements of constant capital, for example the means of production. Let us examine the production of the means of production. The critics' argument is as follows. Consider an initial situation, call it Period 1, such as $80c+20v+20s=120V$. Consider next an increase in productivity in this branch accompanied by the shedding of labour such that $90c+10v+10s=110V$. Call this Period 2. New technologies in Period 2 reduce the rate of profit from 20% to 10% because less labour-power is employed and thus less surplus-value is produced, together with a percentage-increase in constant capital. However, the concomitant increase in productivity reduces the value of the means of production as the output of Period 2 and thus of the same means of production as the inputs of the next period, Period 3. The rate of profit at the end of Period 3 can rise to the level of the rate of profit in Period 1 (20%), according to how much the productivity in this branch has increased and thus according to the size of the decrease in the value of the means of production. If the increase in productivity is such that the value of the means of production falls to the level at which $10v$ can be set in motion by $40c$, then $40c+10v+10s=60V$ and the rate of profit is $10/50=20\%$.

---

[112] Marx 1967a, p. 247.

The increase in productivity and concomitant fall in the value of the means of production have raised the level of the profit-rate from 10% to its level prior to the introduction of the new technologies (20%). Notice that this is always possible because, as the value of the means of production decreases, i.e. as they approach zero, the rate of profit approaches the rate of surplus-value, which is always higher than the rate of profit. If the value of the means of production to be set in motion by 10v falls below 40, the rate of profit rises above the level prior the introduction of the new technologies (20%); if it falls to a level above 40, it rises but does not reach 20%. Thus, whether the rate of profit at the end of Period 3 has climbed back to its level of Period 1 or not depends on whether the technological innovations introduced at the beginning of Period 2 have generated a sufficient increase in productivity and therefore a sufficient decrease in the value of the means of production as the output of Period 2 and thus as inputs of Period 3. The course of the rate of profit is indeterminate.

If this were the whole story, the critics would be right in considering the outcome and thus the law as indeterminate. We would not know whether the fall in the profit-rate prevails over its rise, that is whether the rise is the tendency and the fall the counter-tendency or vice-versa. Unfortunately, in dealing with this question, Marx considers the positive effects on the rate of profit of the cheapening of constant capital due to increased productivity as a counter-tendency, but does not clarify the reasons why. Yet it is possible to submit a reason perfectly consistent with, because implicit in, Marx's theoretical framework.

Let us examine the most favourable case for the critics, that, at each wave of technological innovation, the decrease in the cost (value) of the means of production is sufficient to (more than) compensate the combined negative effect on the average rate of profit of a higher constant capital and of a lower surplus-value percentage-wise. In this case, technological innovations increase rather than decreasing the profit-rate, as in the numerical example above. But this is impossible. The reason is that with each wave of new techniques, while the constant capital decreases due to the cheaper means of production, the labour-power and thus the new (surplus-) value created decrease as well, in such a measure that the decrease in the cost of the means of production cannot compensate the lower surplus-value. In fact, at the limit, the means of production might cost nothing but, if the labour-power employed is also reduced to zero, there are no profits and thus no profit-rate. And, *if it tends to zero, the profit-rate must be decreasing*. The critics' argument is invalid and the numerical example made above illustrates a long-run economic *impossibility* – in other words, it is an example of an episode unwarrantedly extrapolated to a law of development. The effect of the cheaper means of production on the average rate of profit is a counter-tendency that can only delay but not avoid the tendential fall.

It might be objected that the stronger capitals can increase their scale of production because the cheaper means of production allow them to employ more labour-power with the same constant capital. They can absorb the labour-power thrown out by the bankrupt capitals. In the example above, the value of the means of production set in motion by 10v drops from 90 to 40. These 90c can then be used to employ 22.5v instead of 10v. Again, this is the most favourable case for the critics, since we assume that no capital lies unused, that all constant capital can be set in motion at the new, higher profit-rate. However, this increasing capital-concentration affects positively the *mass* of surplus-value produced, but, given the rate of exploitation, does not increase the *rate* of profit ($10/40 = 22.5/112.5 = 20\%$) and further leaves it exposed to the corrosive effect of technological developments.

A third positive factor is given by a different type of cost-reducing technologies. In a different manner from labour-shedding and productivity-increasing technologies, which produce *more* physical output with the *same costs* (only the relative weight of constant and variable capital changes), these types of cost-reducing technologies produce the *same* output with *lower costs.* For physicalism, there is no difference between these two types of technology, as they cannot but increase the average rate of profit. However, in value-theory, a distinction must be made between which costs are reduced. If the cost of constant capital falls, production costs less, the average rate of profit rises. If cost-reduction concerns labour-power, we have two sub-cases. First, less labour-power per unit of capital is employed and thus variable capital falls. If the rate of exploitation is unchanged, surplus-value falls. The share of constant capital rises and the average rate of profit cannot but fall. But, if cost-reduction is due to the same quantity of labour-power being paid lower wages, surplus-value increases proportionally. The average rate of profit increases. Given that these technologies can either increase or reduce the average rate of profit, for the sake of argument here only those cost-reducing technologies that increase the rate of profit will be considered, that is, those technologies that use less (costly) means of production per unit of capital invested or less costly labour-power (lower wages) for the same kind of labour-power.

The reason why this type of cost-reducing technologies cannot hold back the fall in the average rate of profit is that, while the output of the labour-shedding and productivity-increasing technologies rises, the output of the cost-reducing technologies remains unchanged. It follows that the capitalists using the former technologies can sell more outputs per unit of capital invested than the capitalists using the latter technologies. Under the assumptions of price-equalisation within sectors and that only the (surplus-) value produced in a sector can be redistributed within that sector,[113] the former capitalists appropriate value from the latter. The more the labour-shedding and productivity-increasing technologies are introduced, the more the capitalists applying them appropriate surplus-value from the capitalists using cost-reducing technologies, and the more the latter capitalists must reduce the cost of the means of production and of labour-power in order to counter the loss of surplus-value. However, while the costs of these two inputs have a limit, hypothetically zero if the capitalists could pay nothing both for the means of production and for labour-power, the increase in productivity of the labour-shedding and productivity-increasing technologies is, in principle, unlimited. At a certain point, the capitalists using this type of cost-reducing technologies will be unable to further reduce those costs, will suffer losses and will either be forced out of production or have to adopt the labour-shedding and productivity-increasing technologies. At that point, the average rate of profit must fall. The interplay between these two types of technologies accounts both for the indeterminateness within the downward-cycle and for the determinateness of the downward-cycle itself towards a decreasing average rate of profit. Of course, a capital can use both types of techniques. But this does not affect the argument. Here, too, these types of technologies can hold back the fall in average profitability only temporarily. They, too, are therefore counter-tendencies.

Fourth, the credit-system can play a positive role in general profitability but only by creating fictitious capital: 'the self-expansion of capital based on the contradictory nature of capitalist production permits an actual free development only up to a certain point, so that in fact it constitutes an immanent fetter and barrier to production, which are continually broken through by the

---

[113] The assumption that only the value produced in a sector can be realised in that sector simplifies the argument and can be relaxed without affecting the results.

credit system'.[114] Fictitious capital will be a major theme in Chapter 3 below. There, it shall be seen that credit and speculation can only retard the explosion of the crisis but cannot avoid it forever. They, too, can be considered a counter-tendency.

To sum up, in spite of their different *modus operandi,* these four categories of positive factors (which have been called prematurely counter-tendencies because no argument has been submitted yet as to why the negative trend is the tendency) share a common feature. The *more* these positive effects *try to hold back the negative effect of the labour-shedding and productivity-increasing technologies, the weaker they become,* because they approach the limit beyond which they cannot go. Before reaching that limit, they can only temporarily halt or reverse the downward-movement within the upward-cycle, but, when they reach that limit, the downward-cycle sets in. The downward-cycle asserts itself in spite of the contrary (positive) factors. If, and this has yet to be argued for, the former is the tendency, the latter are the counter-tendencies. As Marx puts it, the tendency is only 'delayed', 'checked', 'partly paralyzed', 'retarded', 'not [done] away with...but [simply] impair[ed] [in] its effect' by the counter-tendencies.[115] There are, of course, other factors affecting that particular tendential movement. Given the interconnection of all elements of reality, many more factors play a role in the movement of average profitability. The choice made to leave them out of consideration is justified if the *basic* traits of the movement considered have been explained. This allows us to forecast the repetition of the movement as long as these factors and their interplay do not change.

The above explanation of the cyclical movement could be accepted, but nevertheless, it could be argued that it is the upward-trend that is the tendency and that the downward-trend is the counter-tendency which cannot hold back the manifestation of the tendency. This is the equivalent of orthodox-economics thesis that the economy tends to grow and that this growth is interrupted by periods of crises. This conception has already been addressed above. If one assigns the status of tendency to the downward-trend (from peak to trough), one subscribes to a notion of capitalism as a system tending towards crises, a movement only temporarily interrupted by a contrary

---

[114] Marx 1967a, p. 441.
[115] Marx 1967a, pp. 226 and 232–7.

movement within the business-cycle. The system lacks an inherent (tendency towards) growth and equilibrium. This view provides an objective rationale for labour's struggle. If, on the other hand, one assigns the tendential status to the upward-cycle (from trough to peak), one subscribes to a notion of a system tending towards growth, full employment and (within the context of simultaneism) equilibrium. This cyclical movement is only temporarily interrupted by the downward-movement within it. In this view, labour is deprived of the rationale for its struggle. As mentioned above, it is the class-content of these two opposite views that decides the issue.

It is for this reason that, contrary to the commonly accepted notion in economic theory that the economy exits crises through more capital-accumulation, growth, and so on, for Marx the system regenerates itself in a destructive way, it tends towards its own catharsis, the destruction of excess (because less productive) capital: 'Under all circumstances...the balance will be restored by the *destruction of capital* to a greater or lesser extent.'[116] It is the destruction of capital that gets the system going again. After this destruction has taken place, growth can resume. But it should be noticed that the destruction of capital that makes recovery possible is not so much that caused by technical obsolescence but, rather, the destruction of capital as social relations which results in the diminished production of surplus-value due to unemployment.[117]

There remains a last point, that the law cannot predict 'actual falls in the rate of profit'. This is indeed the case, as mentioned above, *but only within trends*. This is both in line with Marx's text and theoretically and logically consistent with his approach. The law explains why the average rate of profit must eventually fall to a trough, thus unleashing economic crises. After having reached that point, the average rate of profit starts climbing again to a peak (in spite of temporary reversals within this ascending trend), thus temporarily overcoming the tendential (downwards) trend. Having reached a peak, it starts anew to descend. The law's purpose is not to forecast, at any given moment, whether the average rate of profit falls or rises relative to its previous level (the movements within the trend). Rather, the law is meant to explain why the capitalist economy tends cyclically towards crises, in other words why it falls

---

[116] Marx 1992, p. 328; emphasis in the original. The German text reads: 'Unter allen Umständen...würde sich das Gleichgewicht herstellen durch *Vernichtung von Kapital* in grösserem oder geringerem Umfang.'

[117] If capital is a social relation, the destruction of capital can only be the destruction of that relation. See Carchedi 1991 and 2006a. See also Chapter 3 below.

cyclically relative to its previous peak, and why this downward-cycle rather than the opposite upward-cycle is the tendency. Far from being theoretically indeterminate, the law sketches the broad lines of capitalism's development, it accounts for the succession of cycles, and it explains capitalism's objective tendency towards its own supersession.[118]

5. The transformation-'problem'

The debate around Marx's transformation-procedure has become one of the most obscure in the literature. This is unfortunate because Marx's transformation-procedure is nothing else than his theory of distribution and thus of prices. If this can be shown to be internally inconsistent, as the critics hold, then it is the whole of Marx's theory that is called into question, given that the current period's production depends upon the previous period's distribution. It follows that all the specific and fundamental features of Marx's theory are challenged, from exchange-value to exploitation and the theory of crises. The unnecessary recourse to mathematical techniques makes it difficult, if not impossible, for the interested reader to follow the discussion, thus leaving the field to the specialists. This is something that should be avoided, given the aforementioned importance of the issue.

The critique focuses on the difference between values and prices. Let us then, first, set out clearly what they are and how they differ. The *individual value* is 'the labour-time that the article costs the producer in each individual case'.[119] It should be distinguished from the *market-value*, the individual value of the commodities produced under average conditions of production (average efficiency) in each sector. Both the individual and the market-value are *values contained* or *embodied* in the commodity before realisation. The *value realised* by a commodity upon its sale is called its *price*. The *production-prices* are the value *tendentially* realised under the assumption that the rates of profit are equalised among branches. The *market-prices* are the value *actually* realised by those commodities when the rates of profit in the different branches differ according to the profit actually realised. Price is the monetary expression of abstract labour (under capitalist production-relations). Schematically,

---

[118] It goes without saying that labour's subjective struggle is also needed for this objective movement to result in capitalism's supersession. See Chapter 4 below.
[119] Marx 1976a, p. 434.

Table 1. Value contained and value realised (prices) in Marx

Value before realisation, or value contained	Value after realisation, or prices
– Individual value	– Production-price (tendentially realised)
– Market-value	– Market-price (actually realised)

Given that realisation takes place through the sale/purchase of commodities, abstract labour must manifest itself as money. This holds for value both before and after realisation. In order to grasp this, let us anticipate a point of cardinal importance for the temporal approach to be argued for below. The value realised by a commodity as an output of a certain period, that is, its production- or market-price, is the same, by definition, as the individual or market-value of the same commodity as an input of the following period. Thus, not only the values realised by the commodities as outputs of one period, but also the value of the same commodities as inputs of the following period, are expressed in money-terms. There is nothing unclear about 'the value of a commodity [being – G.C.] expressed in its price before it enters into circulation'.[120] The value of the commodity-output before realisation (its value contained) is the price paid for the inputs, plus the surplus-value. The latter can be monetarily quantified before exchange, because we know the price paid for labour-power and the rate of surplus-value. *This is why Marx is perfectly right and consistent in referring interchangeably to value as abstract labour and money.* It is thus mistaken to consider value as labour and price as money, just as it is mistaken to think that, in Marx, there are two different and separated systems of accounting, one in terms of labour and the other in terms of prices.

Table 1 above distinguishes between actually and tendentially realised values, that is, prices. The latter are the values that would be realised if all (average) producers realised the average rate of profit. There are two reasons for computing the average rate of profit and thus production-prices. The first is that the rate of profit for the whole of the economy, the general rate of profit, is the *thermometer* of the economy. In fact, as the economy proceeds towards the crisis, the general rate of profit falls, thus indicating a decreasing production of surplus-value, even though some capitals might increase their rate

---

[120] Marx 1976a, p. 260.

of profit at the expense of other capitals. After the crisis, the average rate of profit rises again (see Chapter 3 below). Notice that, just as social relations are not directly observable but can be observed indirectly through the processes determined by them (see Chapter 1, Section 2.1), so it is also the case that, under conditions of constant-capital movements across branches and constant introduction of new technologies within each branch, the average rate of profit is also a tendency that is not directly observable because, every time a capital moves to a different sector or it introduces a new technology, it changes its value-composition and thus it changes the average profitability. Nevertheless, this tendency is a realised phenomenon because it is an average of realised profit-rates. It is indirectly observable through the constantly changing profit-rates of the individual capitals constantly seeking the highest expedient profit-rates. Notice also, that the average rate of profit refers to the productive sectors of the economy and not to both the productive and the unproductive sectors. As Chapter 3 will argue, the unproductive sectors' profits are not produced in those sectors, but are an inflated measure of the profits appropriated from the productive sectors.

The second reason is that Marx's transformation-procedure (which, as argued below, is free from 'problems') is simply the redistribution of the surplus-value produced at the moment of purchase/sale and thus through exchange. Given a certain total quantity of surplus-value at any given moment, this redistribution depends upon the price at which the output is sold. One can assume the actual prices, the market-prices. However, one can also assume the production-prices, the prices at which each branch realises (or would realise) the average rate of profit. The advantage of using the production-prices is that we abstract from the seemingly chaotic movement of the market-prices. This assumption is further justified by a real movement, the movement of capitals towards the highest possible area of profitability. It is just this movement that justifies the hypothesis of an average rate of profit. In fact, given a certain quantity of value and surplus-value produced, if low-profitability capitals move to higher-profitability areas, the latter's supply increases and the former's supply decreases. Prices and thus profits fall in the high-profitability area and rise in the low-profitability area. The outcome is not a general rate of profit equal to that of the highest-profitability capitals (areas), as sometimes suggested, but, rather, an average profit-rate.

Two points follow. First, the average rate of profit is not an equilibrium-point, because it is immediately upset by further technological innovations that change the organic composition of capital and thus the average profit-rate. *An average profit-rate is inconsistent with equilibrium.* A temporal sequence of production-prices (average profit-rates) is not a sequence of equilibrium-points, because *tendentially* each point is at a profitability-level lower than the previous one, due to labour-shedding and productivity-increasing technologies. Rather, within such a sequence, average profit-rates are signposts towards the crisis. This does not exclude equilibrium at the level of prices and thus of exchange, that is, the equality of demand and supply if all products were sold at their production-prices. It is in *this* sense that Marx refers occasionally to equilibrium, equilibrium at the level of exchange. But equilibrium at the level of exchange hides a profound disequilibrium at the level of the production of surplus-value and thus hides the economy's march towards crises. Second, production-prices cannot become manifest as such, but are nevertheless realised phenomena. It is thus warranted, to rebut the critiques, to assume that the new period starts with the production-prices rather than with the market-prices of the outputs of the previous period. But, of course, one can just as well start with the market-prices. On the basis of the above, let us now consider Marx's transformation of values into prices.

5.1. *The transformation-procedure*

In Table 2 below, both Sector 1 (the producer of means of production, MP) and Sector 2 (the producer of means of consumption, MC) are represented by a modal producer.[121] Let i and o indicate inputs and outputs respectively, so that, for example, MPi stands for the means of production as inputs and let t_1, t_2, and t_3 indicate different and successive moments in time. We consider first the use-value aspect and focus initially on columns 2, 4, and 7. We assume simple reproduction, that is, all the surplus-product is consumed by the capitalists so that no surplus-product is reinvested. The procedure would not change in expanded reproduction, that is, if a part of the surplus

---

[121] We are dealing thus with market-values. For a more detailed analysis in which each sector is composed of modal and non-modal producers see Carchedi 1991, Chapter 3. To simplify matters, in what follows, individual value will be taken to mean the individual value of the modal producers, that is, the market-value, unless otherwise specified.

Table 2. The computation of production-prices in Marx

	t1	t1–t2	t2	t2	t2	t2–t3
(1) Sector	(2) Inputs	(3) Value produced	(4) Outputs	(5) Market- price	(6) Production- price	(7) Inputs
1 MP	60MPi+ 40MCi	60c1 + 40v1 + 40s1 = 140V1	140MPo	150V1	130V1	60MPi+ 40MCi
2 MC	80MPi+ 20MCi	80c2 + 20v2 + 20s2 = 120V2	120MCo	110V2	130V2	80MPI+ 20MCi

product were reinvested instead of being consumed unproductively by the capitalists.

At t1 (Column 2), Sector 1 starts the production-process with 60MPi+40MCi and, at t2, it has produced 140MPo (Column 4). Similarly, Sector 2 starts its production-process at t1 with 80MPi+20MCi and, at t2, it has produced 120MCo. The 140MPo are purchased only by the capitalists while the 120MCo are purchased both by the capitalists and by the labourers.

Point t2 is the end-point of period t1–t2. As an initial assumption (to be relaxed shortly), t2 is also considered to be the starting point of t2–t3 (Column 7), in other words, there is no time-lag between the end of one process and the beginning of the next one. Then, the *same* commodities as outputs of t1–t2 become immediately the inputs of t2–t3. The 140MPo are purchased as inputs at t2 by Sector 1 (60MPi) and Sector 2 (80MPi). Thus, at t2, all means of production are purchased in the same proportions as at t1, the beginning of t1–t2. The 120MCo are purchased by the labourers of both sectors (40MCi in Sector 1 and 20MCi for Sector 2) and by the capitalist (40MCi in Sector 1 and 20MCi for Sector 2). This follows from the assumption of a rate of surplus-value of 100%. In Sector 1, the capitalists pay the labourers 40v1 and extract and appropriate 100% of 40v1, 40s1. Similarly, in Sector 2, the capitalists pay a wage of 20v2 and extract and appropriate 100% of it, 20s2. At t2, all the means of consumption are again used by the labourers in both sectors as at t1 and the rest is consumed unproductively by the capitalists.

Let us now consider the value-aspect. We assume that one unit of abstract labour (value) is represented by one unit of money (so that, as mentioned above, the following figures can be read, as in Marx, both as money and as labour-, or value-, quantities).[122] Each sector invests a certain quantity of money as constant capital (c) to buy means of production and as variable capital (v) to buy the labourers' labour-power and forces the labourers to produce surplus-value (s) so that the total value of the output in each sector is c+v+ s = V. Column (3) gives the value invested at t1 as well as the value produced during t1–t2 by both sectors (140V1 and 120V2). At t2, the producers of MPo and MCo sell their products at their market-price. These commodities are bought by other producers as MPi and MCi of the next production-period at the same prices (if the same commodity is bought and sold at the same time, it must be bought and sold for the same price). *The transformation is thus, first of all, the redistribution of the value contained in the outputs if the value represented by their market-price does not coincide with their value contained.* This is Column 5, where, for example, Sector 1 sells its MPo at 150V1. Given that the total value realised cannot exceed the total value contained, Sector 2 must sell its MCo at 110V2. There is thus a transfer of value equal to 10V from Sector 2 to Sector 1, that is, Sector 1 realises 10V more than the value it produces at the expense of Sector 2. The new production-period begins with means of production and of consumption whose value is 150MPi and 110MCi.

This computation implies the first principle of dialectics set out in Chapter 1 above, namely that phenomena are always both realised and potential. If the value contained in the outputs (140V1 and 120V2) is realised as 150V1 and 110V2, the former set of values realises itself as the latter set of values. *The value contained in the output (140V1 and 120V2) is potential value and the price is value realised.* The quantitative transformation rests on a qualitative, dialectical, transformation from potential to realised quantities. But the reverse is also true. If those outputs enter as inputs in the next production-process, the value realised by them as outputs of t1–t2 (150V1 and 110V2) becomes again the potential value of those same commodities as inputs of t2–t3. This means that the initial assumption in Table 2 that the values contained in the MPi and MCi at t1 are (60+80)c and (40+20)v implies a previous production-period, t0–t1 not shown in Table 2, whose MPo was sold at 140V1 and whose MCo was sold at 60V2.[123] This is the first point at which dialectics comes in, the transforma-

---

[122] To further simplify matters, there is no fixed capital here, in other words, all the means of production (MP) are consumed in one period.

[123] This would seem to imply an endless regression in time. But this is not the case, as Sub-Section 5.2 below will show.

tion of potential into realised and back to potential values. This is not only an application of the first principle of dialectics as set out in Chapter 1. It is also consonant with Marx. The value of the means of production 'is determined not by the labour process into which it enters as a means of production but by that out of which it has issued as a product'.[124] However,

> Suppose the price of cotton to be one day sixpence a pound, and the next day, in consequence of a failure of the cotton crop, a shilling a pound. Each pound of the cotton bought at sixpence, *and worked up after the rise in value,* transfers to the product a value of one shilling; and the cotton already spun before the rise, and perhaps circulating in the market as yarn, likewise transfers to the product twice its original value.[125]

This would seem to contradict the quote that the inputs 'add to the labour time contained in the products only as much labour time as they themselves contained *before* the production process'.[126] If a commodity/input has an original value of six euros, how can it transfer 12 euros to the product after its price has doubled? This can only be the case if it transfers six euros of its own value plus six euros of the value of other commodities. That this is what Marx had in mind is supported by his approving quote of the eighteenth-century Italian economist Pietro Verri to the effect that 'all the phenomena of the universe, whether produced by the hand of man or indeed by the universal laws of physics, are not to be conceived of as acts of creation but solely as a reordering of matter'.[127] Suppose a commodity A is sold as an output at the end of t_0–t_1 at 6 euros. This is its price as an output of t_0–t_1 but also its value contained as an input of t_1–t_2. At t_1, A enters the production-period t_1–t_2 as an input of another commodity, B. As far as the price-structure of B is concerned, at t_2 the producer of B realises the individual value of A, or the value contained in A. This is the value it had at t_1 as an input of t_1–t_2, that is, 6 euros. Suppose now that A doubles its price during t_1–t_2 and suppose that, at t_2, the price of A that rules the market is 12 euros. Then, the producer of B will want to charge, as far as A is concerned, 12 euros. If the purchasers of B are willing and able to pay an extra 6 euros, they will have

[124] Marx 1967a, p. 206.
[125] Marx 1967a, p. 209; emphasis added.
[126] Marx 1988, p. 177.
[127] Marx 1976a, p. 133.

less purchasing power for other commodities. The producers of those com-modities will have to lower their prices by that much. This is consonant with the following: 'Although [the inputs – G.C.] entered the labour process with a definite value, they may come out of it with a value that is larger or smaller, because the labour time society needs for their production has undergone a general change.'[128] Here, too, the theoretical foundation is provided by dialectics. The value of the input A at t_1 is only potential because A realises its value (in a possibly modified quantity) at t_2, when B (of which A is an input) is sold.

This holds also if the output of the previous period (A) is not sold imme-diately upon being completed or, even if immediately sold, it lays unused for some time before entering the production of B. The value realisable by A (the socially-necessary labour) might change during the period it is not sold or used. The value A transfers to B is the value it realises when it is sold as an output of the previous period. The value realised by B on account of A can be different. The loss or gain of the producer of the output B using that input A is then given by the difference between the value realised by A when it is sold as an output of the previous period and the value it has when it enters the production of B plus the difference between this value and the value A realises when B is sold.

It follows that *the complete transformation must take into account not only the redistribution of surplus-value contained in the output but also that of the value of the inputs.* It also follows that, if capitalists who are more productive than the average in their sector realise more than the average rate of profit and vice versa for the less-than-average-productivity capitalists, the surplus-value produced is redistributed among all producers, but in such a way that only the producers who adopt the average technique at the moment of their prod-ucts' realisation receive the average rate of profit.[129] Marx provides the exam-ple of a capitalist using a gold- instead of a steel-spindle. Only the capitalists using a steel-spindle (the average technique) realise the average rate of profit. The capitalist using a gold-spindle realises less than the value of the spindle transferred to the product. The difference is appropriated by the producers

---

[128] Marx 1988, p. 79.
[129] This is not shown in Table 2, because each sector is represented by one producer who is thus the average producer by definition. For detailed numerical examples, see Carchedi 1991, Chapter 3.

using the average technique (steel spindle). While the average rate of profit is computed by dividing at t2 the total surplus-value produced during t1–t2 by the total capital invested at t1 (that is, invested both by average and non-average producers), the production-prices are computed by adding this average profit-rate to the *average* value of the inputs at t1 (which is why the average rate of profit is tendentially realised only by the average producers).

This is Marx's procedure. This procedure has been criticised on two accounts. They are the backwards *ad infinitum* critique and the price-inconsistency critique.

5.2. *The backwards* ad infinitum *critique*

We have seen that, in order to compute the production-price of this period's outputs, we must know the individual value of this period's inputs. But they are the production-price of the previous period's outputs that, in their turn, depend upon the individual value of their inputs. Supposedly, we are trapped in infinite regression. This is the backwards *ad infinitum* critique.[130] This approach, the quest for the origin, is absurd because it would make any science impossible. Moreover, to posit the value of the inputs at the beginning of the period as given can be theoretically justified. The solution hinges on the principle that the value realised is not simply the social evaluation of the expenditure of physical human energy in the abstract. It is its social evaluation *when the output is sold*. Seen from this perspective, there is no need to regress infinitely in time. One step backward in time is sufficient.

Suppose we want to calculate the abstract labour (value) contained in the means of production, for example a machine, entering the t1–t2 period at t1. We can do that only if we start our computation in t0–t1, the period preceding the present one. We can count the hours of labour needed to produce that machine during t0–t1. This is *new* labour (necessary labour plus surplus-labour). The quantity of money paid as wages and profits corresponds to this quantity of labour. Suppose that wages and profits amount to 40,000 euros and that the hours of new labour are 200. The ratio 200 / 40,000 = 0.005 indicates that one euro represents 0.005 of one hour of new labour. Given the *inherent homogeneity of both money and value as abstract labour*, the same ratio applying

---

[130] Robinson 1972, p. 202.

to the new labour can be applied to all the labour realised by the sale of that machine. If the machine is sold at t1 for 60,000 euros, by applying that ratio we obtain the *social valuation* (300 hours) of the abstract labour (value) realised by that machine when it is sold as an output at t1. This is also the labour contained in that machine when it enters as an input in the next production period t1–t2. The individual value of the inputs of t1–t2 is thus obtained not by endlessly counting the hours of past labour but through a *social valuation* of past labour at the end of the previous process (t0–t1). Both the value of the inputs and of the outputs can be expressed in monetary terms. Starting from t1–t2, the labour-value of the output of t1–t2 is also the labour-value of the input of t2–t3, and therefore stepping back in time is no longer needed. Notice that the double transformation of more-skilled into less-skilled labour and of more-intense into less-intense labour need not concern us here because, if money-prices (wages and profits) represent value realised, they represent the hours of labour realised whatever the internal structure of those hours of labour, that is irrespective of whether they have been hours of labour of a certain intensity and skill or not.

5.3. *The price-inconsistency (circularity-) critique*

Even though a first critique was put forward by von Böhm-Bawerk[131] shortly after the appearance of *Capital*, Volume III, by far the most influential attack on Marx's transformation-procedure has been mounted by von Bortkiewicz[132] which was brought to the modern readership's attention by Sweezy.[133] To exemplify, in Table 2 above, the value of the MPo is 140 but their production-price is 130. Similarly, the value of the MCo is 120 but their production-price is 130. The capitalists sell their MPo at 130 but need (must buy) MPi for a value of 140 to start the new production-process on the same scale. The purchasing power needed to buy those 140MPo is insufficient to start a new process. Similarly, the capitalists sell the MCo at 130 but both capitalists and labourers need (buy) MCi for a value of 120. There is excess-purchasing

---

[131] Von Böhm-Bawerk 1973 argued that there is a contradiction between the first and the third volume of *Capital*. For a refutation of this critique see Ernst 1982, Carchedi 1984, Freeman and Carchedi 1996, and Kliman 2007.
[132] Von Bortkiewicz 1971, p. 30.
[133] Sweezy 1970.

power. *Simple reproduction fails*, or so it seems. The reason is that (supposedly) in Table 2 the inputs are bought at their value contained but sold at their production-price. If this were the case, it would be a glaring contradiction because, if the inputs of a process are also the outputs of another process, the same commodity must be bought by the purchaser and sold by the seller at the same price (value). This is the price-inconsistency critique.

It follows that if prices cannot be derived from values, there is supposedly in Marx a value-system in which the value of the outputs is determined by the value of the inputs (Column 4 in Table 2 above) along with a price-system in which the (production-) prices of the outputs are determined by the (production-) prices of the inputs. Consequently, there is a dual system in Marx. It also follows that there are two rates of profit. In the words of Steedman, Marx 'assumes that $S/(C+V)$ is the rate of profit but then derives the result that prices diverge from values, which means precisely, in general, that $S/(C+V)$ is *not* the rate of profit'.[134] In Table 2 above, the value system gives an average rate of profit of 30% (inputs and outputs are valued at their value). But, if the inputs are valued at the production-prices, the MPi are devalued to $130/140 = 0.9285$ so that Sector 1 invests $60 \times 0.9285 = 57.72$ and Sector 2 invests $80 \times 0.9285 = 74.28$ in MP. Similarly, the MC are revalued to $130/120 = 1.0833$ so that Sector 1 invests 43.33 and Sector 2 invests 21.67 in MC. These would be the production-prices of the inputs. Thus, the price-system would be the one in Table 3 below

Table 3. The retroactive valuation of the inputs

C	V	S	V
55.72	43.33	43.33	142.38
74.28	21.67	21.67	117.62
130.00	65.00	65.00	260.00

Now, the average rate of profit is not 30% any more (as in the value-system) but $65/195 = 33.33\%$. The inputs are bought and sold either at their value or at their production-price, but not at both. This is the price-inconsistency critique.

---

[134] Steedamn 1977, p. 31.

Firstly; we must note that the critique rests on a theory whose foundation is hopelessly inconsistent. This system is based on commodities seen purely as use-values and thus as the outcome of purely concrete labour. For Steedman, 'the rate of profit and all process of production can be determined without reference to any value magnitude'.[135] Value is thus redundant. But concrete labours are incommensurable. Steedman is aware of the difficulty. His answer is 'All summations of labour-time are summations of quantities of abstract labour'.[136] But this is a glaring contradiction. If abstract labour is needed for commensurability-purposes, it is not redundant. Until this contradiction is solved, the neo-Ricardian approach is based on quicksand. While it pretends to see the mote in Marx's eyes, it does not see the beam in its own.

Second, the critique is based on a confusion that, even though elementary, has held sway also among Marxist authors. The inputs MPi are bought and sold at t₁ for 140 and the outputs MPo are bought and sold at t₂ at 130. The inputs and outputs of a production-period are *two different commodities* bought and sold at *two different moments at two different prices* (this, in essence, is the temporalist approach). The same for MCi and MCo. By holding that the MPi are bought at 140 (their value) and *at the same time* sold as MPo at 130 (their price of production) the critics discover a 'contradiction'. To escape this 'contradiction', they submit that the prices of the inputs and of the outputs should be determined simultaneously through a system of simultaneous equations.[137] In so doing, time is wiped out. But then, if realisation is instantaneous, if time does not exist, production must also be atemporal, that is, the inputs must be the *same commodities* as the outputs. The inputs of one period become the outputs of *the same period*.[138]

---

[135] Steedman 1977, p. 14.
[136] Steedman 1977, p. 19.
[137] Von Bortkiewicz 1973, pp. 199–221.
[138] It could be argued that the inputs are valued at their replacement-cost at the end of the period. If an input A costs 100 at t₁ but, at t₂, it would cost 80 to replace it, its value contained is said to be 80 (its replacement-cost) at t₂. A value of 20 is made to vanish. In reality, A has cost 100 at t₁ and the producer of B (who uses A as an input) realises only 80 for A, that is, loses 20 to the purchasers of her B because, by t₂, the average price of A and thus of B has dropped by 20. However, in the replacement-cost approach, inputs and outputs have the same prices but are not the same commodities. The replacement-cost of A is the value of another, even though physically identical, A.

The postulate on which the critique rests and builds its simultaneous price-determination is a reality without time. This implies equilibrium. Clearly, Marx's supposed inconsistency is surreptitiously created by injecting the atemporal assumption into an approach that, like reality, oozes with time. This inconsistency disappears if time is reintroduced in the analysis, that is, if two points are kept in mind. Consider the means of production (the same holds for the means of consumption). First, given t1–t2, at the moment of the MP's purchase/sale (t2), their price as MPo of one period (t1–t2) become their value contained as the MPi of the following period (t2–t3). If the end of one period coincides with the start of the following period (t2), the same commodity has, at the same time, both a price, that is, a value (actually or tendentially) realised as the MPo of a period (t1–t2), and a value contained, a value not yet realised, as the MPi of the following period (t2–t3). Second, the means of production bought and sold at t2 and means of production bought and sold at t3 are not the same commodities, even if the latter were perfect copies of the former. Different commodities bought and sold at different times need not have the same value and price.[139] Such simple considerations are sufficient to make the circularity-critique fail.

Marx is said to have been conscious of having made a mistake and that he did not correct it:

> We had originally assumed that the cost-price of a commodity equalled the *value* of the commodities consumed in its production. But for the buyer the price of production of a specific commodity is its cost-price.... There is always the possibility of an error if the cost-price of a commodity in any particular sphere is identified with the value of the means of production consumed by it. Our present analysis does not necessitate a closer examination of this point.[140]

There is no mistake here if one chooses, following Marx, the temporalist approach. Given t1–t2, the output A is valued at its production-price at t2, the

---

[139] The first critique of the simultaneist approach inherent in neo-Ricardianism is Perez 1980. Carchedi 1984 (reprinted in Fine 1986, pp. 215–39) reaches independently similar results and provides the first temporalist counter-critique in English. In a different manner from Perez, Carchedi stresses the need for a dialectical approach, an element that has been disregarded by all other temporalist authors. This work returns to the dialectical origin of the temporalist approach.

[140] Marx 1967, pp. 164–5; emphasis in the original.

moment of sale. For the buyer, the same commodity is the input that enters the new production-process also at t2. Then, the production-price becomes the individual value of the same commodity A as an input of t2–t3. What Marx says is that it would be an error to compute the cost-price of B on the basis of the individual value (rather then the production-price) of A as an output of t1–t2. This does not concern Marx here because he is interested in the production-price of B, so that the production-price of A and its difference with its individual value can be taken as given.[141]

The internal consistency of Marx's transformation-procedure can be defended with different arguments from those used above. For example, Moseley argues that 'The main point to emphasize here is that Marx's key concept of capital is defined in terms of money, not in terms of labor-time....Marx is not talking about the labor-time embodied in the means of production, or the means of subsistence thrown into and withdrawn from circulation.'[142] 'These *'quantities of constant capital and variable capital are taken as given.'*[143] 'The aggregate money capital...is assumed to represent a definite quantity of abstract social labor. The precise quantity of abstract social labor represented by a given quantity of money depends on the value of money, that Marx also took as given.'[144] 'Constant capital...is the money capital invested to purchase means of production, whether or not this quantity of money capital is proportional to the labor-time embodied in the means of production.'[145] Similar considerations hold for variable capital.

Moseley is to be commended for his effort to show that Marx's transformation-procedure is free from internal contradictions. He rightly points out that *Capital*, Volume I is about the production of surplus-value and *Capital*, Volume III about its distribution. This is why the constant capital at the start of the transformation can be taken as given. However, in his article from 2000, Moseley's approach is flawed by a different form of inconsistency. The cardinal feature of his interpretation is not that the starting point is money, which

---

[141] Ramos 1998–9 stresses that Engels omitted a relevant passage and included a numerical example that did not appear in the original and that this omission reduced the strength of Marx's presentation, contributing to the consolidation of von Bortkiewicz's interpretation.

[142] Moseley 2000, p. 289.

[143] Moseley 2000, p. 290; emphasis in the original.

[144] Moseley 2000, p. 294.

[145] Moseley 2000, p. 296.

is assumed to represent value. Rather, it is the qualification as to 'whether or not this quantity of money capital is proportional to the labor-time embodied in the means of production', that is, whether it is its individual value or its production-price. It follows that 'Marx did *not* "fail to transform these inputs" because the inputs do not have to be transformed – instead they remain invariant'.[146] This interpretation retains the distinction between individual value and production-price, only we do not know which one is the value of the inputs when they enter the production-process. The problem here is that, if the outputs are valued at their production-prices, the same commodities as inputs must also be valued at their production-prices. The individual value, that which has to be transformed into a production-price, becomes redundant. But the redundancy of the individual value is inconsistent with the qualification as to 'whether or not this quantity of money capital is proportional to the labor-time embodied in the means of production', because this qualification admits the existence of individual values and therefore implies their difference with production-prices.

It might be for this reason that, in his 2008 article, Moseley discards the notion of individual value as a real, existing quantity and submits that the inputs enter the production-process at their production-price. Why is this so? Because, Moseley submits, while in *Capital*, Volume I, Marx assumes as a first approximation that the inputs are valued at their individual values, in *Capital*, Volume III, 'Marx provides a *more complete explanation*', that is, that the inputs are valued at their production-prices.[147] The transformation, thus, is not any more a real process, a redistribution of the value of the inputs. The transformation is simply a question of approximating a more precise concept: 'what changes is the explanation'.[148] This is a radical reformulation of Marx's problematic. It reintroduces a contradiction between Volume I and Volume 3. But this contradiction disappears if the production-price of an output is considered to be also the individual, not transformed value of the same commodity as an input of the following period. However, Moseley chooses a different approach.

---

[146] Moseley 2008, p. 109.
[147] Moseley 2008, p. 116; emphasis in the original.
[148] Ibid.

At first sight, it might seem as if Moseley's approach were consistent with a temporalist approach. In fact, if the outputs of the previous period are valued at their production-price, and if those outputs are the inputs of the following period, then the inputs are also valued at that production-price. However, consider a t1–t2 period. In conformity with Moseley's interpretation, at t1 a certain machine enters the production-process at its production-price. This is the value it transfers to the product. Suppose now that the production-price of that machine changes between t1 and t2. Suppose it falls because of changed technologies that reduce the labour-time needed on average to produce it. There are two possibilities.

It can be assumed that the value transferred to the output is the production-price the machine had at t1 and that the value realised due to the employment of that machine is the production-price that machine has at t2 when the output is old. The producer has employed a machine whose value (production-price) at t1 is higher than the average at t2. The producer loses the difference to the purchasers of the output. In this case, the production-price of the input at t1 has been transformed at t2. But, then, it is incorrect to call the value of the machine at t1 its production-price, because, at t1, that value has still to be transformed. That value is transformed at the time of the sale of the output of which that machine is an input and is therefore its individual value. The notion of individual value re-emerges necessarily after having been banned. Alternatively, it can be assumed that the value transferred to the product is the production-price of that machine at t2, that is, its replacement-value at t2. In this case, that machine does not have two values, the individual value at t1 to be transformed into its production-price at t2. Rather, it has only one value, at t2, and this is the value it transfers to the product. In this case, the production-price of the inputs is determined simultaneously with the production-price of the output and one falls into a simultaneist approach, with the consequences highlighted above. The consequence of discarding the notion of individual value and of retaining only that of production-price is simultaneism.

There is a point at which Moseley seems to discuss the transformation of the individual value of the means of production into their production-prices. In discussing fixed-capital goods, Moseley notes that 'the money recovered from the depreciation component of all capital goods is used to purchase the subset of newly-produced fixed capital goods'.[149] Supposedly, in this case,

---

[149] Moseley 2008, p. 112.

'two different bundles of fixed capital goods are exchanged for one another'.[150] Since different goods exchange at the same production-prices, and since different goods have been produced with different organic compositions, there is an exchange of different quantities of labour embodied (transfer of value). This implies that there is a transformation of individual values into production prices. The notion of individual value emerges again.

Moseley's interpretation has been criticised by Ravagnani, but from a different, neo-Ricardian, perspective. Contrary to Moseley, Ravagnani argues that Marx takes as the starting point of his analysis not the money-quantities but the physical quantities of the means of subsistence and of the means of production and then derives the constant and variable capital (money-quantities) from these physical quantities. Both authors can produce textual evidence to support their interpretation. This is not without reason, given that Marx starts from the value embodied in the means of production and of consumption, and thus from the money-expression of those physical quantities, as in Table 2 above. The alternative between Moseley's interpretation, on the one hand, and Ravagnani's interpretation, on the other hand, is thus false. The relevant passages can be thought to be 'ambiguous'[151] only because the two opposite interpretations capture only one aspect of Marx's theoretical richness.[152] But this aside, Ravagnani's critique is misdirected because it does not get to the heart of Moseley's position. The specificity of Moseley's position is not that constant and variable capital are given; rather, its core feature is the denial that the value of the inputs needs to be transformed. The critique, however, is the logical extension of the physicalist nature of the neo-Ricardian theory. The inconsistencies and adverse ontological features of this theory have been pointed out above, especially the incommensurability of different use-values and the theorisation of capitalism as an equilibrium-system.

---

[150] Ibid.

[151] Moseley 2008, p. 115.

[152] In an attempt to find common grounds with the neo-Ricardians, Moseley submits the following: 'I would suggest that we revise Marx's theory, or "reconstruct" it, along the lines of...the "monetary" interpretation presented here: that the magnitudes of constant capital and variable capital are initially presupposed in the theory of surplus-value and then are eventually explained in successive stages by the values and the prices of production of the presupposed quantities of means of production and means of subsistence' (Moseley 2008, p. 118). Given that this is Marx's position, it is surprising to read that 'With this one revision, which is entirely reasonable and for which there is substantial textual evidence, Marx's theory would be transformed from a logically contradictory mess to a logically coherent whole' (ibid.).

Finally, it could be held that the analysis of a static, atemporal situation can be the starting point for a more realistic analysis based on time. But this is inadmissible. One can start from a simplified depiction of reality in order to proceed to a more and more complex and realistic one, but on condition that each further step should retain the basic, fundamental assumptions upon which the previous stage of research rested, rather than on their rejection. In other words, the further made assumptions should not conflict with the initial ones. If, at a later stage of the analysis, one rejects those initial assumptions and replaces them with other, incompatible ones, one rejects the previous analysis (the more simplified one) and creates a disjuncture rather than a bridge between the different stages of the analysis. If one starts from a static analysis based on simultaneism, one should proceed to a dynamic analysis also based on simultaneism. If this cannot be done, the analysis of a static situation is severed from, and becomes useless for, further analyses of real, dynamic situations, because the initial postulate of an absence of time conflicts with the further postulate of the existence of time. Either one postulates time or one does not. It follows that a timeless dimension cannot be the starting point of an analysis of reality, because it denies reality (time) rather than distilling from it its most pregnant aspects and using them as the starting point of the inquiry.

5.4. Reproduction-prices and simple reproduction

Let us now see how, contrary to the critics, the production-prices of the outputs are consistent with the requirements of simple reproduction.[153] Consider again Table 2 above. At t2, the unit production-price of the MPo is $130/140 = 0.9285$. 80MPo are bought as MPi by the capitalists of Sector 2 at the unit production-price of 0.9285 and 60MPo are bought as MPi by the capitalists of Sector 1 at the same price. All MPo are sold at the unit production-price. Similarly, the unit production-price of the MCo is $130/120 = 1.0833$. 40MCo are bought by the labourers of Sector 1 and 20MCo are bought by the labourers of Sector 2 at the unit-price of 1.0833. The values spent for the MPo and MCo needed to start a new cycle at t2 are

Sector 1: $(60 \times 0.9286 = 55.714) + (40 \times 1.0833 = 43.333) = 99.05$
Sector 2: $(80 \times 0.9286 = 74.286) + (20 \times 1.0833 = 21.667) = 95.95$

---

[153] The following example is taken from Carchedi 2005b, p. 132.

Given that both sectors must realise 130V, the profit the capitalists have in order to purchase the remaining 60MCo is

Sector 1: 130–99.05 = 30.95V
Sector 2: 130–95.95 = 34.05V

With this 34.05 + 30.95 = 65V, the capitalists of the two sectors can purchase 65/1.0833 = 60MCo. Thus, 140MPo are supplied and demanded at their production-price and the same holds for the 120MCo. All output is sold at its production-prices and simple reproduction is ensured. Notice that the capitalists of Sector 1 receive 30.95/1.0833 = 28.6 means of consumption instead of 30 and that those of Sector 2 receive 34.05/1.0833 = 31.4 means of consumption instead of 30. The difference with the simultaneist approach is that these production-prices apply to the MC and MP as inputs of the following period rather than of the same period.[154]

5.5. *Simple reproduction with production-prices and purchasing-power parity*

One aspect remains to be considered. In Table 2 above, there are two sectors, one producing means of production (MP) and the other producing means of consumption (MC). In it, all MP are exchanged for MC and vice versa. But, at a lower level of aggregation, some MP will be exchanged with MP and some MC will be exchanged with MC. Sector 1 exchanges internally 60 MP for a value of 60c1 and buys 80MC from sector 2 by selling 80MP for a value of 40v1 and 40s1 (for a total value of 80). Sector 2 exchanges internally means of consumption for a value of 20v2 and 20s2 and buys means of production from Sector 1 by selling 80MC for a value of 80c2. As Marx discovered in *Capital*, Volume II, the condition for simple reproduction is then c2=v1+s1. If products are exchanged at their values, a value of 80 is exchanged for a value of 80. This concerns inter-sectoral exchange. However, if 80MP are exchanged for 80MC at their production-prices,

Sector 1 sells 80MP at 80×0.9286 = 74.288 while
Sector 2 sell 80MC at 80×1.0833 = 86.664.

---

[154] Screpanti's 'proof' that the temporal approach is mistaken is based upon a computational mistake that, if correct, proves that the temporal approach is indeed correct. See Screpanti, 2005. For the rebuttal of Screpanti's 'proof', see Carchedi 2005b.

By selling its 80MP, Sector 1 receives 74.288 from Sector 2 but needs 86.664 to buy 80MC. It lacks a value of 12.376. Conversely, Sector 2 has a value of 12.376 in excess. The purchasing powers of the two sectors (the value obtained by each sector through the sale of its commodities and available for the purchase of the other sector's commodities) do not coincide. Simple reproduction with prices of production would seem to be inconsistent with the purchasing power needed for inter-sectoral exchange. But this is not the case.

If the problem changes, the conditions must change too. For the purchasing powers to be equal, the capital invested to produce MP and MC for inter-sectoral exchange must be *equal*. In this case, the same profit-rate on the same capital gives the same value realised and thus the same purchasing power. This is the case in Table 2 if all commodities are exchanged inter-sectorally (in that case, both the 140MP and the 120MC exchanged inter-sectorally are produced with a capital of 100), but not if we assume that only 80MP are exchanged for 80MC (because those 80MP and 80MC require different quantities of capital for their production). Thus, Table 2 is unsuited to exemplify the case at hand. A different numerical example is thus required, one in which the same capital is invested in both sectors for inter-sectoral exchange. If the further assumption is made that capitals producing for inter-sectoral exchange cannot produce for intra-sectoral exchange, the average rate of profit is the same for the whole of the economy only under the assumption that the average capitals producing for intra-sectoral exchange use the same organic composition of capital as that of the capitals producing for inter-sectoral exchange.

5.6. *Negative values*

Consider the case of an economy in which ten bushels of seed-corn (input) are planted by farmers who perform a certain quantity of labour. Owing to a drought, only nine bushels of corn (output) are harvested. For simultaneism, given that the price (value) at the beginning of the period is equal to the price (value) at the end of it, the output is worth less than the input. In this case, labour subtracts value instead of adding it. Kliman objects to this conclusion because, in terms of Marx's value-theory, (abstract) labour added must increase the value produced. The output (nine bushels) is worth more than the input (ten bushels).[155] Actually, both positions are erroneous. In

---

[155] Kliman 2007, pp. 81–2.

Marx's theory, abstract labour creates value *if as concrete labour it transforms use-values into new use-values*. If concrete labour *destroys* use-values, abstract labour cannot create new value, it destroys the value contained in the seed-corn. This would be the case mentioned by Baran of a bakery paying a worker to add chemicals to the dough in order to increase the bread's perishability, thus destroying a part of the bread's use-value.[156] This is what I have called value-destroying labour.[157] The case mentioned above is similar, only that the destruction of value is achieved by nature rather than by labourers. The abstract labour gone in the corn destroyed by the drought has been destroyed and cannot create value, which is why, if nature destroyed all corn, one would be left without value, no matter how much labour the production of that corn had cost.

5.7. *The hidden dimension*

Dialectics is the hidden dimension that both makes Marx's transformation procedure intelligible and constitutes it as an element of a theory of radical social change. Consider first the dialectics of the relation between abstract labour and value.

(i)   If the capitalist production-process has been started but is not yet finished, the labourers are performing abstract labour and are thus creating the commodity's value embodied. However, that abstract labour is not yet realised value, it is, rather, value in formation, potential embodied value, because the commodity itself, not being finished, is being created and thus it exists only potentially.

(ii) If the production-process is completed and thus the commodity is finished (but not yet sold), the abstract labour which has gone into it becomes the value *contained* or *embodied* in it, whose material substance is abstract labour. Since a commodity must be sold in order to realise its value, its value contained is also its potential realised value.

(iii) When the commodity is sold, the value embodied in it becomes *realised* value (either tendentially or actually realised value) whose substance is

---

[156] Baran 1968, p. xx.
[157] Carchedi 1987, p. 228 and Carchedi 1991, pp. 138–9.

the value contained in it.[158] The labour embodied determines the value realised, because the former calls into existence the latter from the realm of its potentialities and because the latter reacts upon the former but in the following period.

(iv) Since commodities are produced in order to be sold for money, the labour-value realised (labour-price) becomes itself a substance that takes necessarily the *monetary form* of value. Money is the form of existence of, and thus represents value.

(v) The realised value (price) of the output becomes the non-realised value, or value contained, or potential realised value of the same commodity as an input of the following period. Here, too, the former determines the latter for similar reasons.

(vi) Finally, this potential value becomes again realised when the following period's output containing that input is sold. Here, too, the same reasons hold. It is from this point that the cycle of determination starts again.

The transformation seen as a dialectical process is a temporal succession of transformations, from potential to realised values and vice versa, and from determinant to determined values and vice versa. Dialectics is the *necessary qualitative* dimension that accounts theoretically for the quantitative transformation. The transformation seen as a dialectical process is thus an instance of the dialectical view of social reality as a temporal flow of determining and determined contradictory phenomena continuously emerging from a potential state to become realised and then going back to a potential state in a cyclical and tendential movement towards capitalism's supersession. It is a manifestation of the class-determined view of social reality. It is thus perfectly consistent with labour's world-view.

As argued in Chapter 1 above, dialectics does not reject but makes use of the tools of formal logic. From the perspective of temporalism immersed in dialectical logic, Marx's theory is perfectly consistent. This shows that temporalism is the principle upon which that theory rests and that simultaneism, even though internally consistent, is foreign to it. A simultaneist critique is

---

[158] Realised value is usually referred to as social value (also by Marx), as opposed to individual value. Since value always has a social content, *individual* value is here set against *realised* value.

an internal critique neither of temporalism nor of Marx. Simultaneist theories are not an 'improvement' of Marxism, but, rather, they represent different theories with their own class-content. As argued above, simultaneism implies equilibrium and thus a view of the economy tending towards its equilibrated reproduction. From this angle, the capitalist economy is an inherently rational system and any attempt to supersede it is irrational. That is simultaneism's social content. Temporalism, if immersed in a dialectical context, reaches the exactly opposite conclusions: the economy is in a constant state of non-equilibrium and tends towards its own supersession. From this perspective, capitalism is inherently irrational and any attempt to supersede it is rational. It is from this perspective that the four above issues have been analysed. From this perspective, the choice between temporalism and simultaneism turns out to be the choice between formal logic on the one hand, and dialectical logic on the other. This is much more than a personal preference; it is a class-determined choice based on a class-determined principle. If one is interested in radical change, one should choose temporal dialectics.

This is the *real significance* of the dialectical (and thus temporalist) approach.[159] Both temporalism and simultaneism should move on from being only a critique and counter-critique of each other, applying only formal logic to the issue of consistency, towards showing how their view of consistency fits into a wider theory of radical social change, thus grounding the choice of their initial postulate into labour's perspective. Neither of the two camps has done this and this has been the limit of the debate, on both sides. The time has come to change course and the challenge is to overcome this limit. This chapter has attempted to do that on the basis of a dialectical method of which temporalism and thus non-equilibrium is an integral part. It is only a beginning.[160] It is to be

---

[159] Kliman holds that the temporal single-system interpretation (and within it temporalism) cannot prove that 'Marx's theory is true' and that all it can prove is that it is logically consistent (Kliman, 2007, p. 168). This is correct if temporalism is immersed in formal logic. Kliman does an excellent job within this framework. But this is also the limit of his work and more generally of the temporalist approach as it has evolved over the years. Temporalism immersed in dialectical logic can indeed prove Marx's theory 'true', that is correct from the perspective of labour.

[160] In discussing replication as a principle of verification, Mohun holds that, 'What is required is not an assessment of rival interpretations, but a theory for today's world and its use in empirical analysis' (Mohun 2003, p. 100). Actually, this chapter has argued that what is required is an assessment of rival interpretations' consistency in terms both of formal and dialectical logic (and thus in terms of class-content). Dialectical

hoped that simultaneist authors will accept the challenge and show how their approach to the issue of consistency based on simultaneism and equilibrium is an aspect of a broader theory furthering the liberation of labour. Regarding both approaches, what Marx once said holds: *Hic Rhodus, hic salta!*

6. The alien rationality of *homo economicus*

The sections above have argued that Marx's theory is irreconcilable with a static notion of a reality in which time is banned and equilibrium rules. Since this notion is that upon which orthodox economic theory, in its many manifestations, is based, the argument above comes down to the irreconcilability between Marxist economics and orthodox economics. But are these two opposite approaches equally internally consistent in their own terms? Of course, orthodox economics claims to be free from internal contradictions. The character in charge of showing that this is the case is *homo economicus*, the first acquaintance of every student of economics. This section will show that it is the rationality of *homo economicus* and thus of orthodox-economic theory, rather then Marx's own, that fails the test of formal logic, the only mode of reasoning it knows.

According to the dominant economic theory, of which neoliberalism is an offspring, the capitalist economy, if let free to function unencumbered, tends naturally towards equilibrium. This tendency is based on *homo economicus*, the rational being *par excellence*. This rationality can be exemplified by the supply-and-demand curves: if the demand for a good rises, its price rises and vice versa; if the supply of a good rises, its price falls and vice versa. It follows that the two curves have different slopes, one has a rising slope, the other a falling slope. Therefore, they can intersect, thus fixing the equilibrium-price, that is, the price at which demand and supply coincide. This is the alpha and omega of *homo economicus'* rationality.[161]

This theoretical setting can be criticised on several grounds. However, the critique should be accurate. For example, it has been said that this rationality

---

verification is, at the same time, an element of 'a theory for today's world'. The ball is in now in Mohun's court and in the court of Marx's critics as well.

[161] For the sake of simplicity, I deal only with partial equilibrium-theory. For a more complete treatment which includes the problem of general equilibrium, see Carchedi 1991.

is egoistic because individuals maximise their own welfare independently of the others, as if they were monads for whom society does not exist.[162] This is not quite correct. *Homo economicus* is an egoist because he is rapacious and exploitative, qualities which do presuppose the existence of other people as well as his interest for those people. Let us take only one example, the behaviour behind the demand-curve. If the demand for a good rises, that is, if those who do not have that good have a greater need for it, those who do have that good take advantage of the situation (the greater need) and raise that good's price. *Homo economicus* maximises not independently of, but at the cost of, the others. He is an egoist because he exploits the needs of others.

The objection can be raised that, in reality, economic agents can (and do) behave differently, that is, altruistically. But the orthodox economist can easily refute this critique by subsuming altruism under egoism: if individuals maximise their pleasure by acting altruistically, they do not give up their egoistic rationality. However, aside from the obvious ideological advantage for capital of subsuming altruism under egoism, there are at least two reasons to reject this option. First, if human beings are both egoistic and altruistic, if they maximise their welfare by behaving both egoistically and altruistically and, if this maximisation is rational, then they are *always* rational, no matter what they do. If there is no longer any irrationality, the notion of rationality becomes meaningless and one ends up by explaining nothing. Secondly, an altruistic behaviour is inconsistent with the larger theoretical setting. An altruistic behaviour would lower (rather than increasing) prices if needs (demand) rise in order to make possible the satisfaction of those greater needs. But such a behaviour implies that the demand-curve can have both an upward and a downward slope. There is no guarantee any longer that it can intersect the supply-curve. In this case, the whole neoclassical construction, including the notion of equilibrium, would collapse like a house of cards. Altruism is logically inconsistent with neoclassical theory: they exclude each other.

Thus, egoism is the only behaviour consistent with neoclassical theory. What is the empirical evidence that human beings actually behave like *homo economicus*? Aside from some exceptions which – with some goodwill – could be disregarded, the amount of deviant behaviour is enormous. There

---

[162] Tsakalotos 2004, p. 142. For a critique along the lines of this section, see Carchedi 2006b.

is a whole range of goods, such as status-goods and financial goods, whose demand can rise if their price rises and fall if their price falls. While the former category might be quantitatively relatively unimportant, the same cannot be said of the latter. Already in the 1990s, the financial markets were fifty times bigger than the export of goods and services. Or, to mention another example among many, at the beginning of the 1990s, the one hundred biggest pension-funds of the USA, Japan and Europe were managing one third of the world's income. Not bad for an exception! But this is not all. The behaviour of demand is strongly influenced by the economic cycle. For example, in the upward-phase, capitalists increase their purchases of means of production and labour-power even though their prices rise. In the downward-phase, they can decrease their demand even if prices fall. The same holds for consumption-goods. It follows that all goods, from consumption- to investment-goods, from financial to status-goods, can behave as presupposed by *homo economicus* or not. Therefore, a huge slice of reality is irrational for *homo economicus* and thus cannot be explained in terms of the theories based upon him. Moreover, the slope of the demand-curve is indeterminate and the notion of equilibrium (in exchange) unfounded.

But there is more. The slope of the demand-curve, and thus the rationality of *home economicus*, cannot be empirically tested either. If I want to know how a person's demand for a good changes as a result only of a price-change, I must assume the *ceteris paribus* condition, that is, that this person has the same interest (preference) for that good after as well as before the change. In other words, my preferences must not change in that time-period or I will not be able to test whether and how my demand changes as a result of only that price-change. But we cannot be sure that this is the case, that is, the hypothesis can be tested only if we assume *a reality without change, that is, without time*. Marshall was aware of this: 'We do not suppose for time to be allowed for any alteration in the character of tastes of the man.'[163] If the theory must be testable, it is irrelevant because it has to rule out time. If time is introduced into the analysis, the theory ceases to be testable. In terms of Popperian methodology – to which orthodox economics adheres – the theory is pure metaphysics. Moreover, the consequences in terms of class-content of a theory based on the

---

[163] Marshall 1920, p. 94.

presupposition of the absence of time (and thus of equilibrium) have been made clear above.

But there is still more. *Homo economicus* is not only egoistic and rapacious, he is also arrogant. He asserts that his rationality is nothing less than the manifestation of human nature. The hypothesis that human nature is egoistic is based on a skilful ideological move. This is more easily seen if one considers marginalist theory. This theory rests on the notion of decreasing marginal utility, that is, the decreasing satisfaction the consumer derives from the consumption of an extra unit of a certain good. In equilibrium, the ratio between the marginal utility and the price must be equal for all goods. Then, if the marginal utility of a good rises, more is demanded of that good. But, at the same time, the ratio between that marginal utility and that price rises too. To re-establish equilibrium, its price must also rise. The same goes for a fall in marginal utility. Three features stand out. First, demand hinges upon the utility derived from the consumption of an extra unit of a good, that is, demand falls because of increased satiety (even if satiety increases at a decreasing pace). Second, a comparison between utilities implies that they are related to prices, that is, prices do not indicate purchasing power but are simply the factor which makes comparison possible. Third, it is on the basis of the comparison between these ratios that both the shape of the demand-curve (that is, the egoistic and rational nature of economic agents) and equilibrium are founded.

This theory can be criticided on several grounds. Here, it suffices to stress its class-content. If demand decreases with increasing satiety, the movement of demand is biologically, rather than socially, determined. It is with regard to this trait of human biology that the egoism inherent in the demand-curve is founded. But this 'explanation' of demand is class-determined – it reflects the view of those very few for whom purchasing power is no problem (for whom the limit to their consumption is only their satiation) rather than the view of the working class and of by far the greatest majority of the world's population, whose purchasing power is insufficient (even though the quantification of 'insufficient' varies from situation to situation). For them, if the price of the goods they need increases, their demand can fall but this fall is due to the decreasing purchasing power (value) left, given their limited and more often than not absolutely insufficient income. If this is the case, both the shape of the demand-curve (people's behaviour) and its theorisation (its reflection of human rationality) are socially, class-, determined. Marginalist theory super-imposes the view of the super-rich, and thus of capital, upon that of the rest of the world's population. The power of this ideology is that it tells a lie which seemingly corresponds to our daily experience.

The consequences are far reaching. The 'rational' (that is, exploitative and egoistic) behaviour of *homo economicus* (as depicted in the demand-function) is determined by capitalist society and is functional for the reproduction of this society. There is nothing rational about this behaviour, except that, under cap-italism, people learn to be, and are obliged to be, egoistic. From Marx's per-spective, human nature is neither egoistic (as the critique of *homo economicus'* supposed egoistic rationality shows) nor altruistic. Human beings tend to the maximal realisation of their potentialities, which can be realised only within a specific social setting where the ownership- and thus the production-rela-tions are determinant (see Chapter 1, Section 2.2 above). Consequently, they can strive towards their full development either *together with*, or *at the expense of*, each other. *This* is the choice and this is the difference between capital-ism and socialism. A notion of socialism in which scarcity has become less acute or even conquered does not capture the truly radical difference inherent in this change. The reason why this change is possible is that human beings are formed by the contradictory social relations in which they are born and through which they develop (something which, as shown in Chapter 1, Sec-tion 3 above, does not exclude but requires their individuality as concrete individuals). Under capitalism, egoism is functional for the reproduction of the system, altruism (in the sense of co-operation, solidarity and equality) is functional for its supersession. In this society, one can be an egoist or an altruist (in various degrees) simply because the social relations within which individuals are born and raised are contradictory, because the system – being based on contradictory social relations – creates the conditions for its own reproduction as well as for its own supersession.

The legitimacy of the capitalist system is based on a purportedly exploit-ative and egoistic human nature, so that this egoistic and exploitative system is supposedly the most suitable, and thus the most rational, to be justified in terms of this very nature. Any other system, such as a communist one based on co-operation, solidarity and equality, becomes then irrational because it is contrary to this supposed human nature. But, if one acknowledges that *homo economicus* is a creature of the capitalist system and that he reflects the essence of this system, his legitimacy simply vanishes. *Homo economicus* turns out to be nothing more than an ideological construction. Even an apparently harmless choice, as the use of a Latin term, has an ideological flavour because it tends to suggest that the last stage of human evolution is not *homo sapiens* but homo *economicus*.

Capitalism can be defended on other grounds. For example, as Milton Friedman suggested, orthodox-economic theory can be defended not on the grounds of its realism, but rather because of its forecasting power. This is not only a recognition of the lack of realism (and thus impotence) of the theory, it is also its own methodological own goal. In fact, the forecasting power of *homo economicus* is nil. As seen above, *homo economicus* forecasts the behaviour of the economic agents in cases when they behave so and fails to forecast such behaviour in all other cases. These latter instances are so many and are, indeed, so important that they could just as well be the rule rather than the exception. But this is not the main point. The point is that, even if the forecast is correct (for example, a price-rise as a consequence of a rise in demand), *homo economicus* has no valid explanation of it because the explanation is based on a supposed ahistorical egoistic human nature. If the explanation is lacking, the occurrence is a chance event. The same holds for the so-called exceptions.

As for the relationship between the realism of the assumption and the validity of a theory, we have seen in Chapter 1, Section 7 that the crucial point is the method of abstraction. In a sense, all theories are based on assumptions that are not realistic, because they are extreme simplifications of reality. Consequently, the problem as to whether a theory is realistic or unrealistic depends on the type of assumptions on which it rests. There are two types of assumptions, both of which are different and opposite from each other because they have been reached through two different and opposite methods of abstraction. There is a type of assumption-formation that allows us to build a realistic theory because the assumptions to be found there represent the *end-point* of a process of abstraction of the essential and determinant characteristics of the segment of reality that one wants to analyse. This is Marx's process of induction discussed in Chapter 1, Section 7. The notions reached through this process are, so to speak, an extract of reality that contains the other, more concrete and detailed aspects of reality. The process of deduction (discussed in Chapter 1, Section 7) starts from these notions and proceeds backwards, from higher to lower and ever lower levels of abstraction. This method allows for the possibility of reaching a more and more realistic (concrete) view of reality – what Marx calls 'the concrete in thought'. If, on the other hand, one starts from assumptions which are not realistic because reality has been irremediably eliminated from them, the theory based upon them cannot but be separated from reality by an unbridgeable gap. This is the case of *homo economicus*, whose theoretical existence (whose testability) depends upon the absence of time. Once time is introduced into the analysis, *homo economicus* has no reason to exist any longer because his existence and testability depends on this very absence. All the theories, and not only the neoclassical one, whose basis is *homo economicus* are characterised (whether they are aware of it or not) by the fundamental assumption that time does not exist. But, once this assumption is made, it cannot be dropped and one is trapped in a model, or notion of reality, that is anything but real. The fundamental conclusion within this context is that, in the absence of time and therefore of change, society and thus the economy are in a state of equilibrium. Equilibrium and timelessness thereby presuppose one another.

Chapter Three
Crises

Section 4 of Chapter 2 above has sketched some of the essential elements of a theory of crisis based on the tendential fall of the average profit-rate. The following sections will deal with this topic in greater detail by examining the present crisis. What is first required is an evaluation of the most influential theses that purport to reveal its causes, consequences and possible remedies. There are five alternative explanations.

1. Alternative explanations

The first holds that the crisis has originated in the financial/speculative sphere, due to extremely high levels of debt, rampant speculation, a permissive monetary policy, the loosening of rules governing borrowing and lending due to deregulation, and so on. In short, the crisis is the outcome of policy mistakes. The implication is that the crisis could have been avoided if different policies had been chosen. For example, Robin Blackburn states that 'The source of the problems which surfaced in 2007 – though some had warned about them years earlier – did not lie only in the US deficits or the Fed's easy money policy. It also lay in an institutional complex and a string of disastrous incentives and agency problems riddling an over-extended system of financial intermediation'.[1] The obvious question is: since crises are a recurrent and constant given of capitalism, if crises were merely due to the policy-makers' mistakes, why would these mistakes be recurrent and constant? If crises were epiphenomena, why would they recur regularly? Why would their amplitude grow to such a scale that they nowadays affect the whole of the world? Why would they accompany the introduction of capitalism whenever and wherever it penetrates and changes other modes of production? Why cannot policy-makers learn from their mistakes? Obviously, there must be some structural reasons that prevent them from learning from their past mistakes, that is, that force them to continue making these very mistakes.

A second thesis, one that is presently enjoying wide currency within the Left, is underconsumption. In this view, crises are caused by a long-term fall in wages against a rise in labour's productivity. In the words of Ollman, the workers 'can buy ever smaller portions of what they themselves produce...leading to periodic crises of overproduction/underconsumption'.[2] As for the present crisis, the underconsumptionist thesis holds that the cause of crises has been a long-term fall in wages. Lower wages, it is submitted, instead of increasing the rate of profit, cause it to fall because of failed realisation, first in the consumer-goods sector and from there to other sectors. This is so because, in underconsumptionist fashion, the economy is driven in the last instance not by the movement of the average rate of profit but by aggregate demand. This is demand for consumption-goods by consumers, for investment-goods by the capitalists and for both types of goods for public expenditure by the state. The argument is that the demand for consumer-goods is the crucial element. A fall in the demand for consumer-goods provokes a chain-reaction, because the demand for the means of production needed to produce those consumer-goods falls as well; this fall, in its turn, provokes the fall in the demand for means of production needed to produce those means of production. If wages decrease, a part of the consumption-goods, and thus of the investment-goods, cannot be sold and capital suffers a loss. Consequently, the average rate of profit falls. Lower wages are thus the cause of the crisis. Lower wages, in their turn, have been the result of neoliberal policies. If correct, this thesis would be a powerful critique of neoliberalism. Unfortunately, this is not the case.

---

[1] Blackburn 2008, p. 72. Blackburn only mentions in passing Baran and Sweezy's theory of overproduction in footnote 44 without elaborating.
[2] Ollman 1993, p. 16.

Marx had invalidated this thesis already in the second volume of *Capital* by noticing that

> It is sheer tautology to say that crises are caused by the scarcity of effective consumption....That commodities are unsaleable means only that no effective purchasers have been found for them.... But if one were to attempt to give this tautology the semblance of a profounder justification by saying that the working-class receives too small a portion of its own product and the evil would be remedied as soon as it receives a larger share of it and its wages increase in consequence, one could only remark that crises are always prepared by precisely a period in which wages rise generally and the working-class actually gets a larger share of that part of the annual product which is intended for consumption. From the point of view of these advocates of sound and 'simple' (!) common sense, such a period should rather remove the crisis.[3]

That crises are preceded by a period of high wages and thus of relatively high consumption and realisation of commodities was true in Marx's times as it is nowadays. In the high-growth period following post-WWII, wages grew at a sustained pace. As Table 1 below shows, in the US wages grew by 2.5% annually from 1967 to 1973. After that year, suddenly the US economy started to experience increasing difficulties and the rate of growth of wages fell substantially (with the exception of the 1995–2000 quinquennium) until it became negative in the 2000–4 period

Table 1. Trends in average wages, 1967–2004

Annual wages (thousands of 2005 dollars)		Wages: annual growth-rates:	
1967	25,509	1967–73	2.5%
1973	29,672	1973–9	0.1
1979	29,891	1979–89	0.9
1989	32,718	1989–2000	1.3
1995	33,657	–1989–95	0.5
2000	37,860	–1995–2000	2.4
2004	37,424	2000–4	–0.3

Source: Bernstein, Mishel and Shierholz 2006–7, Table 3.1.

---

[3] Marx 1967b, pp. 410–11.

Table 2. Value of minimum-wage, % change

1979–89	−29.5%
1989–2000	14.6
2000–5	−11.8
1967–2005	−25.7

Source: Bernstein, Mishel and Shierholz 2006-7, Table 3.40.

If the minimum-wage can be seen as a proxy for the value of de-skilled labour-power, Table 2 indicates a rise in that value only in the 1989–2000 period and a fall before and after that period. For the whole 1967–2005 period, the value of labour-power falls by 25.7%.

Empirical observation, however, is insufficient to definitively reject a theory. The underconsumptionist thesis, if wrong, should be rejected on theoretical grounds. Marx was obviously aware of the possibility that not all the output produced could be sold:

> The entire mass of commodities...must be sold. If this is not done...the labourer has been indeed exploited, but his exploitation is not realised as such for the capitalist.... The conditions of direct exploitation, and those of realising it, are not identical.... The first are only limited by the productive power of society, the latter by the proportional relation of the various branches of production and the consumer power of society.[4]

If commodities are unsold, capital suffers a loss and the average rate of profit falls. Could lower wages, then, reduce the average rate of profit and act as the cause of crises?

The average rate of profit rises with a rise in surplus-value and falls with a rise in the organic composition of capital (the ratio of constant to variable capital) per unit of capital invested.[5] If wages are reduced, profits increase and the average rate of profit rises. This is always the case for the individual capitalist. It applies also to the economy as a whole *only on one condition*: that the commodities not purchased by labour (due to lower wages) are purchased by capital (thanks to higher profits and thus to higher purchasing power). It is capital's purchasing power that ensures the realisation of the commodities

---

[4] Marx 1967c, p. 244.
[5] The (average) rate of profit = $s/(c+v)$.

not purchased by labour in case of wage-reductions. Therefore, if capital lacks sufficient purchasing power, some commodities will not be sold. A loss follows. Let us see what the consequences for the average rate of profit are.

Let us consider the most favourable case for underconsumptionism. Suppose that all the commodities not purchased by labour cannot be purchased by capital either. Labour's purchasing power falls by the amount of the wage-cut and this is a loss for the producers (capitalists) of wage-goods. This wage-cut is then the maximum-loss for capital due to lower wages. The extra surplus-value accruing to capital due to lower wages is cancelled because the commodities, being sold neither to capital nor to labour, represent a loss: 'the labourer has been indeed exploited, but his exploitation is not realised as such for the capitalist'. Gain and loss cancel each other out and the numerator (the surplus-value) returns to its pre-wage-cut level. As for the denominator, the capital saved thanks to lower wages is idle capital. Given that the rate of profit is computed on all the capital available for investment and not only on the capital actually invested, the denominator is unchanged and the average rate of profit returns to its pre-wage-cut level. However, if some of the goods not purchased by labour are purchased by capital – an assumption consonant with a positive conjuncture – the average profitability rises. In any case, the average rate of profit does not fall because of lower wages; at most, it is unchanged.[6]

------

[6] Suppose an initial situation such as 80c+20v+20s. The average rate of profit is 20%. If wages are reduced by 10, the extra profit is cancelled by the loss of an equal amount due to unsold wage goods. The numerator is unchanged. The denominator is also unchanged because 10 is both the decrease in the variable capital invested and the increased unused capital (reserves, R). The average rate of profit is unchanged. However, the average hides important differences. Suppose that the economy is divided into Sector I, producing means of production, and Sector II, producing means of consumption. Both sectors have invested 80c and 20s. Thus, Sector I suffers no loss because it does not sell means of consumption. Its situation is as follows: 80c+10v+10R+30s and π_1 = 30%. Sector II suffers a maximum loss equal to 20L and its situation is 80c+10v+10R+(30s-20L = 10s) and π_2 = 10%. π is still 20% but both the capitalists in Sector II and the labourers lose to the capitalists in Sector I. If some of the consumption-goods are sold to the capitalists, π_2 increases up to a maximum of 30%. Then, π = 30%. The assumption that capital cannot purchase those means of consumption implies that capital has already entered a downward-phase.

Two conclusions follow. First, if lower wages cannot decrease the average rate of profit, they cannot be the cause of crises. This disproves the under-consumptionist thesis. Second, if capitalists resort to lower wages in times of depression and crises, these wage-cuts are a counter-tendency holding back only temporarily the fall in the average rate of profit, rather than being its cause. This cause, as we shall see shortly, must be sought elsewhere.

The reason for the fall in the ARP (average rate of profit) is not difficult to find. As the formula for the profit-rate indicates, this rate's movement is determined by two factors: the rate of exploitation (and thus by lower or higher wages) and the organic composition of capital, that is, the ratio of constant to variable capital. If the organic composition of capital increases, the average rate of profit decreases.[7] The reason is that a percentage-increase in constant capital and/or a decrease in variable capital decrease the quantity of labour employed and thus (given that only labour produces value) the quantity of value and surplus-value produced per unit of capital. This explains the tendential fall in the average rate of profit, which is tendential because of many counteracting factors (see Section 4 of Chapter 2) of which lower wages is one example. Underconsumptionism observes only the relation between the falling average rate of profit and falling wages and, by ignoring the smaller production of surplus-value due to the increase in the organic composition of capital, draws the wrong conclusion that crises are due to low wages.

The consequences of subscribing to the underconsumptionist theory are far-reaching. First, if lower wages were indeed the cause of crises, in principle the economy could exit the crisis through higher wages. But, as we shall see shortly, higher wages increase the realisation by labour of commodities but decrease profits. Second, if the economy could exit the crisis through higher wages (a lower rate of exploitation), crises would be due to harmful distributional policies, and could thus, in principle, be avoided. If crises can be avoided, the economic system does not tend towards depressions and crises, as Marx holds, but towards recovery and booms and prosperity, as it is held almost unanimously even by many Marxists. The consequences for labour are disastrous. If the system tends (or can be made to tend) towards prosper-

---

[7] The rate of profit is $s/(c+v)$. If the organic composition of capital is c/v and if the rate of surplus-value is $s'= s/v$, then $s/(c+v) = (s/v)/[(c+v)/v] = s'/[(c+v)/v] = s'/(1+c/v)$.

ity and growth, even if through economic cycles with periods of depressions and crises, the system is rational. But if the system is rational, the struggle to replace it with a different system becomes irrational, because it is a fight against a rational system, and a pure act of will not based on an objective movement. Labour is deprived of the theoretical basis upon which to base its struggle. This is the class-content of underconsumptionism. Underconsumptionism is not only irreconcilable with Marxism, it is also (and for this reason) deeply inimical to labour.

As a variation on the underconsumptionist theme, it could be argued that the peculiarity of this crisis is that the rest of the world has been able to postpone the realisation-difficulties due to labour's underconsumption by exporting consumer-goods to the US. US-consumers have been able to purchase those goods by incurring higher and higher levels of debt. However, the thesis continues, US-consumers have recently become unable to absorb those goods due to collapse of the credit- and debt-system heralded by the collapse of the subprime-mortgages and loans (see below). This is why realisation-problems have re-emerged in the rest of the world. Whether this is a correct rendition of the present situation or not (the financial crisis will be dealt with later on), the origin of the crisis is still sought in labour's insufficient purchasing power and the temporary postponement of these difficulties is provided by the US-consumers' debt. The *debt*-dimension accounts for the *delay* in the explosion of the crisis which is caused by decreasing possibilities to realise all the consumer-goods as a result of lower wages. The critique above applies here too. Without the absorbing function of the US-consumers based on debt, the rest of the world, as well as the US-consumers, would have been faced with realisation-difficulties long ago. But this does not mean that these difficulties, whether delayed by debt or not, are the source of crises. Actually, the above has shown that this is not the case. This critique applies also to the case in which the level of wages is made to depend on class-struggle. In this view, the present crisis has been caused by excessively low wages due to labour's failure to stop capital's offensive. The implication is that the economy could exit the crisis if a labour-offensive could impose higher wages. The cause of the economic cycle is then the political cycle, the ups and downs of the class-struggle. This thesis must also answer the critique above, namely, whether the class-struggle explains the level of wages or not, lower wages cannot explain this or any other crisis because the effect of lower wages on the average rate of profit can only be positive even if the maximum realisation-failure is considered.[8]

If lower wages cannot be the cause of lower profit-rates and crises, the theoretical possibility opens up of reversing the relation of causation, that is, for the crisis to be the cause of lower wages. This brings us to the third alternative explanation, one that identifies the cause of crises in higher, rather than lower, wages. This is the profit-squeeze Marxist approach to crises, but, curiously, it is also the essence of the neoliberal view of crises. This approach was in vogue in the 1970s in the US and is now undergoing a revival. It views the cause of the decline in the US rate of profit in greater workers' power and higher wages and thus lower profits. More recently, Peter Gowan wanted to break with the orthodoxy that claimed it was the 'real-economy' actors that caused the crisis. The orthodoxy purportedly argued and argues that the changes in the financial system that caused the speculative bubble were, in their turn, caused by the need to reduce the share of labour in the national income.[9] Yet he neither specified what 'the orthodoxy' was nor argues why it should be abandoned. To the contrary, for the *Monthly Review* school, the long-term wage-reduction is also a consequence rather than the cause of depression: 'Stagnation in the 1970s led capital to launch an accelerated class war against workers to raise profits by pushing labor costs down. The result was decades of increasing inequality.' However, in contrast to the present approach, stagnation is seen as 'the *normal state* of the monopoly-capitalist economy, barring special historical factors' and the post-WWII stagnation is the manifestation of the petering out of the temporary historical factors that had caused the prosperity of the 1950s and 1960s. The authors, following the works of Paul Baran, Paul Sweezy, and Harry Magdoff, identify these historical factors as

> (1) the buildup of consumer savings during the war; (2) a second great
> wave of automobilization in the United States (including the expansion
> of the glass, steel, and rubber industries, the construction of the interstate
> highway system, and the development of suburbia); (3) the rebuilding of

---

[8] For Joan Robinson 'the maldistribution of income is quite as deeply embedded in the capitalist system as Marx believed the tendency to falling profits to be, and cannot be eliminated without drastic changes in the system' (1962, p. 72). If, by maldistribution, Robinson means simply the distribution between wages and profits, this is indeed a permanent feature of capitalism. If maldistribution refers to the underconsumptionist thesis, the above has refuted this thesis.

[9] Gowan 2009, p. 24.

the European and the Japanese economies devastated by the war; (4) the Cold War arms race (and two regional wars in Asia); (5) the growth of the sales effort marked by the rise of Madison Avenue; (6) the expansion of FIRE (finance, insurance, and real estate); and (7) the pre-eminence of the dollar as the hegemonic currency.[10]

The profit-squeeze argument runs more-or-less as follows. During recoveries and booms, wages increase. At a certain point, they become too high, the higher costs of production indent on profitability and the rate of profit falls. The system is pushed over the edge and growth turns into depression. Then, if wages are sufficiently low, profits start increasing again. In this theory, falling profitability is caused neither by the percentage-fall in the production of (surplus-) value (as in Marx) nor by failed realisation (as in underconsumptionism) but by the higher costs of labour-power. This approach also comes in for a number of criticisms.

To begin with, empirical research refutes this thesis. In a recent paper, Alan Freeman tests the relative weight of the organic composition of capital and of the wage-share on the rate of profit by using regression-analysis.[11] The author uses macroeconomic categories as proxies for the Marxian ones. The argument is that, if the capital/output ratio is shown to dominate over all else, including the wage-share, (a) the profit-squeeze thesis is empirically undermined and (b) Marx's thesis is substantiated even in terms set by his detractors. Charts 1 and 2 show the results.[12]

---

[10] Foster and Magdoff 2008.
[11] Moseley 1997, Appendix 1, p. 172, shows a very similar movement in the average rate of profit from 1948 to 1994.
[12] In macroeconomics, the rate of profit is usually defined as π/K where π is annual profits and K is accumulated fixed capital plus variable capital. Following a common procedure, this formula can be re-written as $(\pi/Y)\times(Y/K)$ where Y stands for annual net output $(\pi+v)$. In this formula, the first term is the capitalists' share of income, or profit-share, and the second is the output/capital ratio that Freeman prefers to call the maximum profit-rate. It should be mentioned that the notions of π, K and Y diverge from Marx's own. On the one hand, K does not take into account constant circulating capital. On the other hand, for Marx, the rate of surplus-value is $s'=\pi/v$. But, here, it is $\pi/Y = \pi/(\pi+v)$. Moreover, the figures are those provided by official statistics. These figures are the monetary expression of *use*-values rather than of value (a point to be discussed in more detail below). If these corrections could be made, the figures of the average rate of profit would diverge from those in the two aforementioned charts. But the point is not the exact measurement of the average rate of profit. The point is to gauge the relative weight of the two components on the average rate of profit.

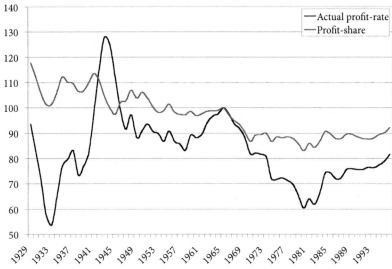

Source: Alan Freeman.

Chart 1. US profit-rate and US profit-share
Index: 1965=100

Source: Alan Freeman.

Chart 2. The US actual and maximum profit-rate ('output-capital' ratio)
Index: 1965=100

Keeping the above in mind, the results are summarised by the author as follows: 'Chart 1 shows what would have happened if the only thing affecting the profit rate was the profit share – that is, if the output-capital ratio (maximum profit rate) were held constant. Chart 2 shows what would have happened if the profit share had no effect at all – that is, if the profit share is held constant'. Chart 1 shows that the profit-rate line and the profit-share line do not exhibit the same general features. Given that income is divided into profits and wages, if the profit-share has almost no explanatory power, the same holds for the wage-share. On the other hand, Chart 2 shows that, with the sole exception of the five years of decline from 1965 to 1970, the output/capital ratio accounts for almost the whole variation in the profit-rate since 1929. Regression-analysis cannot prove causation, yet these data provide substantial empirical support for the thesis that the movement in the wage-share or in the profit-share are largely unrelated to the movement in the rate of profit. Further empirical substantiation will be provided by Charts 3 and 4 below.

Empirical refutation is important, but even more important is theoretical invalidation. Two points can be mentioned in this connection. First, profit-squeeze theory, just as the underconsumptionist conception, is a redistributional theory which, as with all similar theories, implies a constant quantity of new value produced (wages plus profits). Clearly, then, the rate of profit decreases because it is implicitly assumed that the total value to be redistributed remains the same (or falls). However, to explain the turning point from the high to the low phase, that is, the inception of the crisis, one has to assume the upward-phase, when the new value produced rises. To assume the downward-phase would mean to assume what has to be explained. But in the upward-phase, it is perfectly possible and it actually occurs that both profits and wages increase. If we assume that profit can only increase if wages decrease, we assume implicitly either stagnation or the downward-phase of the cycle. The profit-squeeze theory, then, cannot explain the inception of the depression and crisis because it presupposes a stagnant or decreasing production of surplus-value. Therefore it presupposes what has to be explained. As Marx claims, 'nothing is more absurd...then to explain the fall in the rate of profit by a rise in the rate of wages'.[13]

---

[13] Marx 1967c, p. 240. Anwar Shaikh's critique of the profit-squeeze school is that it fails to consider the difference between surplus-value and 'the bourgeois category

Second, aside from this critique, we should consider the profit-squeeze's class-content. It has been pointed out by many commentators that this theory ends up by giving ammunition to the employers' claim that crises are due to excessively high wages and thus that, in order to avoid/exit the crisis, lower wages are necessary. Indeed, we have seen above that lower wages do increase the average rate of profit but also that the rise can only be a counter-tendency. Thus, what explains recoveries and booms is not an increase in the share of profits relative to that of labour within the context of an unchanged production of surplus-value, it is not an increase in the average rate of profit due to redistribution, but that increase is a consequence of an *expanded production* of value and surplus-value. For lower wages to spur a recovery, then, the extra surplus-value must be invested. But, in the downward-trend, capital eschews investments in the productive sphere where the profit-rates are falling. They resume investing vigorously only when the turning point in the cycle has been surpassed. After that point, lower wages contribute to the recovery but cannot start the recovery before that point.

In addition to this, there is a deeper objection that has escaped, to the best of my knowledge, the commentators' attention. This objection is similar to that raised against the Okishio's theorem (see Section 4 of Chapter 2). Contrary to Marx, in profit-squeeze theory, *labour is seen as a cost rather than as the source and content of value*. But, in the upward-phase, we witness the growth not only of the wage-rates but also of employment and thus of the surplus-value created. The standpoint that sees only a cost in the increasing share of labour relative to income is the standpoint of the individual capitalist, for whom labour is indeed a cost. For the individual capitalist, higher costs (including wages) cause the average rate of profit to fall and lower costs (wages) cause the average rate of profit to rise. If this is extrapolated to the whole of the economy, that is, if only the positive effects of lower costs (wages) on the profit-rate are seen, capitalism's inner dynamic is tendentially towards growth rather than crises. The consequences for labour's struggle are the same as those of under-consumptionism. Labour's struggle for the abolition of capitalism becomes both irrational (because it aims at superseding a rational economic system,

---

of profit (net operating income). See Shaikh 1978a. This critique is insufficient in that it does not provide a theoretical, internal critique.

a system tending towards economic growth and thus welfare) and a pure act of voluntarism (because it is no longer the conscious manifestation of the system's inherent tendency towards crises and thus towards its own super-session). This view's theoretical horizon, as well as of any view that abandons the analysis in terms of value in favour of an analysis in terms of costs, is that of capital. Only value-analysis makes possible an economic theory consonant with labour's interests and struggle. As was already shown to be the case for underconsumptionism and for the Okishio-theorem, profit-squeeze theory is not only inconsistent with Marx, not only does it introduce an alien class-content into Marxism, but it is also a powerful demotivating factor for labour.

2. The cyclical movement

If distributional changes cannot cause crises, there is only one alternative left: to look for the cause of crises in the sphere of production. A commonly-held view, and this is the fourth thesis concerning the cause of crises, holds that crises are caused by decreasing productivity-levels. This is contrary to Marx's conception that crises are determined by the decreasing production of value and surplus-value coupled together with increasing productivity-levels, in other words by labour-shedding and productivity-increasing new technologies. If the decreasing-productivity thesis were correct, we should be able to observe approximately a decrease in productivity on the basis of which to explain the decrease in the average rate of profit shown in Chart 2 from 1945 to 1980. However, as Table 3 below shows, the whole of the 1959–2007 period is one of increasing productivity (with only some occasional drops lasting only one year), whether the average rate of profit increases or not.

Table 3. Output/hour in the non-farm business-sector, 1992=100

1959	51.3	1985	87.5
1960	51.9	1990	94.5
1965	61.4	1995	102.0
1970	68.0	2000	115.7
1975	76.2	2005	134.1
1980	80.6	2007	135.9

Source: Council on Foreign Relations 2008, table B49. Data for 2007 refer to the first quarter. Output refers to GDP in that sector.

Notice that this refutation rests on the use of the categories used by the opponents of Marx, in other words it is based on official statistical data that collect the monetary expression of *use-values*. The data does not measure the value contained in those use-values. Since the decrease in the value produced is lost sight of, only the direct relation between physical productivity and the average rate of profit is perceived.[14] Table 3 above, then, provides the basis for an empirical internal critique of the thesis. The only alternative left, and this is finally the fifth view, is Marx's thesis, in other words, the inverse relation between productivity and the average rate of profit. Let us then attempt to set out briefly the cyclical movement.

As anticipated in Section 4 of Chapter 2 above, new means of production, that is, innovations, increase labour's productivity, defined as units of output (use-values) per unit of capital invested. But they, at the same time, usually replace people with means of production. They are *labour-shedding and pro- ductivity-increasing innovations*. The economy's organic composition of capital, that is, the proportion of constant capital (invested in means of production) to variable capital (invested in labour-power) and thus of machines to labourers rises. If less labour-power is employed, less (surplus-) value is created by the innovating capitals. But this smaller quantity of (surplus-) value is embodied in a greater quantity of use-values, units of output. The economy as a whole produces more use-values (a greater output) but less (surplus-) value. This is the contradictory outcome of technological innovations and, at the same time, the *ultimate cause of economic crises*.

Due to the tendential price-equalisation within sectors, the innovators sell their greater output per unit of capital at the same unit price as the price of the smaller output (also per unit of capital) of their less-efficient competitors. The former realise a higher rate of profit. But, if they produce less surplus-value, their greater profitability cannot but come from the appropriation of surplus-value from the other producers (laggards) in their own branch, that is, through the price-mechanism. At the same time, given that capitals migrate across branches searching for the highest possible rate of profit, the several branches' profit-rates tend to equalise into an average rate of profit.

---

[14] Occasionally, the money-profits computed in this way are confusingly called surplus-value. But these profits are not the monetary expression of Marx's surplus-value.

But, as pointed out in Chapter 2, Section 4.1, there is equalisation even in the absence of capital-movement because the innovators' higher profit-rates are obtained from the rest of the economy and because they are eroded as soon as the laggards catch up in the technological competition. There is thus also a transfer of value across branches whenever a branch as a whole realises more or less value than that produced by it. If, due to technological innovations in a branch, less surplus-value is produced in that branch and, if that branch realises the average or a higher-than-average rate of profit, the innovators in that branch appropriate value both from the laggards in that same branch and from other branches.[15]

In short, for Marx, technological innovations tend to decrease the average rate of profit because they tend to replace labourers with machines. Since only labour creates value, the output per unit of capital increases while the value incorporated in it decreases. As Marx writes, 'The value of a commodity is determined by the total labour-time of past and living labour incorporated in it. The increase in labour productivity consists precisely in that the share of living labour is reduced while that of past labour is increased, but in such a way that the total quantity of labour incorporated in that commodity declines.'[16] It follows that 'The rate of profit does not fall because labour becomes less productive, but because it becomes more productive.'[17] Or, capital itself is the moving contradiction.

It is this contradictory outcome, an increasing output of use-values incorporating a decreasing quantity of (surplus-) value, that is the ultimate cause of crises: 'periodical crises...arise from the circumstance that now this and now that portion of the labouring population becomes redundant under its old mode of employment'.[18] In other words, ultimately, crises are the consequence of labour-reducing but productivity-increasing technological innovations. Therefore,

> the ultimate reason for all real crises [as opposed to financial and speculative
> crises – G.C.] always remains the poverty and restricted consumption of the
> masses [due to the expulsion of labour as a consequence of labour-decreasing

---

[15] See Carchedi 1991 for detailed numerical examples.
[16] Marx 1967a, pp. 260–1.
[17] Marx 1967a, p. 240.
[18] Marx 1967a, p. 264.

and productivity-increasing technologies – G.C.] as opposed to the drive of capitalist production to develop the productive forces [the productivity of labour through those technologies – G.C.] as though the absolute consuming power of society [rather than the poverty and restricted consumption of the masses – G.C.] constituted their limit.[19]

In the light of what has been argued above, it is now clear that this quotation should not be interpreted in an underconsumptionist light, as if it were impossible to realise all the (surplus-) value produced. Even assuming that all products are sold, the average rate of profit would still fall as a consequence of the decreased production of surplus-value.

Under the pressure of increased competition and the financial difficulties that arise as a consequence of it, some of the laggards introduce the new (or newer) productive technique. They too increase their organic composition of capital and thus their productivity. But they too contribute to the rise of unemployment. A further decrease in the (surplus-) value produced follows. The average rate of profit falls further. Lower average profitability plus higher unemployment mean that the downturn has set in.

If the fall in average profitability goes far enough, some firms, among the technological laggards in whatever sector, start going bankrupt. Further unemployment follows. Sales fall due not only due to the labourers' reduced purchasing power but also as a result of the capitalists' reduced purchasing power. The reason why the absorption-capacity of capital decreases is rooted in the explanation just highlighted: in the downward-phase, the weaker capitals go bankrupt. Consider three capitals, A, B and C. Capital A exchanges its products with both B and C. For the sake of simplicity, the latter two capitals do not exchange their respective outputs. Capital A produces a value of 200 which exchanges for a value of 100 produced by capital B and a similar value produced by capital C. If capital C goes bankrupt, a value of 100 produced by capital A cannot be sold to C. Capital A suffers a loss due to failed realisation of its products. At the same time, capital C's labourers, having become unemployed, cannot purchase wage-goods. The sector producing wage-goods also starts experiencing greater difficulties. But sales fall also because, due to an uncertain future, the employed labourers increase their hoardings and because productive capitals invest less, that is, a part of productive capital is kept idle. A further fall in demand and more bankruptcies follow. The downturn has become a crisis. On the one hand, capital as a social relation has been destroyed: the relationship between workers and capitalists has been severed. On the other, money-capital lies idle. This is matched by unsold commodities. Excess-money and commodity-capital has been created. *Crises generate both excess-capital* (in its money- and commodity-forms) *and a lack of capital* (as a social relation).[20] If crises are ultimately determined by contracted production of value and surplus-value per unit of capital invested as expressed by a fall in the average rate of profit, recoveries should be fuelled by an expanded production of (surplus-) value also per unit of capital invested, as expressed by a rising average rate of profit. But, as we shall see below, this is possible only after sufficient capital (the less productive units) has been destroyed.

The rise in the organic composition of capital following the introduction of labour-shedding and productivity-increasing technologies is a regular and inevitable factor in the development of capitalism, a factor that acts sometimes openly and sometimes subterraneously. Given that the new technologies, percentage-wise, replace labourers with means of production, and given that only the labourers produce value and surplus-value, the average rate of profit falls. If the economy is still in a period of high growth, the labour-power liberated by the bankrupt capitals can be absorbed by the stronger capitals that are still expanding the scale of their production. In spite of the decreasing average rate of profit, the rate of capital-accumulation is sufficiently strong to ensure enlarged reproduction. The mass of surplus-value increases but, under conditions of an increasing organic composition of capital, an increase in the rate of accumulation *decreases* the average rate of profit. What ushers in the economic depression is not simply a fall in the average rate of profit, but rather *what is crucial is that this fall is the result of a decreased production of value and surplus-value.* Thus, the course of the cycle is determined not by the average rate of profit for the economy as a whole but by the average rate of profit *for the productive (of surplus-value) sectors only.*

As this movement progresses, as more and more of the technological laggards leave the scene, unemployment starts surfacing and less and less value and surplus-value is produced. This is *destruction of capital as a social relation,*

---

[20] Very generally speaking, in the downturn-phase, supply increases due to technological innovations but demand and the average rate of profit fall. In the crisis, supply also decreases, due to closures and bankruptcies.

the severing of the relation between capital and labour.[21] At this point, the *mass* of value and surplus-value produced falls too. This reinforces the fall in the average *rate* of profit, given that it is the low organic-composition (low-productivity) capitals that usually go bust. According to many commentators, the weakest capitals stop their operations when their rate of profit becomes too low for them to justify production, for example, when their profit-rate falls below the rate of interest they can gain on treasury-bills. While these factors and personal and psychological considerations might play a role, their ceasing operations is not so much a matter of choice but one of choiceless necessity. The average rate of profit is an average of the high rate of profits of the innovators and of the low rates of profit of the laggards. It moves downwards because the innovators realise higher profits that are more than offset by the lower rates of profit of the laggards, in other words at the expense of the laggards. If the average rate of profit moves downwards, some laggards will be forced out of production, because their profits turn into losses. The fall in the mass of surplus-value produced is further reinforced by the decreasing capital-utilisation as a conscious means to reduce production. If fewer means of production are used, less labour-power is used and less surplus-value is produced. The numerator of the average rate of profit falls, but the denominator is unchanged, given that the average rate of profit is computed on the basis of the whole of the capital available for investment and not only on that actually invested and in operation. The capitalists try to hold back this downward-movement by reducing wages, but, in and of themselves, lower wages cannot start a new upward-movement. Lower wages are a counter-tendency which, as was argued for in Chapter 2, can hold back the tendency only temporarily.

Chapter 2 has also indicated that, besides lower wages, there is another counter-tendency which is of the greatest relevance for our purposes. During depressions and crises, it becomes increasingly difficult for borrowers to invest in the productive (or surplus-value) sphere, given that produc-

---

[21] In a recent paper, Kliman 2009 claims that by destruction of capital 'Marx meant…not only the destruction of physical capital assets, but also, and especially, of the value of capital assets…debts go unpaid asset prices fall, and other prices may also fall, so the value of physical as well as financial capital assets is destroyed'. These factors become the condition for the next recovery. But unpaid debts are a loss for the creditors and a gain for the debtors. There is no destruction of value, only a transfer of value from the creditor to the debtor. Similarly for falling prices.

tive capital itself experiences increasing profitability and thus realisation-difficulties. As a result, this money flows to the commercial, the financial and speculative sectors where higher profits can be made. But these sectors are unproductive.

As the production of surplus-value decreases due to decreasing employment in the productive sectors, firms start closing down and the working class' purchasing power decreases as well. Some wage-goods remain unsold. Equally, the capitalists' purchasing power for means of production decreases as well. Some investment-goods remain unsold. To stimulate the sale of the unsold commodities (mistakenly perceived as the prime cause of crises), and possibly for the purpose of increasing new production, the monetary authorities stimulate credit by increasing the quantity of money. Moreover, capital flows from the productive to the unproductive sectors. This makes possible an artificial inflation of profits in these unproductive sectors. Debt (and speculation) start growing disproportionately compared to the production of value and surplus-value incorporated in the commodities (and thus relative to purchasing power). The process snowballs and acquires a dynamism of its own. But this cannot go on indefinitely. Sooner or later, debts must be repaid. As unemployment surges, an increasing number of debtors default on their debts. This applies both to the productive and to the financial sector. But it is in the financial and speculative sectors that the crisis erupts at first, because it is in these sectors that the bubble has increased the most. The present crisis manifested itself first in the banking sector. If the value of some banks' assets falls below the value of their liabilities, those banks become (or threaten to become) insolvent, with the result that depositors will rush to withdraw their funds. If the run on the banks cannot be stopped, those banks go bankrupt. As long as the phenomenon is limited, the crisis can be contained. The present financial crisis exploded when a few giant banks with a predominant weight in the financial sector saw their equity shrinking and eventually becoming negative. We shall return to this point later.

The basic point is that financial crises are caused by the shrinking productive basis of the economy. A point is thus reached at which there has to be a sudden and massive deflation in the financial and speculative sectors. Even though it looks as if the crisis has been generated in these sectors, the ultimate cause resides in the productive (of surplus-value) sphere, that is, in the shrinking productive basis of the economy and in the attendant falling profit-rate *in this sphere*, even though this downward movement manifests itself at first in the financial and speculative sectors.[22] It is not the case that decades of low wages have lead to realisation-problems and, finally, to the bursting of the financial bubble (at present, the dominant view also within the Left). Rather, decades of shrinking production of new value have forced capitalists (1) to lower salaries (something that is mistakenly seen by some as the cause of the crisis) and (2) to shift to highly profitable financial and speculative investments which, however, being based on fictitious capital, could only conceal the true state of the productive basis of the economy (something that is mistakenly seen by others as the cause of crisis). The reduction of both classes' purchasing power is *revealed* in a *gradual* way, and the collapse of the financial and speculative sectors *reveals* in a *sudden* and abrupt way, the continuously shrinking productive basis of the economy that had been concealed through increasing levels of debts.

But the crisis creates the conditions for the next recovery. If sufficient capital as social relations has been destroyed, capital can start expanding again. A number of factors make this reversal possible. First, wages are lower and rates of exploitation higher, due to labour's weakness following the economic crisis. Second, the price of the means of production is also lower because the crisis has caused a fall in prices, because the new technologies have made possible the production of cheaper means of production, and because some means of production have been taken over by the survivors at a price lower than the remaining value (that is, net of amortisation). Moreover, given the previous low capacity-utilisation, unutilised means of production can be brought back into production. Third, the level of debt has become lower due to the explosion of the financial bubble. And, fourth, the survivors have further advantages, namely they face less competition due to the laggards having left the scene so that they can fill the share of the market left void by the bankrupt competitors and are better equipped to penetrate the new branches of production that have come into being and that initially have a lower organic composition of capital. These factors spur the surviving capital to start enlarged reproduction. This is made possible not only by easily avail-

---

[22] A similar conclusion is reached by Foster and Magdoff but within a different perspective, the stagnationist one: since financialisation can be viewed as the response of capital to the stagnation-tendency in the real economy, a crisis of financialisation inevitably means a resurfacing of the underlying stagnation endemic to the advanced capitalist economy. See Foster and Magdoff 2008.

able and cheap labour-power willing to accept higher rates of exploitation, but also by large quantities of money-capital that has been set aside during the crisis. As employment starts increasing, new purchasing power is created and thus labour's absorption-capacity rises. The mass of surplus-value grows together with a higher rate of surplus-value. Capital-absorption capacity rises as well. The realisation-difficulties decrease progressively and eventually are minimised. Recovery and boom follow.

These, as well as other factors, spur on the capitals that have weathered the storm to resume and increase production. However, as soon as new labour-shedding and productivity-increasing technologies are introduced in the ascending phase of the cycle, the conditions are re-created for a new phase of depression and crises. As long as the mass of new value grows to such an extent that the surviving capitals absorb the labour-power 'liberated' by the weakest capitals that have gone bankrupt, the decreasing rate of profit and the possible closure of the less-efficient capitals does not affect economic growth, even if the average rate of profit might decrease due to the higher organic composition of capital of the surviving firms. But, when the new technologies start provoking generalised bankruptcies and spreading unemployment, the mass of profits starts falling as well. A lower rate of profit, as a consequence of a lower mass of profits, ushers in a new period of depression and crisis.

The features just sketched can be found in all the major crises that have battered the world-economy since capitalism has become the dominant socio-economic system. Even though each crisis has its own forms of appearance and consequences,[23] it is important to stress the common characteristics because they fundamentally reveal the unchanged nature and working of the capitalist system. This holds for the great 1929–33 depression as well.[24]

The Wall Street crash of 1929 was preceded by a recession in the real economy, a feature common to the other leading capitalist countries Germany, Belgium and Britain. In the US, the 'Big One' was preceded by a period of intense speculation, huge expansion of credit, enormous concentration of

[23] A momentous consequence of the present crisis is, as David Laibman (2009) stresses, the re-proletarianisation of the US-labourers through the crisis of homelessness. Strictly speaking, proletarianisation refers to the expropriation of the means of production rather than of the labourers' homes. However, Laibman makes an important point here. Homelessness, is a powerful means to further weaken labour. This process has gone further in the US than in the European countries.
[24] The following two paragraphs rely heavily on Harman 2009, to which the reader is referred for further details.

wealth in a tiny fraction of the population and the destruction of the trade-unions. The similarities with the present crisis are obvious. At the same time, the US average rate of profit had been falling by about 40% between the 1880s and the early 1920s, while the organic composition of capital had been rising by about 20%. Profitability recovered briefly through the 1920s, but only due to an increased rate of exploitation. This does not mean that investments declined everywhere. In 1928 and 1929, output increased three times faster than consumption, partly due to the completion of investments started in the previous period and their coming into operation at the onset of the crisis (Ford's River Rouge auto-plant was completed in 1928) and partly due to investments in new sectors that seemed to offer higher profitability (the radio-set sector). Nevertheless, investments in the productive sphere as a whole kept declining. The upsurge in luxury-consumption was utterly insufficient to fill the gap between production and consumption basically because capital needs to capitalise profits rather than consume them unproductively. Capital flowed massively into the unproductive sectors, primarily into the sales-efforts (by the end of the 1920s, these expenditures had grown to two thirds of total surplus-value) and into the financial and speculative sector (that caused a succession of speculative booms and great increases in the price of stocks and real estate). To counter the falling purchasing power, the upsurge in the sales effort had to be supported by growing debt. When the debt could not be serviced any longer, the speculative bubble burst. Banks had to resize their balance-sheets. Successive waves of bank-failures followed. Developments in Germany followed basically the same pattern while Britain showed specific characteristics that, nevertheless, fit well in this scheme.

It is instructive to review briefly also the Japanese crisis of the 1990s. When Japan entered the financial crisis in the 1990s, it had had a period, from the 1950s to the late 1980s, of a rapidly rising ratio of capital to workers. In the 1980s, this ratio grew four times as fast as that in the US. Consequently, the profit-rate fell from 36.2% in the 1960s to 14.5% in the 1990s. At the same time, real wages were low (exploitation was high), something that limited the internal market's absorption. Within the new international setting, the logical thing to do was to find outlets in the export-markets. But, in the late 1980s, the long-term fall in the profit-rate finally made itself felt. The opportunities for domestic investments shrank and export-channels came under pressure due to the international economic depression. To encourage both investments and consumption, the government resorted to massive injections of liquidity by encouraging the banks to vastly increase their lending. This liquidity found its way in speculation. Bank-loans fuelled steadily increasing prices both in the real-estate market and in the stock-exchange. But, when prices collapsed in these markets, the banks got into trouble. The use of public money in 1995 to rescue the bank-system did not have the desired effect. Neither did it help to resort to Keynesian policies through enormous investments in the public sector. The relatively large role assumed by the state (state-expenditures amounted to 8% of GDP and the proportion of the labour-force employed by the state to 10% of the total) avoided the collapse of the system but did not rescue it from its malaise.

Let us now return to the present. Similar to the two crises dealt with above, the present financial crisis finds its prime cause in the shrinking production of surplus-value as the other side of the coin of increased efficiency. Chart 3 shows the growth of fixed capital per worker, which corresponds to Marx's organic composition of capital.[25]

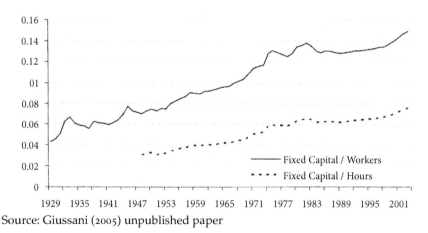

Source: Giussani (2005) unpublished paper

Chart 3. Fixed capital per worker or per hour of work, 1929–2003

---

[25] Actually, the organic composition of capital is the ratio of constant (that is, both fixed and circulating) capital to variable capital, while the following two tables relate only fixed capital to variable capital. But this does not significantly affect the argument.

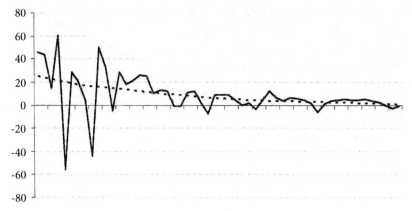

1950 1950 1958 1962 1966 1970 1974 1978 1982 1986 1990 1994 1998 2002
Source: Giussani 2005, unpublished paper

Chart 4. US incremental labour/fixed capita ratio

and Chart 4 shows that this phenomenon is coupled with the replacement of labour by capital. More specifically, each incremental unit of fixed capital generates a lower percentage-increase in employment and even a negative absolute increase (if the percentage-increase is negative). In other words, more and more constant capital creates fewer and fewer jobs.[26]

As mentioned above, one of the consequences of the declining profitability in the productive sector is the migration of capital to the unprodutive sectors. This is shown in Table 4.

These data are only indicative. For example, given that, under certain conditions (see Chapter 4, Section 6 of this work), the production of knowledge can be productive of surplus-value, the category 'information' could be added to the productive sectors. Or, to the extent that the firms in the productive sector, say, advertise their own products, they perform unproductive labour. The reverse is true for the firms in the unproductive sphere which hire labourers for the maintenance of buildings, computers, etc. – they perform productive labour. More information could be gathered if the category services (that increases from 26% in 1979 to 39.3% in 2005) could be broken down.

---

[26] In the UK, the number of economic inactive rose from around 1 per cent in 1970 to figures lying between 10 and 20 per cent, depending on the years involved (Ticktin 2008). However, Ticktin seems to think that the cause of this has been a deliberate policy of containment of the working class. Again, this might have been the intention of the capitalists as a means to counter the crisis, but it is not its cause.

Table 4. US-employment percentage-share by sector, 1979–2005

Industry sector	1979	1989	2000	2005
Goods producing	27.8%	22.3%	18.7%	16.6%
– Mining	1.1%	0.7%	0.5%	0.5%
– Construction	5.1%	4.9%	5.2%	5.5%
– Manufacturing	21.6%	16.7%	13.1%	10.7%
– durable	13.6%	10.2%	8.3%	6.7%
– nondurable	8.0%	6.5%	4.8%	4.0%
Services producing	72.2%	77.7%	81.3%	83.4%
– trans. utilities	4.0	3.8	3.8	3.7
– wholesale trade	5.0	4.9	4.7	4.3
– retail sale	11.3	12.1	11.6	11.4
– information	2.6	2.4	2.8	2.3
– fin., ins., real estate	5.4	6.1	5.8	6.1
– services	26.0	31.8	37.0	39.3
Total	100.0	100.0	100.0	100.0

Source: Bernstein, Mishel and Shierholz 2006-7, Table 3.27

Nevertheless, this table provides interesting clues. If the goods-producing sector is identified with the productive sector in Marxian terms, the productive basis of the US-economy falls from 27.8% in 1979 to 16.6% in 2005 while the unproductive sector rises from 72.2% to 83.4% in the same period, that is, the productive sector falls from 38.5% of the unproductive sector to 19.9%. Thus, the decline in the US-economy's capacity to produce value and surplus-value dates back to the 1970s. It is at that time that industrial capital begins to shift to financial capital. The US is by no means an exception: 'Some 31 million manufacturing jobs were eliminated between 1995 and 2002 in the world's 20 largest economies. Manufacturing employment declined during a period when global industrial production rose by more than 30%.'[27]

Similar results are reached by Moseley. The author finds that, in the 1947–77 period, the US profit-rate falls from 22% to 12% in spite of an increase in the rate of surplus-value from 1.40 to 1.63. The causes are an increase in the organic composition from 3.58 to 5.03 as well as increase in the share of unproductive labour relative to productive labour. In fact, the ratio of the flow of unproductive capital to variable capital grows from 0.54 to 0.94 and the ratio of the stock of

---

[27] Gold and Feldman 2007, p. 24.

unproductive capital to variable capital grows from 0.30 to 0.66.[28] Starting from the mid-1970s, the rate of profit changes course and starts rising again. In the 1975–94 period, it rises from 12% to 16%. The reason is two-fold. First, the successful offensive of the employers against labour and the resulting decrease in wages, as clearly shown by Table 1 above. The rate of surplus-value jumps from 1.71 to 2.33. Wage-decreases are the classic counter-tendency against the tendential fall in the profit-rate. Second, the composition of capital falls from 5.39 to 4.61 as a result of the slowing down of the introduction of new technologies. However, the rate of profit rises moderately, from 12% to 16%, because of a further shift from productive to unproductive labour. The ratio of the flow of unproductive capital to variable capital grows from 0.98 to 1.46 and the ratio of the stock of unproductive capital to variable capital grows from 0.69 to 0.83.[29] This explains the relatively moderate rise in the rate of profit, a rise which remains well below the previous peak of 22%.[30]

We have now all the empirical data supporting Marx's thesis. Chart 3 shows the increase in the organic composition of capital accompanied by productivity-increases (Table 3) and by capital's decreasing absorption-capacity for labour (Chart 4), while Table 4 shows the decreasing share of employment in the productive sectors, that is, the decreasing production of new value. These data fully support Marx's thesis as to the cause of the long term fall in the average rate of profit as shown in Chart 2 and thus affirm Marx's theory of crises. This highlights the basic contradiction leading to economic crises and, consequently, to falling wages and labour's decreasing purchasing power as an attempt to halt the fall in profitability. As for the rise in the profit-rate, starting in the 1980s (see Chart 2), in spite of the rising organic composition of capital (see Chart 3), this is probably due to the liberalisation of the financial and capital-markets and to the great speculative boom starting around the beginning of the 1980s, which led to a much greater rise of profits in the financial than in the non-financial sector, as shown in Chart 5 below.

This chart shows a dramatic rise in non-financial profits but a much greater rise financial profits. The explosion of profit in the non-financial sphere can be

---

[28] Moseley 1997a, Table 1.
[29] Moseley 1988a, Table 2.
[30] Moseley remarks: 'The "profit squeeze" theory . . . cannot explain why two decades of higher unemployment and lower wages have not fully restored the rate of profit' (1997a, p. 34).

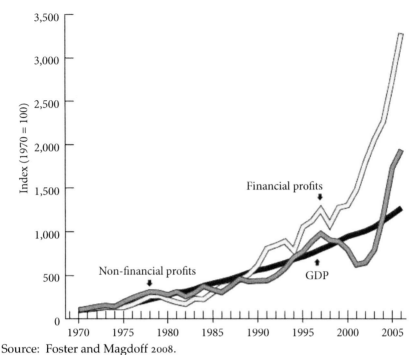

Source: Foster and Magdoff 2008.

Chart 5. Growth of financial and non-financial profits relative to GDP
(1970 = 100)

explained by the increasing investments by non-financial corporations in the
financial sector (by buying, among other things, their own shares and those
of other companies). The line indicating profits in the non-financial sector is
thus a mixture of financial and non-financial profits. But this indicates a rise
in indebtedness rather than in the production of surplus-value.

As mentioned above, the downward pressure on the average rate of profit
is augmented by the decreasing capacity-utilisation. This is graphically illus-
trated by Chart 6 below.

3. The subprime debacle

The long-term decline in the average rate of profit in the productive (non-
financial) sectors has provoked a series of financial crises, the last one being
the present crisis. This crisis exploded in 2007. In the previous years (2003–5),
the government had pursued an easy monetary policy to limit the economic
damage following the technological bubble of 1990–1. To reiterate one of

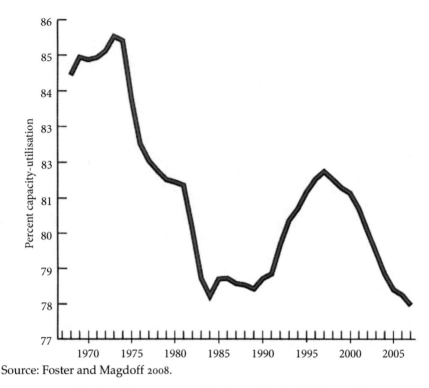

Source: Foster and Magdoff 2008.

Chart 6. Percentage-utilisation of industrial capacity

the main theses of this chapter, easy credit was one of the immediate causes
of the present crisis (in the housing sector), but it was certainly not its ultimate cause. Also, lower interest-rates were needed to stimulate demand, but
demand-stimulation was in its turn needed due to the long term profitability-
crisis of the US-economy. Further, mortgage-standards had been severely
curtailed to allow purchases by people who otherwise would have been seen
as unreliable borrowers. Hundreds of thousands of US home-owners had
been lured into buying a home even if they lacked the financial means (these
were the so-called subprime mortgages). That was why the housing prices
skyrocketed, even if, on the one hand, wages and more generally income
kept decreasing, and, on the other hand, the number of new houses built kept
increasing. This price-rise generated a speculative bubble. This was a sure
recipe for a future mortgage-crisis. But the danger did not come only from
subprime mortgages. A price-rise for even a relatively low number of houses
is sufficient to push upwards the estimated value of all other (unsold) houses

and thus the borrowing capacity of those home-owners. It easily increased the creditworthiness for them. It is on these grounds that a second mortgage could be obtained on the basis of highly overestimated collateral. This extra credit (referred to, in a somewhat slanderous fashion, as a spending spree) was actually used by the home-owners to support their declining purchasing power, but, at the same time, being based on overvalued creditworthiness, it further weakened the possibility of the home-owners to repay their mortgages. In addition, millions of home-owners profited from lower interest-rates for the purposes of refinancing their mortgages. Many borrowers were not told that payments were fixed for two years and that they would become higher after that period and furthermore, that they would be dependent on the level of Fed interest-rates, which also rose substantially starting from 2004. Higher interest-rates plus increasing unemployment sparked a wave of defaults and repossessions. Millions lost their houses. This, in turn, had a dramatic effect on house-prices, reversing the housing boom of the previous years. The effects spilled over to the broader economy with the building industry expected (in November 2007) to cut its output by half.

The first signs of the coming crisis appeared in 2006 when defaults started to increase. Nevertheless, lending proceeded at a sustained pace. Banks had invented financial instruments (basically, contracts) that allowed them to shift the insolvency-risks to other institutional investors and thus to insure themselves against those risks. We shall see below a couple of examples of what these instruments actually were and why they failed. In 2007, more and more of those loan-holders became insolvent. Foreclosures followed. The crisis finally exploded in 2007 in the United Kingdom when Northern Rock, experiencing difficulties in keeping its business going, approached the Bank of England on September 12 to obtain credit. This provoked a generalised concern about the bank's solvency. In spite of the Bank of England's and the Government's assurance about the financial soundness of the Bank, thousands of customers withdrew more than 1 billion pounds from their savings. The government was forced to nationalise Northern Rock on 17 February 2008, to avoid its bankruptcy. On 8 October 2008, the UK-government announced a 500 billion pound bank rescue-package. The main feature was that the government, by using tax-payers' money (that is, by borrowing from the public) and upon request of the banks themselves, could buy shares in banks experiencing financial difficulties, thus partly nationalising them. The nationalisation of Northern Rock added 87 billion pounds to the public-sector debt.[31]

In the US, the crisis erupted when two hedge-funds owned by one of the US major investment-banks, Bear Stearns – which had invested heavily in the subprime market – collapsed. Massive withdrawals by clients and lenders caused a liquidity-crisis which, in its turn, raised the risk of failure. However:

> It would have been highly risky for other Wall Street firms if Bear Stearns had been allowed to go under because Bear is tightly interconnected with them as both a borrower and a lender. Any firms that are owed a lot of money by Bear would have fallen under suspicion, on grounds that they might not be able to pay their own debts if Bear failed to pay them. That could have triggered a dangerous wave of defaults.[32]

Eventually, failure was avoided because another major investment-bank, J.P. Morgan, agreed to provide a line of credit that, however, was secured by the Federal Reserve. In case of failure, the US-taxpayer would have paid for the bailout.

On 11 July 2008, the Independent National Mortgage Corporation went bankrupt. Before its failure, it was the largest savings and loan association in the Los Angeles area and the seventh largest mortgage-originator in the United States. Its failure was the fourth largest bank-failure in United States history. On 8 September 2008, the Treasury department placed Fannie Mae and Freddie Mac, two government-sponsored enterprises backing single mortgages, into conservatorship. Between the two of them, they backed nearly half of the $12 trillion mortgages outstanding as of 2008. Given their size and key role in the US housing market, they could not be allowed to go bankrupt. The government took over their management. On September 15 2008, dubbed Meltdown Monday, Bank of America acquired Merrill Lynch for 50 billion dollars. On the same day, the government refused to bail out Lehman Brothers, which had to file for bankruptcy after it failed to find a buyer for the entire company. Lehman Brothers' failure helped triggering financial difficulties for the huge

---

[31] Chote 2008.
[32] Goldstein 2008.

insurer AIG. The Fed had to provide a 85 billion-dollar emergency-loan to rescue it. As *Business Week* reported:

> The problems at AIG stemmed from its insurance of mortgage-backed securities and other risky debt against default. If AIG couldn't make good on its promise to pay back soured debt, investors feared the consequences would pose a greater threat to the U.S. financial system than this week's collapse of the investment bank Lehman Brothers.[33]

On 26 September, it was Washington Mutual's turn to declare bankruptcy. The holding company's primary operating subsidiary, Washington Mutual Savings Bank, was closed and placed in receivership. This was the largest US bank-failure in history. On 29 September, Wachovia Corp., the fourth biggest US-bank by assets, was sold to Wells Fargo. As these examples indicate clearly, more and more banks and other institutional investors found out that they had in their portfolios derivatives based on insolvent loans.[34] This further deflated the housing prices. In early 2009, the situation was sketched as follows by the Congressional Research Services as reported by *New York Times*:

> Some of the largest and most venerable banks, investment houses, and insurance companies have either declared bankruptcy or have had to be rescued financially. In October 2008, credit flows froze, lender confidence dropped, and one after another the economies of countries around the world dipped into recession. The crisis exposed fundamental weaknesses in financial systems worldwide, and it continues despite coordinated easing of monetary policy by governments, trillions of dollars in intervention by governments, and several support packages by the International Monetary Fund.

As was seen above, some of the biggest banks and insurance-companies had to be rescued by the government through infusions of liquidity. By June 2009, 'The breadth of these interventions was substantial: almost half of the world's largest 20 banks received direct government support'.[35] Or, as of July 2009, 'government interventions in the USA, in the UK and in the Eurozone

---

[33] *Business Week*, 16 September, 2008.
[34] For the notion of derivatives, see below.
[35] Bank of England 2009, p. 17.

since the beginning of the present crisis amount to $14,810bn.'[36] But this did not stop the financial crisis that, in the meantime, had expanded to prime mortgages, due to the generalised fall in housing prices as a consequence of foreclosures, and then to the real economy, affecting the three biggest auto-makers, due to the increasing difficulty firms had to finance their operations and to refinance their debts. Let us then see how the financial measures needed by the system in a futile attempt to at least postpone the crisis only contributed to inflating the speculative bubble thus making the crisis worse when the bubble eventually burst.

To stimulate demand in spite of decreasing wages, the monetary authorities increased the quantity of money. This is achieved by basically printing money with which the US Federal Reserve purchases treasury-bills from the public. The sellers of the treasury-bills partly spent it and partly deposited it in their bank-accounts. The banks granted credit for a multiple of those deposits. As a consequence, interest-rates fell. But, more importantly, the banks started to use the inter-bank deposits, whose function had been clearance on a daily basis, for speculative purposes, that is, to fund speculative activities. Also, credit was stimulated by financial deregulation, which effectively allowed banks to create credit at a multiple of their reserves well above the safe level. On the other hand, the financial system (banks) needed to find new ways to invest that extra supply of money and to grant credit in a situation in which incomes were falling and the creditworthiness of the borrowers as well as the possibilities to find outlets for investments were decreasing. The way to stimulate demand this time was found in the mortgage-market and in the securitisation of mortgage-loans. It is here that the subprime mortgages and crisis come into play. In order to comprehend this more clearly, three notions must be briefly highlighted, namely mortgage-backed securities, collateralised debt-obligations, and the credit-default swaps.

Suppose a commercial bank grants a loan to a borrower for the purchase of a house. Traditionally, the commercial bank could use the depositors' money to grant a loan that would be paid back by the debtors. They were the bearers of the risk in case of the borrower's default. With the ballooning of the speculative sector, banks have resorted to a different strategy in order to shift the risk of default to others, namely, to the general public. A commonly used

---

[36] Ibid.

practice is as follows. The commercial bank (or a broker) bundles together many mortgages and sells them (it sells the right to collect principal and interest) to another bank, an investment-bank. The commercial bank renounces the right to collect the mortgages' principals and interest-payments from the home-buyers but acquires the right to receive the capital it needs from the investment-bank. The commercial bank accepts a discount on its loan because it can collect now rather than in the future and, at the same time, it avoids the risk of possible defaults on mortgage-payments. The commercial bank thus loans capital which is not its own. The investment-bank must provide the capital for the commercial bank, but it does not have it. In order to find that capital, the investment-bank creates a corporation to which it transfers those loans in exchange for the capital it needs to pay the commercial bank. To get that capital, this corporation issues bonds which the investment-bank sells to the public. They can be private individuals, but also hedge-funds, pension-funds, and so on. In this way, the company gathers the money that it transfers to the investment-bank. It, in turn, uses that capital to pay the commercial bank, which then loans that money to the home-purchasers. The bond-holders provide indirectly the capital for the home-loans and the home-owners repay the loans to the stock-company that, in turn, uses it to pay principal and interest to the bond-holders. If the demand for those stocks is sufficiently high, their price exceeds the value of those assets (the future stream of payments for principals and interests) and the bond-issuer makes a profit. These bonds are *mortgage-backed securities*, that is, the loans that have been securitised. They are one of the many forms of *derivatives*, that is, contracts that derive their value from an underlying asset (the mortgaged houses, in this example).

Table 5. Mortgage-backed securities

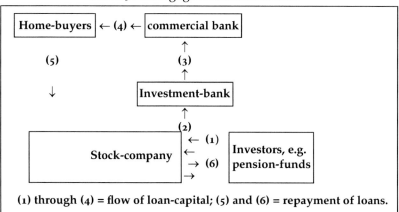

(1) through (4) = flow of loan-capital; (5) and (6) = repayment of loans.

Their advantage for the purchasers of these bonds is that they, in theory, can easily be sold (or, at least, so it is believed) if, for example, the housing market gets into trouble. But, in case of default, if the stream of payments to the company that has issued those bonds stops, the bond-holders' demand for credit-restitution cannot be met by that company. If the company goes bust, the stock-holders lose their capital.

The danger inherent in this example of 'financial engineering' was that the investment-bank, given that it collects substantial fees on loan-issuance and runs no risk in case of homeowners' default, underplayed the solvency of the loan-takers. The credit-criteria became looser and looser, even to the point where a borrower was not even required to have a job or a stable income to be able to purchase a house. This process was further facilitated by the failure of credit-rating agencies to properly rate the solvency of the loan-takers. The drive to grant even more mortgages was reinforced by transforming those mortgage-backed securities into collateralised debt-obligations. This means that the bonds are divided by the issuer (the corporation) into three different tranches. The investors looking for a less risky investment get lower interest, but are the last to lose in case of default. The opposite for those who seek higher returns and are willing to accept a higher risk. The third tranche lies in the middle of the other two tranches. In this way, more funds could be collected than if only one type of investor had been targeted.[37] However, in practice, to hide the insolvency of a good deal of the collateralised debt-obligations from the public eye, banks repackaged different collateralised debt-obligations with different ratings into bonds whose degree of riskiness was unknown and eventually proved to be worthless. In the words of Peter Gowan

> The products bundled in cdos [collateralised debt-obligations – G.C.], however, came from hundreds of thousands of unidentifiable sources, whose credit-worthiness and cashflow capacity was not known; they were sold 'over the counter', without any secondary market to determine prices, far

---

[37] The behaviour of the loan-issuer, who has only to gain and nothing to lose by issuing loans to potentially insolvent mortgage-takers, has been called a 'moral hazard'. But, aside from whether this behaviour is moral or immoral (it depends on the class-determined standpoint) the question is that this behaviour is determined in general by the need to make profits and, in this particular case, by the extra pressure on capital to find those high levels of profitability that are no longer available in the real economy.

less an organised market to minimize counterparty risk. In short, they were at best extremely risky because more or less totally opaque to those who bought them. At worst they proved a scam, so that within a few months of late 2007 the supposedly super-safe super-senior debt tranches within such cdos were being downgraded to junk status.[38]

Those collateralised debt-obligations found their way into the banking system. Banks have now large quantities of these financial instruments as assets on their balance-sheets. Once it became known that many of these collateralised debt-obligations were based on worthless mortgage-backed securities (due to defaults in the housing market), the market-price of these collateralised debt-obligations collapsed and the market for them dried up. The banks knew that their assets did not reflect their financial solidity because the collateralised debt-obligations on their balance-sheets were grossly overestimated. Given the banking system's overexposure to collateralised debt-obligations, failure to realise the collateralised debt-obligations held by a bank could have meant bankruptcy. This was a very real danger. Given that banks had debts to each other, a given bank's failure implied the impossibility to renew its loans to other banks. They, too, would have thus faced the threat of bankruptcy. This would have ignited a domino-effect. Banks became scared and less willing to renew their reciprocal debts. Every bank wanted to have as much cash as possible to offset the negative effect of the writing off of the collateralised debt-obligations they held as assets. Each bank wanted to keep liquidity for itself and thus was unwilling to renew the credit it had granted to other banks. This meant that they had to start selling their assets. Since the market for the collateralised debt-obligations had dried up, they had to sell their better assets. When this became insufficient, some of those banks were faced with the danger of insolvency. The depositors became concerned and began asking their money back. But this was difficult, if not impossible, not only because of the illiquidity of the assets, but also because credit had been overextended thus increasing the danger of a run on the banks. This process spilled over to the real economy. Banks became unwilling to grant loans also to non-financial companies. These companies too started to have financial difficulties and this resulted into a generalised crisis, especially in

---

[38] Gowan 2009, p. 15.

those companies and branches which were highly leveraged. While the size of this domino-effect has been contained by the central bank's intervention and injection of liquidity into the ailing financial institutions, massive writing off of the collateralised debt-obligations in the ailing institutions' balance-sheets has been necessary. The banking sector is now facing huge losses as many of the mortgage-bonds backed by subprime mortgages have fallen in value.

The third feature specific to the present speculative bubble are the credit-default swaps. Suppose a pension-fund has money to invest. By statute, it can only invest in very safe concerns. At the same time, the pension-fund wants high interest-rates on its investments. But safe investments usually pay low interest-rates. For example, suppose that pension-fund would like to invest in (buy the bonds of) an investment-bank. But, suppose that the investment-bank's rating by a rating agency is less than that required by the pension-fund's statute. Given this relatively negative rating, the pension-fund cannot buy the bonds of the investment-bank. It is here that credit-default swaps come in. The pension-fund can take out an insurance on its credit (the purchase of bonds from a poorly-rated company) with an insurance-agency specialised on debt-default. A necessary condition is that this insurance-company has been given a high rating by the rating agency. Then, the pension-fund pays a fee to the insurance-agency and this latter pays the pension-fund if the investment-bank defaults on its debt. In this way, the investment-fund's bonds have been upgraded because they are insured by a highly-rated insurance-company. Or so it seems.

The problem is that the insurance-company, just because it has received a very good rating from the rating agency, is not required to set aside the money it would need if the investment-bank were to default. It might keep enough

Table 6. Credit-default swaps

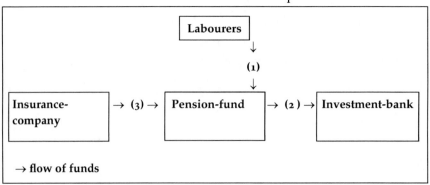

capital aside according to some model that computes the probability that a debtor defaults, but does not have to put aside the whole or even a reasonable part of the capital ensured. One of the reasons is that these models do not provide for the possibility of a generalised credit-default. Moreover, the insurance-company ensures many other institutions like that pension-fund. As long as it does not get downgraded by the rating agency, it can go on insuring investors that buy bonds from poorly-rated loan-issuers without any limit. The reason, of course, is that it can keep collecting interests on the debts it ensures. But the insurance-company itself is not ensured against a financial collapse. If the bubble bursts and the borrowers default, the insurance-company cannot cover a part or the whole of the lenders' (the pension-fund's) credits and the lenders lose their capital. If the lender has not invested its own capital (as in the case of the pension-fund which collects and invests the labourers' pensions) it is those who have provided that capital that suffer the loss. It is in this way that the labourers' pensions have been (sometimes drastically) reduced.[39]

The problem is further exacerbated because the insurance-company, due to the disbursement of capital to the creditors (for example, the pension-fund in the example above) might become undercapitalised and thus might lose its status as a highly-rated company. Then, all those lenders (for example, other pension-funds) that relied on this insurance-company to lend to low-rated borrowers (the investment-bank in the example above) will have to unwind their contracts. This cannot but mean added financial difficulties for the borrowers. The bankruptcy of one borrower has thus a domino-effect. It causes financial difficulties not only for the lender (for example, the pension-fund) and the loss of capital for those who have provided capital to the lender (the labourers), but also for all other lenders that had relied on the high rating of the insurance-company and thus for the borrowers that had relied on the lenders' loans.

But the ingenuity of the 'financial architects' does not stop here. Consider again the example above. The insurance-company ensures the pension-fund against the risk of the investment-bank's default, because its assessment is

---

[39] 'Also suffering huge losses are the bondholders, such as pension funds, who bought [indirectly – G.C.] sub-prime mortgage bonds. These have fallen sharply in value in the last few months, and are now worth between 20% and 40% of their original value for most asset classes, even those considered safe by the ratings agencies'. BBC 2007.

Table 7. Credit-default swaps with hedge-funds

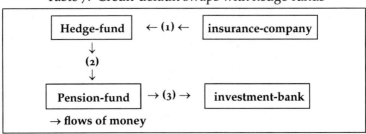

that the latter will not default. A hedge-fund, on the other hand, might have a different view and considers the probabilities of default to be much higher. The hedge-fund buys the credit-default swaps. Now, the pension-fund is not ensured by the insurance-company but by the hedge-fund and the hedge-fund buys an insurance from the insurance-company in case it has to pay the pension-fund. In case of default by the borrower (the investment-bank), the hedge-fund pays out to the pension-fund and is paid by the insurance-company. The hedge-fund bets on the borrowers' default. It can thus insure the lender for the amount it has lent the borrower, but buys an insurance from the insurance-company for a larger amount. If the bet turns out to have been accurate, the hedge-fund pockets the difference. But this might cause the downgrading of the insurance-company with all the ramifications just sketched out above.

In Table 7, (3) is the pension-fund's investment in the investment-bank and (1) and (2) are the flows of money to the pension-fund in case of the investment-bank's default. In case of default, the hedge-fund pays the pension-fund and is itself paid by the insurance-company.

As these examples indicate, in the years preceding the burst of the financial bubble, the financial and speculative sectors have mushroomed into an extremely large and amazingly complex Byzantine construction of derivatives, whose underlying 'assets' have been almost everything under the sun because almost everything lends itself to speculation. This process has been made technically possible by new financial techniques like the one discussed above, the so-called financial engineering, which followed financial deregulation. Speculative debt and transactions have been blown to levels out of proportion with the productive basis and this has made it impossible for debts to be paid back. This is a virtual growth, not a real one, based on ruthless speculation and fraud. The inflation of the bubble is accelerated by the financial institutions' corrupt and deceitful lending and accounting practices and a hidden system of account. The true amount of the bubble has been hidden by the banks' practice of packaging the subprime mortgages with other forms of more reliable credit and selling these financial 'products' to investors as highly-rated bonds. But there is also an international dimension. As more low-income people obtained subprime mortgages, an increasing volume of these assets (in fact, insolvent debts) has been repackaged with debts of a better quality, rated as high quality financial 'products', and sold globally.[40] In this way, large amounts of worthless credit were sold on worldwide markets. As a consequence, the financial crisis extended from the US to other countries which both had bought US 'poisoned' financial instruments and they themselves had engaged in the same financial practices.[41] But, aside from this, the financial crisis in the West has deep effects on the real economies in other countries. For example, the US negative balance of trade with China and other Asian countries expanded those countries' foreign reserves (in dollars) with which they bought US Treasury-bills. The money flowed back to US financial institutions that loaned it to consumers and homebuyers. With the implosion of the US credit-market, those economies' exports feel the crunch and are resized.

To sum up, both theoretical and empirical investigation has provided substantiation for the thesis that the crises' ultimate cause is the tendential fall in the average rate of profit of the productive sectors. Wage-movements can explain neither the crisis nor the cycle. The explanation is to be found in Marx, not in Keynes's underconsumptionism. But, internal critique aside, one should be aware of each of the two views' political and ideological ramifications. If lower wages determine crises, higher wages are the way out of crises. And, if higher wages determine crises, lower wages are the way out of crises. Crises are, at least in principle, *avoidable*. If they are not avoided, it is because 'mistakes' have been made in wage, fiscal, monetary, and so on and so forth policies, or because labour has not been able to impose better work and living conditions on capital. The reformist matrix of this redistributional view is clear: if the system is reformable, a different system is not needed. However,

---

[40] As Pagliarone (2008, p. 79) reports, the mortgage-backed securities are sold also to foreign investors, mainly to the central banks of Japan, China and the UK.

[41] As of November 2008, the world's financial firms had lost 1,000 billion dollars (Giacché 2008, p. 46). The same author reports that the ratio between world-debt and world GNP increased from 130% in 1980 to 350% in 2007, a record maximum high (Giacché 2008, p. 48).

if crises are a constant feature of capitalism, we need a theory that theorises their unavoidability, their necessity. This is exactly what the Marxian explanation does by focusing on the decreased production of (surplus-) value due to technological innovations and the concomitant rising organic composition of capital as the ultimate cause of crises. Given that this is a constant of capitalism, the necessary, constant and unavoidable way capitals compete with each other, *crises are unavoidable*. Stated differently, in the former case (basically, a Keynesian perspective), if crises can be avoided, the system does not tend objectively and necessarily towards crises. The possibility is created to conceptualise capitalism as a system being or tending towards growth and equilibrium (even if at a level lower than full employment). In the latter (Marx's) case, the system tends towards crises through the economic cycle. In the former case, the system is inherently rational (it tends towards equilibrium and growth) and labour's fight to supersede it is therefore irrational. Labour is deprived of the objective, rational base for its fight. This fight becomes a pure act of voluntarism. In the latter case, the system is irrational and labour's fight to abolish it is then both rational and the conscious expression of an objective movement, the tendency the system has to supersede itself. The choice of one crisis-theory rather than another is an individual one. But, given the different class-content of the different theories, this choice places the individual theorist on one side rather than another in the struggle against capital.

4. Either Marx or Keynes

If neither neoclassical theory nor Keynesian theory can find the real cause of the crisis, it stands to reason that neither one of them can find the means to jump-start the economy again. The former theory, with its absolute belief in the self-correcting quasi-magical powers of the market, has been disproved time and again by recurrent crises, of which the present one seems to be, at the time of this writing, one of the gravest. The decennial reduction of real wages as documented above, should be sufficient grounds to disprove the neoliberal belief that the cause of crisis is an excessively high level of wages. But there are also sound theoretical reasons to jettison this theory. It has been shown that high wages cannot be the cause of the crisis, because they cannot explain the turning point at which the high phase of the cycle turns into depression. However, high wages can certainly affect profitability and thus contribute to the worsening of the depression and crisis once it has set in. Neoliberalism is not only wrong about the cause of crises, it is also wrong about the medicine, which in its limited imagination it identifies in lower wages. Lower wages do increase profitability. But this cannot be the cause of the recovery. The increase in the profit-rate that reactivates the economy is the one associated with an increase in the *mass* of profit. The basic mistakes inherent in neoliberalism's recipe are that (a) high wages cannot be the cause of the crisis, because they cannot explain the turning point from the upward- to the downward-phase of the cycle; and (b) that lower wages cannot be the cause of the recovery, because lower wages cannot hold back the fall in the average rate of profit (they are a countertendency) i.e. because, in the descending phase, the extra profits deriving from lower wages are basically invested in the unproductive sectors.

While neoliberalism's dream world is one in which capital sets the frame for capital to reduce wages *ad libitum* with as little government-intervention in the economy as possible (except that, when capital is in serious difficulties, as in major crises, the government's help to the ailing economy is more than welcome), Keynesian theory, having mistakenly identified the cause of crisis in excessively low wages, advocates high wages and government-intervention. There are essentially two ways the government can intervene: through *redistributive measures* and through *Keynesian policies proper*. Let us begin with the former. Keynesian authors argue that redistribution should go *from capital to labour* given that (1) the economy exits the crisis through increased spending (rather than the production of surplus-value); (2) labour should be the recipient of this transfer because labour's propensity to spend is higher than capital's propensity; and (3) this initial expenditure stimulates demand by a multiple of itself through successive, even though decreasing, cycles of spending and thus economic growth. This is the multiplier. However, there are at least four reasons why the multiplier cannot start a new upward phase. First, as seen above in this chapter, a distribution from capital to labour (e.g. higher wages) decreases the rate of profit. Second, the multiplier does not increase the mass of profits either. Irrespective of the size of the multiplier, without an increase in the production of (surplus-) value, *only what has already been produced but not yet sold can be purchased*, in other words there can be only induced realisation. Thus, what the multiplier says is that the injection of money (higher wages) that might be necessary in order to sell all the commodities that have remained unsold might be smaller than the price of those commodities. Third, the assumption that private individuals and firms will spend and invest that extra money is far from being self-evident in a period of crisis. Fourth, even if (part of) that extra money were invested, it would not necessarily be invested in the productive sphere, due to falling profitability in that sphere.

The statistics on the extent of the multiplier do not measure the extent of the induced production of wealth (value). Rather, they measure the extent to which goods previously lying unsold have been sold, that is, value previously produced has been realised. Neoclassical economists criticise the multiplier by arguing that its size is far smaller than what the Keynesians think. This critique, whether substantiated empirically or not, remains within the Keynesian framework. On a more theoretical plane, it is argued that deficit-spending does not create new wealth, inasmuch as the state must pay back the interest on the borrowed capital by appropriating that value from private capital. The state-sector grows at the cost of private capital (the crowding-out effect). The point, however, is that, even if the state could borrow free of interest from private capital in order to finance redistributive policies, there would be no increase in wealth but only the realisation of already produced value.

It is at this point that the state comes in not simply as an agent of redistribution (of induced realisation) but also as a factor spurring new investments and thus new production of surplus-value. These are the *Keynesian policies proper*. They are defined here as the appropriation and/or borrowing by the state of idle capital, in other words, capital's reserves, and/or of labour's idle savings in order to produce, or commission the production of, public works and/or weapons while guaranteeing the realisation of the output. These policies mobilise real resources that would otherwise remain unutilised and stimulate the production of new (surplus-) value while, at the same time, guaranteeing its realisation by the state. They provide means for capital to produce and realise profits and increase employment, thus giving extra purchasing power to labour. All in all, by being an anti-cyclical measure, they contribute to the reproduction of the system. The question, however, is whether the state-induced and state-guaranteed production of extra (surplus-) value and output provides a way out of crises, besides improving labour's working and living conditions – in other words, whether these policies are effective anti-cyclical measures in the sense that they cause an inversion of the trend. Before answering, a few qualifications are in order.

What follows is based on the following assumptions. First, capital is sub-divided into capital owned by private companies and capital owned by the state, into private capital and state-capital. Second, the state can either commission public works and/or weapons to the private sector or carry out these activities itself, through state-owned companies. The assumption here is that the state commissions private capital.[42] Third, the production of public works and weapons is, to a certain degree, independent of crises and depressions. But its extent is certainly conditioned by the phase of the cycle. What follows focuses on Keynesian policies as an anti-cyclical measure. Fourth, even if it is usually held that Keynesian policies should be capital-financed, in practice it is also the labourers who pay for them. Therefore, the case of labour-financed anti-cyclical measures is also considered.[43]

Consider first the case of *capital-financed* (civilian or military) Keynesian policies. This case presupposes the existence of reserves accumulated by the capitalists. Suppose the state appropriates the reserves of capitals A and B (private capital) and with that capital commissions public works or weapons to capital C. Capitals A and B suffer a loss equal to that appropriation which is offset by the gain by the state. Capital C sells its product to the state and is assured the sale of its product.[44] The state becomes the owner of public works or weapons. The final effect on the average rate of profit depends basically on two factors. First, the question is whether capital C's organic composition of capital is higher or lower than the average rate of profit (the average of A and B, in this example). If C's organic composition of capital is lower than the average rate of profit, the average rate of profit rises on this account. Second, the question is whether sufficient reserves are shifted from A and B to C via the state. The lower the organic composition of C relative to the average, the smaller the quantity of reserves to be appropriated in order to increase the average rate of profit. It follows that a positive effect on the average rate of profit, in the sense that the average rate of profit is restored to its pre-crisis level or increased to

[42] 'By the early 2000s a large part of the arms industry was privately owned in most major arms-producing countries.' This applies also to 'the provision of services (outsourcing).' (Stockholm International Peace Research Institute 2002, p. 341.)

[43] To simplify matters, the capital invested in public works is made to include not only the capital needed for their construction but also that for their maintenance during the whole span of their life.

[44] To make the example as simple as possible, we disregard the fact that the state must appropriate more reserves, the difference being the profits to be paid to capital C.

a level higher than its pre-crisis level, depends on whether the appropriation of reserves by the state is sufficiently high and/or the organic composition of C is sufficiently low for this investment into capital C to produce a surplus-value sufficiently high to raise the average rate of profit.

In principle, then, capital-financed Keynesian policies can work even if at the expense of private capital. But, even if they do, their effect is only temporary. In fact, if the average rate of profit keeps decreasing as a result of labour-shedding but productivity-increasing new technologies, the state has to further appropriate reserves. The further this process proceeds, the smaller becomes the pool of reserves that can be appropriated by the state. At the limit, this economic basis dries up and no Keynesian policies are possible any longer.[45] But the process stops a long time before this limit point is reached. In fact, inasmuch as the state chooses high-organic-composition-of-capital firms, it defeats its own aim. Inasmuch as it chooses low-organic-composition-of-capital firms, it puts a premium on technological backwardness. This is contrary to capital's logic. Then the state has to choose firms with high technology, with a high organic composition of capital. The state creates economic activity and employment but is unable to lift the average rate of profit and thus the economy out of the crisis. This form of anti-cyclical measures is a modern (relative to Marx) counter-tendential measure. It too can retard the explosion of the crisis but cannot avoid it.

The Keynesian approach submits that Keynesian policies should be capital-financed. In practice, they are also, and often mostly, labour-financed.[46] Suppose that the state appropriates labour's savings. The transfer of value

---

[45] This is similar to Marx's argument concerning the limit to the extension of the working day. See Chapter 2 above.

[46] In Sweden, over half the housing stock was replaced between 1965 and 1975. However, the funds came from the workers', rather than from the capitalists', pension-funds. The high taxes needed to finance the so-called welfare-state were applied only to the working class, while taxes on profits were among the lowest in the world. To take another example, Shaikh (2003) constructs a net social wage as 'the difference between the value of total social benefits received and total taxes directly paid' by labour (pp. 537–8) and finds that, in the post-WWII period, it is slightly negative for the US but slightly positive for other OECD-countries. On a more fundamental plane, it is labour, and only labour, that produces value. Thus, even if the share of social benefits (net of taxes) received by labour were to increase, there would not be a greater transfer of value produced by other classes to labour but, rather, a greater restitution to labour of value previously produced by the labourers themselves and then appropriated by other classes.

Table 8. Outstanding consumer-debt as a percentage of disposable income in the US (in billions of dollars)

1975	62.0%
1980	69.5
1985	73.0
1990	83.8
1995	89.8
2000	96.8
2005	127.2

Source: Board of Governors of the Federal Reserve System 2006.

from labour to capital has definitely a positive effect on the average rate of profit, but this cannot be an antidote to the crisis because it does not increase the mass of surplus-value produced (in other words, there is no economic growth). For this to happen, the state must commission public works or weapons to capital C. But, here too, the process comes up against a barrier. As the crisis proceeds, labour can save less and less and actually first uses its savings and then gets increasingly indebted so that there are no or insufficient savings to be capitalised by the state. A graphic illustration is provided by Table 8, in which disposable income is the income after paying taxes.

Moreover, as in the case of capital-financed Keynesian policies, sufficient savings must be appropriated (assuming they are available) by the state, and capital C must have a sufficiently low organic composition of capital. But, the state will prioritise modern, that is, high-organic-composition-of-capital firms. It is for these reasons that labour-financed Keynesian policies also can hold back the crisis at best only temporarily. They too are a conscious counter-tendential measure that could not be anticipated by Marx.[47] Inasmuch as labour-financed Keynesian policies work, they are only another way to raise the rate of exploitation and they do exactly the opposite of what they are supposed to do, that is, they transfer value from labour to capital rather than the other way around.

Finally, the state usually borrows to finance its Keynesian policies. But the lenders must be paid back their principal plus interest. The state can resort to

---

[47] These conclusions do not change substantially if the question is introduced as to who pays for the use (rather than the construction) of public works. If private capital pays, its profits decrease and those of state capital increase by that much. If labour pays, the greater profits by state-capital are at the expense of labour's wages.

further credit, but this makes its financial situation increasingly fragile. Eventually, it has to resort to taxation or to some other forms of debt-reduction, such as inflation or default, that is, to the appropriation of value. At that point, private capital and/or labour lose their reserves and savings. The crisis has been merely postponed.[48]

Contrary to the thesis submitted here, it is generally believed that military expenditures are the flywheel of the US economy and not simply a counter-tendency, even though an important one. As Giussani and Pagliarone note, an inspection of the US rate of military expenditures to GNP from 1929 to 2001 shows that the maximum rate (43%) was reached in 1944, in the midst of WWII, and that it has ever since fallen with short-term increases, as for example, during the 1950–3 Korean War until it reaches the minimum of 3.77% in 2000.[49] As for more recent data:

> Since 2001 US military expenditure has increased by 59 per cent in real terms, principally because of massive spending on military operations in Afghanistan and Iraq, but also because of increases in the 'base' defence budget. By 2007, US spending was higher than at any time since World War II. However, because of the growth of the US economy and of total US Government spending, the economic and financial burden of military spending (that is, its share of GDP and of total US Government outlays) is lower now than during previous peak spending years in the post-World War II period.[50]

In short, if US gross national product grows and military expenditures fall as a percentage of gross national product, those expenditures cannot be the flywheel of the economy. Military Keynesianism is just as civilian Keynesianism a counter-tendential measure that cannot prevent the tendential fall in the average rate of profit to manifest itself. It is, however, a constant counter-tendency.

---

[48] The argument that, after the Second World-War, Keynesian policies have made possible a long cycle of growth reverses the order of causation. It is the great post-WWII economic upsurge that made Keynesian policies possible. As expansion lost its momentum, and with it the production of surplus-value, the basis of Keynesian policies waned. See Carchedi, 2003c.

[49] Giussani and Pagliarone 2004.

[50] Stålenheim, Perdomo and Sköns 2008, Chapter 5.

Left Keynesians agree that Keynesian policies cannot ward off crises, but for different reasons. For example, the greater the state-induced investments and thus state-property, the greater the state-bourgeoisie, and the greater the resistance of private capital to a further enlargement of the state-bourgeoisie. Or, the closer the economy gets to full employment through Keynesian policies, the greater the threat (for capital) of higher wages and thus private capital's resistance. Or, Keynesian policies are limited by politics of budgetary balance that restrict borrowing.[51] In reality, the limits of Keynesian policies are of a different nature. They are counter-tendencies that, as such, cannot hold back the tendential movement. Whether Keynesian policies are labour-financed or capital-financed, whether they are financed through direct appropriation or indirectly through state-deficit, whether they are civilian or military, the cause of their ultimate failure is that they can at best postpone but cannot avoid the crisis. Only a massive destruction of capital as a social relation can provide that cathartic moment at which the downward trend turns into its opposite.

Up to this point, the stress has been placed on the similarities between civilian and military Keynesian policies. But there are differences, specific disadvantages and advantages for capital. Concerning the former, the production of weapons is even less likely to restore profitability than public works because it is usually very technologically advanced, with a higher value-composition than that of the rest of the economy. Also, as distinct from public works, weapons are non-reproductive goods. Their production hampers the physical reproduction of the economy. And, finally, weapons are commodities that, in times of peace, are mostly not used. The labour that has gone into them (value) is thus wasted. This is a loss that weighs negatively on the average rate of profit. But there are also advantages (for capital). First, if weapons are exported and if profit-rates tend to equalise internationally, the producers of weapons appropriate international value from other, foreign, capitalists due to the formers' higher value-composition (unequal exchange). Second, science and technology-based military innovations are the basic driving force in, and directly support, the development of civilian science and technology. Since the Second World-War, practically all the major innovations in the civilian sphere have been first generated by military research and development. This gives the technological leaders a competitive advantage which makes possible the appropriation of international surplus-value. Third, the use of public works can become part of the goods considered to be necessary for the reproduction of labour-power, and thus it can lead to an increase in real wages. This 'danger' is avoided if resources are channelled into the military industry. Fourth, military might is a necessary condition for imperialist policies, and thus for value-appropriation from weaker countries (not least for the plunder of natural resources, such as oil, and the protection of foreign investments, and thus of the consequent repatriation of foreign profits). Once imperialism is introduced into the analysis, the positive effects on the average rate of profit attributed to civilian Keynesianism in the imperialist countries can be seen to be in fact, at least partially, the result of the appropriation of surplus-value from the world working class, thanks also to military Keynesianism. Disregard of this fundamental point gives Keynesian policies much more credit than they deserve. There is thus no contraposition between civilian and military Keynesianism. The former can be made possible by the appropriation of international value inherent in the latter.

Fifth, the use of weapons in time of wars is a specific, powerful, method of destruction of capital in its commodity-form and, even more importantly, of the means of production and thus of capital as a social relation. Applied to the countries whose average rate of profit exhibits a long downward-trend, this creates the basic condition for an economic upturn. At the same time, wars make possible the cancellation of the debt contracted with labour (for example, inflation destroys the value of money and thus of state-bonds) and the extraction of extra surplus-value (the labourers, either forced or instigated by patriotism, accept lower wages, higher intensity of labour, longer working days, and so on). Capitalism needs wars and thus weapons.[52]

If capitalism needs wars, wars need enemies. The imperialist nations display great ingenuity in finding, or creating, new enemies. Before the fall of the USSR, the pretext for the arms-industry was international Communism.

---

[52] The paradigmatic case is given by the huge US military expenditures. The US accounts for almost half of the world total. After a period of reduction after the fall of the USSR and of a moderate increase, this proportion has abruptly increased in 2002 and 2003.

After the fall, international Communism has been replaced by Muslim fundamentalism and international terrorism. As the wars against Afghanistan and Iraq show, the substitution is now complete. The attacks of 11 September 2001, have been a golden opportunity for the arms-industry and US-imperialism. The figures for North America are clear. The military expenditures for that region have increased by 24% from 1994 to 2003. However, if this period is broken down, we see that these figures have decreased almost constantly from US$344bn in 1994 to US$313bn in 2001 but have skyrocketed to US$350 in 2002 and to US$426 in 2003.[53] These data, as well as a wealth of others, show that political and ideological factors are of paramount importance for the modes and timing of the conflagration. But they themselves are determined by economic factors. In terms of the results reached in Chapter 1, the capitalist economy is determinant of wars, in the sense that the capitalist economy is the condition of the existence of wars and that wars are the condition of reproduction (or of supersession) of the capitalist economy. Moreover, as Chapter 2 has argued, changes in the determinant instance change the potential contradictory, sectoral, tendential and cyclical manifestation of the determined instance, but cannot predetermine their specific form, time of occurrence and class-content. The notion that wars are caused by 'extra-economic' factors is simply wrong. The Western world has exported (created) countless wars in many dominated countries and has engaged in military-Keynesian policies for the above-mentioned reasons.

After the war is over, a period of reconstruction follows. In the countries hit by wars, production can restart with an increased rate of exploitation. The two basic conditions for economic recovery, the destruction of capital and the increase in the rate of exploitation, have been created. This is the general principle. However, to understand the present conjuncture, a specific sub-case should be mentioned, that of the imperialist countries (especially the US) waging wars against, and on the territory of, the dominated countries. In the former countries, only those weapons that have been used to wage the war elsewhere are destroyed. This might provide an insufficient impulse for recovery unless, as shown by the Second World-War, (a) the war-effort is of such a scale that it absorbs the labour-power and means of production unemployed

---

[53] Stockholm International Peace Research Institute 2004, Appendix table 10A, 10A.1 and 10A.3.

because of the crisis and (b) the former countries provide the commodities as well as the capital needed by the latter's reconstruction. By first destroying another country and then offering 'aid' to rebuild it, they create outlets for the production and export of their own goods without themselves having to undergo destruction and misery. But this would work only if the scale of reconstruction were massive, as for example in the post-WWII Marshall Plan. As for the assaulted dominated countries, what are reconstructed are only those elements of their economy needed by the imperialist countries.[54] Keynes once said: 'Pyramid-building, earthquakes, even wars may serve to increase wealth.'[55] Aside from moral considerations, this is usually theorised as if it were applicable to any country. In reality, it can work only for the imperialist countries. The theorisation of the beneficial (for capital) effects of wars is thus a cynical and immoral apology of imperialism.

This leaves us with the question: should labour fight for Keynesian policies? It is obvious that labour should reject war and thus military Keynesianism. However, whether labour should opt for civilian Keynesianism is a much more hotly debated question. The above has stressed the limits of civilian Keynesianism. Pro-labour and thus capital-financed purely redistributive policies, which are incorrectly defined as Keynesian policies, in the form of higher wages and salaries, better services, better housing, better retirement-schemes, and so on, are obviously favourable to labour, and especially to the less well-paid sectors of it. These policies should be fought for. Keynesian policies proper can increase employment, total wages and, under very stringent and improbable conditions, the average rate of profit, but these effects are of relatively short duration. There should be no illusions that they in and of themselves can contribute to exiting from the crisis. The argument, shared also by many Marxists, that the failure of Keynesian policies is due to their insufficient application is thus wrong.[56] In the long run, they reproduce the emergence of the downward-phase of the cycle and thus are inimical to

---

[54] During the New Deal, civilian state-expenditures grew from US$10.2bn in 1929 to US$17.5bn in 1939. However, in the same period, GNP fell from US$104.4bn to US$91.1bn and unemployment grew from 3.2% to 17.2% of the total labour-force. It was only in December 1941, when the US went to war, that the US-economy exited from the crisis. See Giacché 2001, pp. 111–12.
[55] Keynes 1964, p. 129.
[56] See Wolff 1999.

labour. The real importance of these policies is that, inasmuch as they can postpone the crisis, they can be used to 'buy social peace'.

It follows that the dilemma that is posed between labour-financed, capital-financed, or credit-financed Keynesian policies is false. By focusing on this false choice, Keynesianism implicitly undermines labour's ability to develop a programme 'for change beyond all forms of capitalism'.[57] Labour should have no illusions about these policies' potential for a long-run improvement in their working and living conditions, let alone for radical social change. To hold that, in the long run, we are all dead – in other words, let labour profit from whatever positive effects Keynesian policies might have here and now, waiting for better times to come – ignores the fact that possible short-term gains are at the same time the causes of the weakening of the economy in the longer run and serve to deter labour's capacity to envisage radical alternatives to capitalism. If it were only up to Keynesian policies, better times would never come.

Clearly, to call for a rejection of Keynesian policies in a political and ideological conjuncture in which these policies seem to be the best the European 'Left' can think of is bound to be an unpopular stance. Yet, if the criticism above is correct, the alternative is neither for, nor between one type or another of, Keynesian policies. Rather, given the ideological content of these policies, labour should fight for some of those policies but from a totally different perspective. Labour should fight for redistributive measures (that is, higher wages and pension-benefits, a minimum-wage for the unemployed, and so on), for more labour-friendly labour-legislation (for example, concerning capital's power to dismiss labourers), for state-induced, capital-financed, public works (for example in the education-sector and in the health-services) as well as for the reconversion of the weapons-industry – in general, for labour-friendly reforms. But it should fight for these reforms not from the perspective of Keynesian policies (as if they were labour-friendly, effective anti-crisis policies) but from the perspective of, and thus by introducing whenever possible, thoroughly different social (and, to begin with, production-) relations, that is, relations based on co-operation, equality, and solidarity. This is the perspective which secretes not only different forms of consciousness and insights into possible and radically alternative futures, not only radically different forms

---

[57] Wolff 1999, p. 78.

of political structures with which and through which to conduct the fight, but also concrete policies consonant with the supersession of capitalism. For example, labour should reject an educational and training system aiming at supplying a flexible labour-force to the labour-market and should try to implement a system in which all have equal opportunities to learn to develop all aspects of their personality, not at the cost of but together with everybody else, that is, from the perspective of co-operation, equality and solidarity.

Needless to say, this is not only a hugely difficult task, it is *the most difficult* task for labour, especially in the present conjuncture. Nevertheless, the development of strategies of resistance as well as long-run alternatives within this perspective is the only way out of barbarism. One of the pre-conditions for its success is that labour becomes fully aware of the class-nature of Keynesian policies (their being temporary palliatives ultimately functional for the reproduction of capitalism as well as of its crisis-ridden nature), in other words that the real alternative is: *either* Marx *or* Keynes.

Chapter Four
Subjectivity

1. Crisis-theory and the theory of knowledge[1]

A work on the crisis that focuses only on its objective causes and operations without considering how this contradictory objectivity emerges at the level of the individuals' consciousness, is only half the story. The other half requires the development of a theory of knowledge consistent with Marx's wider theoretical opus, suitable for the development of an account of those aspects left unexplored by Marx, in tune with contemporary reality, and appropriate to foster radical social change. One of the features of this work is that it inquires not only into the crisis-ridden nature of the capitalist economy, that it not only discerns the causes of its recurrent crises and the reasons why they must occur irrespective of the intentions and behaviour of the economic agents, but that it also relates the objective working of the economy to the subjectivity of the social agents, that is, to the subjective manifestations of the contradictory objective foundations of the economy. Within this framework, two areas of a Marxist theory of knowledge will be explored.

---

[1] Some parts of this Chapter are a reworked version of Carchedi 2005a.

The first one concerns the relation between the crisis-ridden nature of the capitalist economy with the subjective and necessary manifestations of these objective developments at the level of social consciousness. It requires the development of a theory of individual and social knowledge. In the process of providing answers to these questions, other debated issues will be explored, such as the problem of whether and when the production of knowledge is the production of value and surplus-value. This issue is of great importance for a theory of crises since there is nowadays a widespread notion that in contemporary capitalism the economy rests more on the production of knowledge (mental production) than on 'material', or better said, objective production.

The term 'material' has been put within quotation-marks, because, to anticipate a point to be expanded upon later on, all production (including mental production) is material in the sense that it is the expenditure of human energy, which is material. The difference is in the outcome, that is, whether the outcome is an objective transformation of the reality outside us (and, in this sense, it is an objective production) or a transformation of our perception of that reality (transformation), and, in this sense, it is a mental production. Thus, the correct terminology is *objective* production versus *mental* production both of them being material production.

A second area of research will deal with the question as to whether the knowledge produced under capitalist relations is suitable for the application to a period of transition towards a socialist society. An especially important role is ascribed to a specific type of knowledge, the natural sciences and techniques. In this connection, it should be mentioned that the theorisation of the production of knowledge both in general and in particular under capitalism has been impaired by the acceptance of two epistemological dogmas, namely, that the working of the mind (knowledge-production) is independent (a) of the body and (b) of society.[2] Orthodox-Marxist theory avoids these theoretical pitfalls, but, in its dogmatic rendition, has created some problems of its own, principally the idea (a) that knowledge-production is a reflection in our minds of material and natural processes and (b) that social knowledge is a simple summation of individual knowledge. The rejection of 'reflection-theory' and the emphasis placed on the class-determination of knowledge to be submitted below, however, seems to run into the difficulty that classes apparently do

---

[2] Ferretti 2004.

not express necessarily a theorisation of their own interests and that knowledge (especially the natural sciences and techniques), being amenable to be used by different classes, is, in fact, class-neutral. These are deemed to be sufficient grounds to reject the Marxist thesis, defended and developed in this work, of the class-determination of knowledge. Instead of class, information or services are deemed to be the specific and characteristic features of modern societies. Accordingly, the notion of a class-divided society has been displaced by that of 'information-society' or 'service-society'. But, if knowledge is not class-determined, then the working class cannot or does not necessarily produce its own view of reality and thus of the crisis-ridden nature of this system, which, in turn, deprives the working class of the theoretical guide in its struggle against capitalism. The thesis of the class-neutrality of knowledge has thus devastating effects on the struggle for a radically alternative form of society.

2. Neither information-society nor service-society

It is currently fashionable to hold that capitalism has been replaced by the information-society or by the service-society, in other words by a world-system in which, supposedly, the developed countries are not dependent any longer on objective production. Rather, allegedly, their main activity has become the provision of services, which – confusedly – are made to include the production of natural sciences and techniques as well. The production of wealth (value, in Marxist terms), then, is ascribed principally to the service-, natural-scientific and technique-sectors in the imperialist countries and the economy is thought to have become 'immaterial'.[3] Concomitantly, these two sectors are seen as being constituted by either a new working class or a new middle class. As we shall see, these theses catch some elements of novelty, but in an erroneous and highly ideological manner. They rest on an injurious confusion between knowledge (including natural sciences and techniques) and services as well as on the highly heterogeneous and thus utterly useless category of services. The notions of information and services are usually lumped together, not only because they allegedly are both immaterial, but

---

[3] The notion of immaterial production will be dealt with and criticised in Section 7 below.

also because both are said to be 'produced' as commodities. Nevertheless, for the sake of convenience, these two theses will be assessed separately. Let us begin with the information- or knowledge-society.

This thesis is multifaceted. To begin with, it is argued that knowledge has become a commodity.[4] But this has always been the case under capitalism, starting from the production and popularisation of the printed book. The difference is only quantitative, even though extremely significant. It is also argued that the new technologies require the separation of software from hardware.[5] But, again, this was also the case for old technologies, for example, which at that time existed in the form of manuals for the operation and maintenance of machines. Again, the difference is only quantitative, even though of major importance. It is also said that software (knowledge), as opposed to material outputs, can never wear out since the value of the labour embodied in the software becomes subdivided between a potentially infinite number of products.[6] But the material shell in which knowledge is embedded does wear out. Moreover, and most importantly, knowledge is subjected to technological obsolescence. Actually, in this phase of capitalism, knowledge loses value due to obsolescence at an unprecedented pace. Also, presumably, information, unlike material goods, needs to be produced only once and can then be copied and transferred. But information also has costs associated with its reproduction, even though they might be less than the costs for the reproduction of objective commodities. Again, the difference is quantitative. Another opinion submits that knowledge can realise its value only if its owner has a monopoly on it. But this is common to all commodities, including objective ones. Only the owner of a commodity can realise its value. It is also argued that new technologies mark the end of labour or, in the words of Mandel, represent the 'absolute limit of capitalism'.[7]

Such opposing views disregard the cyclical pattern of capitalist development, whereby today's new technologies will be obsolete tomorrow and the replacement of people by machines is only a tendency; one of its counter-tendencies being the development of new products and the opening up of new branches marked by a low organic composition of capital.

---

[4] See the various contributions in Davis, Hirschl and Stack (eds.) 1997.
[5] Ibid.
[6] Morris-Suzuki 1997a, p. 18.
[7] Mandel 1978, pp. 207–8.

Another view claims that it is the knowledge embedded in a commodity that creates its value. But knowledge does not create value. Rather, it is the productive labourers who create value and it is the value of the labourers' labour-power, which is partly determined by the past value gone into the production of their knowledge, that determines the quantity of value created. Others hold that the production of knowledge relies on a constant improvement of the intellectual capabilities of workers and technicians.[8] This disregards the constant dialectical process of tendential dequalification and of counter-tendential requalification of labour-power.[9] But, as May remarks, by considering the production of knowledge as a highly skilled and 'empowering' activity, the 'still Taylorised ranks of the service class' are swept under the rug.[10] Finally, it is often heard that knowledge is produced by the capitalists.[11] This is capitalist self-deception, masterly spread among all social classes. In reality, knowledge is the product of the mental labourers' productive powers. As this chapter will argue, it is the social content of knowledge that bears the imprint of capital even though knowledge itself is the product of labour. This casts a light on the question of intellectual property-rights which is different from what capital would have us believe. Intellectual property-rights are actually the capitalist's appropriation of the outcome of the labourers' mental labour rather than being the product of the capitalists themselves. The capitalists can not only decide which knowledge should be produced, how it should be produced, and for whom. They can also make a profit out of it.

All these views disregard two basic points. *First*, capitalism is still capitalism. Its essence, the ownership of the means of production by the capitalists, and thus the ensuing division between capital and labour, is unchanged. If anything, the owners/non-owners divide is growing, as indicated by the growth of privatisations.[12] What has changed and is changing is the forms of appearance of the capitalist ownership-relations, and thus of the two basic classes, as shown by capital's unprecedented freedom to subject labour to old and new forms of domination (for example, displacement by automation, de-skilled, flexible, temporary, casual, off-the-books, and on-call jobs),

---

[8] See Section 7 below.
[9] Ibid.
[10] May 2000.
[11] See Sections 8 and 9 below.
[12] This does not imply that state-ownership necessarily implies workers' ownership.

188 • Chapter Four

by capital's penetration of realms of activities previously not subjected to capitalist (ownership-) relations (for example, the commodification of previously free activities), and by the growing sector of mental labour employed by capital in the capitalist centre. Contrary to notions such as the 'new economy' and the 'information-society', which are based on a supposedly generalised 'empowerment' along with so-called creative mental work, most mental labourers are not self-employed but subjected to the rule of capital and thus to the just-mentioned old and new forms of domination to which all labour is subjected. For example, mental labour, just as objective labour, is subjected to continuous waves of technological innovations and restructuring that tendentially de-qualify positions.[13] This is a tendential movement. While existing positions are dequalified (the tendency), new and qualified positions might be created (the counter-tendency). The former, tendential, process continues until the skills are incorporated into the machines, while the new, qualified positions will sooner or later be subjected to dequalification. A new wave of technological innovations will repeat the process. This is a far cry from self-fulfilment through work (see Section 7 below). The so-called information-society, or, better said, this new stage of capitalism, is far from having made class-relations, the production of surplus-value, and thus the law of value redundant. As Section 6 will argue, the production of knowledge can be the production of value and surplus-value.

Second, while the production of natural sciences and techniques is highly concentrated in the imperialist world, objective production has not become less important in these countries. It has only been partly shifted to the dependent countries but the beneficiaries of this shift are mainly the capitalists in the advanced capitalist countries: 'At present, only 1% of patents are owned by persons or companies in the Third World and, of those, 84% are owned by foreigners and less than 5% are actually used for production in the Third World.'[14] The shift of some objective production to the dependent countries is a new and crucial aspect of the continuing domination of those countries by

---

[13] The debate on the labour-process that followed the publication of Braverman 1974 suffered from the sterile opposition between the dequalification and the requalification theses. In fact both theses are part of a dialectical view. See Carchedi, 1977, 1983, 1987 and 1991.

[14] Mihevc 1995, p. 172.

the imperialist ones through the retention by the latter of the production of advanced, productivity-enhancing, natural sciences and techniques. But this form of mental labour is also subject to international relocation, something that affects the working and living conditions of the mental labourers in the imperialist countries as well. The less-qualified sectors of mental labour are threatened by international relocation and thus by increased exploitation. This does not exclude the fact that some dependent countries might achieve, in some branches, levels of production of knowledge and technological development comparable to those of the imperialist countries. But this, in and of itself, is not sufficient for those countries to break free of their condition of dependency. And, even if some countries emerge from the status of dependency to that of imperialist countries, the imperialist system nevertheless continues unabated.[15] Moreover, given the high concentration of unproductive, financial, and speculative activities in the service-sector of the developed countries and given the appropriation of value from the dependent countries by the imperialist ones, the information-society thesis reduces both the value produced by the dominated countries and inflates the value produced by the dominant ones. It is thus a *rationalisation of capitalism and imperialism*. Finally, as May has pointed out, certain tasks, which used to be carried out within the processes of objective production, such as security and advertising, are now undertaken by firms specialising in those activities.[16] Statistically, what used to be categorised as an industrial activity is now defined as a service. But this is a statistical change, not a real, economic one.

Closely related to the information-society or knowledge-society (or economy) thesis is the service-society. This thesis rests on the category 'services'. This category is highly ideological. In fact, supposedly, the capitalists provide a service to the workers, by supplying them with the means of production, and the workers provide a service to the capitalists by making available to these latter their labour-power. The exchange of services replaces exploitation. But this category cannot explain the production of value either. In fact, as Marx remarks: 'A service is nothing other than the useful effect of a *use* value, be it that of commodity, or that of labour. But we are here dealing

---

[15] See Carchedi 2001.
[16] May 2000.

with *exchange* value.'[17] Since this category pertains to the realm of use-values, it cannot explain exchange-value, and thus the production of value. Finally, this category is spurious. In fact, let us recall from Chapter 2 that labour (as abstract labour) is productive of (surplus-) value if employed by capital and if it (as concrete labour) transforms existing use-values into new use-values. Consequently, the problem as to whether a service produces value depends on whether that particular concrete labour, as employed by capital, transforms existing use-values into new ones. However, this category encompasses activities that both transform and do not transform use-values. Let us review them keeping in mind that the assumption is that these 'services' are provided by workers working for capital.

Public utilities. The extraction of gas, the production of electricity from coal, the purification of water, and so on, are all examples of objective transformations of use-values and thus, under capitalist production relations, of the production of (surplus-) value. In addition, the production of use-values is not complete until it reaches the user, otherwise those use-values could not realise themselves as use-values. Therefore, the transportation of objective goods (including the just mentioned commodities) is productive labour. The labour used for the provision of postal services, telephone and telegraph, and so on is an example of the transmission of knowledge. It too is similar to the transportation of objective products. But this is mental production. That knowledge has to be transmitted if it is to realise its use-value. The labour needed to transmit this knowledge (not to be confused with the knowledge being transmitted) produces value because this is the last step in the transformation of knowledge.

Social services. The labour used for the provision of social insurance, of health-care (for example, hospitals, family help), of entertainment, of old-age pensions, and so forth, participates in objective production for the same reason as that adduced by Marx, for example, in his discussion of the maintenance of machinery. Maintenance prevents the deterioration of use-values and thus is equivalent to a phase of their (re)production. The difference is that here the use-value preserved is the labourers' labour-power.

Financial services. The labour used for these activities, like those provided by banks and other financial institutions, is often referred to as immaterial

---

[17] Marx 1976a, pp. 299–300; emphasis added.

production. However, as it was anticipated above and as it will be argued for below in Section 3, immaterial labour/production does not exist. All labour is material because of the expenditure of human energy, which itself is material. The labour performed in financial services pertains to the realm of exchange, that is, to the redistribution of value. This, for Marx, is unproductive labour. The purchases and sales of commodities (both objective and mental) and all the (financial, speculative and so on) activities derived from them do not change the use-value of those commodities and thus are unproductive. These labour-processes deal with use-values but are unproductive because they deal with use-values without however changing them.

The army. Private armies (for example, mercenaries) when engaged in battles destroy use-values. Thus, this labour can be neither productive nor unproductive of (surplus-) value. Rather, it is an example of what has been called elsewhere 'value destroying labour'.[18]

The police and more generally the 'services' provided by repressive apparatuses. These are examples on a societal level of what Marx calls 'non-labour' that is, the work of control and surveillance within the production-process. They do not extract (surplus-) value directly but are part of a generalised system whose function is that of preventing the labourers from ridding themselves of the rule of capital. That is one aspect. However, the police are productive of value inasmuch as they help prevent the destruction of use-values (which is similar to the transformation of use-values). The analogy is with Marx's analysis that deals with the work of the maintenance of machines. Sometimes the demarcation-line is blurred.

Tax-collection. This too is an example of non-labour, the extortion of surplus-value from the working class as a whole after surplus-value has been produced, realised and appropriated by the capitalist class. This case should not be confused with the subsequent redistribution of the taxed (surplus-) value, which, being a redistributive activity, is unproductive labour, rather than non-labour.

Finally, *the production of knowledge.* Marx mentions only two possible cases of knowledge-production, the mental activity inherent in the production of books, works of art, and so on, and in teaching (and thus, by extension, modern educational services). Marx refers to the production of knowledge as

---

[18] See Carchedi 1991.

'immaterial' production[19] but this is imprecise and should not be taken literally, given that, for Marx, all labour is expenditure of human energy which is a material activity. As already mentioned, this theme will be developed in the following sections.

To sum up, services comprise a whole range of economic processes: processes of production of (surplus-) value based on the transformation and delivery of objective goods and of knowledge, as well as of the preservation of labour-power and the prevention of the destruction of use-value; processes of redistribution of (surplus-) value, that is, unproductive processes; processes of destruction of (surplus-) value based on the destruction of objective use-values; processes of extraction of surplus-value; processes of production of knowledge which, as it will be argued, can be production, or redistribution, or extraction, or destruction of value. Given this heterogeneity, the category 'services' can only hinder value-analysis.[20] But, even more importantly, by ascribing a productive nature to all these activities, the service-society thesis minimises the production of surplus-value by, and thus the exploitation of, the productive labourers. One important consequence is that, as argued in Chapter 3, by ascribing the role of productive labour to the financial and speculative sectors, which are only an empty simulation of a real process of valorisation, the understanding of the real causes of crises is impaired.

Having cleared the way of the notions of information-society and service-society, we can now start our analysis of a modern theory of knowledge. First of all, the boundaries between individual and social knowledge must be drawn and the differences highlighted.

3. Individual knowledge

The distinction between concrete and abstract individuals introduced in Chapter 1, Section 3, is the basis for a theorisation of individual and social knowledge. *Individual knowledge* is the view of reality from the perspective

---

[19] Marx 1976a, pp. 1047–8.

[20] In the 1960s and 1970s, 'services' were basically provided by public institutions. The question, therefore, was whether state-institutions could produce value and surplus-value. On this point, see Carchedi 1977, Chapter 2. Nowadays, most services are being or have been privatised. The point is then under which conditions they are productive when provided by private capital.

of the concrete individual. It is his or her specific view of reality. This will be the topic of the present section. Social knowledge is the view of reality of social groups. This will be analysed in the next section.

Characterisations such as 'intellectual labour' versus 'manual labour' are inadequate and theoretically unfounded. All labour is intellectual, because it involves the working of the brains and all labour is manual, including the writing down of one's thoughts on a piece of paper. Likewise for the distinction between 'mental' versus 'material' labour. As we shall soon see, all labour is material because the expenditure of human energy is itself a material entity. At the same time, all labour is intellectual, the result of conception, because conception is produced by the whole body (without which the brain could not work) and because humans are not automata who can act without thinking. We must change our perspective. The following paragraph introduces the basic notions and definitions that will guide the analysis in this and the following section.

Let us introduce the notion of transformations. We can distinguish between two types, objective transformations and mental transformations. *Objective transformations* are the transformation of objective reality, of reality existing outside our consciousness, while *mental transformations* are the transformations of knowledge, be it knowledge of objective reality or of previous knowledge.

It could be thought that objective transformations are material and that mental transformations are non-material. However, *both objective and mental transformations require the expenditure of human energy and* (given that human energy is material as shown by human metabolism, see Chapter 2 above), *are thus material processes*. The opposition between material and mental labour is incorrect.[21] It follows that, for the same reason, material labour cannot be contrasted to immaterial labour. The latter does not exist. Marx does refer to 'immaterial labour', to the best of my knowledge, only once,[22] but it is clear from his opus that this should not be taken literally. One could hold that mental transformations are material processes, but that the new knowledge produced is not (see below). This thesis would imply that the first law of thermodynamics, that is, that energy can neither be created nor destroyed but can only change form, can be dispensed with. Since the first law of thermodynamics cannot be

---

[21] I also used this incorrect terminology in my previous writings.
[22] Marx 1976a, pp. 1047–8.

dispensed with, new knowledge too must be material. More specifically, the reason why knowledge is material is that thinking, the learning process, is an expenditure of human energy that causes a change in the nervous system. This is a change in synapses, the functional connections between neurons in the brain, that is, information from one neuron flows to another neuron across a synapse. 'Recent studies have shown that synapse and spine densities are altered following learning....Synaptic change clearly occurs with learning.'[23] This is a material change. New knowledge is the *outcome of a material process, of synaptic changes. It is this synaptic modification that changes our perception of the world*, that is, our knowledge of it. To deny materiality to knowledge production and to knowledge means to ignore the results of neuroscience. But, as we shall see, new knowledge is much more than synaptic changes.

It follows that objective transformations are material transformations of the reality outside us and mental transformations are material transformation as well, synaptic changes, occurring with learning, that is, with changes in human cognition and consciousness both of the reality outside us and of our previous knowledge.

Let us consider these two types of transformations in more detail (see relations (1) and (2) in Appendix 2). Objective transformations, for example the production of a car, are the transformations by labour-power of the *means of objective transformation,* for example machines, and of the *objects of objective transformation,* for example iron and plastic. In this case, labour-power is the capacity to transform objective inputs into objective outputs. Mental transformations, or transformations of knowledge, are the transformations by labour-power of the knowledge contained in the labourers' labour-power, their *subjective knowledge,* and of *objective knowledge,* into the new knowledge. Objective knowledge is both the knowledge contained in the objective means of mental transformations, for example the information stored in computers, books, and so on, and the knowledge contained in other mental producers' labour-power, inasmuch as it has not become (yet) an input of our subjective knowledge, that is, inasmuch as we have not (yet) known it. The knowledge contained in labour-power (subjective knowledge) is both the *means* of mental transformation and one of the two mental *objects* of mental transfor-

[23] Woolf 2006, pp. 66–7.

mation (the other one being objective knowledge).[24] Mental transformations are the self-transformation of knowledge. Here, labour-power is the capacity to transform knowledge. Mental transformations can be either individual or social. *Individual mental transformations* transform the individual knowledge and consciousness (the knowledge of concrete individuals) into a different individual knowledge. They transform individual subjectivities. This is the topic of this section. *Social mental transformations* transform social knowledge, the knowledge shared by the members of a social group, into a different social knowledge. They transform social subjectivities. They will be analysed in the next section.

To sum up, individual knowledge is subjective knowledge. But new individual knowledge is a mental transformation and thus the transformation by labour-power of subjective and (possibly previously incorporated) objective knowledge. Since thinking is a constant process, individual knowledge is a constant process of becoming something different from what it has become. This applies also to social knowledge, knowledge shared by many concrete individuals. Consider now again objective knowledge. From a person's or a group's perspective, the (individual or social) knowledge of other individuals or social groups is objective knowledge, inasmuch as that person or group does not know it. But, from the point of view of other persons or groups, our knowledge, inasmuch as it is unknown to them, is objective knowledge which is transformed by them into their subjective knowledge when they use it as an input in their production of knowledge. The moment we transform objective knowledge by making it our own, we transform it into our individual or social knowledge, into our individual or social subjectivity. But, when we interact with other individuals, our subjective knowledge (which up to this point was for them objective knowledge) becomes part (an input) of their subjective knowledge which then exists outside us and from that moment on, becomes independent of our knowledge and thus becomes objective knowledge for us. Thus, mental transformations are a two-way process: they are transformations of objective knowledge into subjective (individual or social) knowledge and back from (individual or social) subjective knowledge into objective knowledge according to who is the producer of knowledge.

---

[24] We shall see in Section 8 below that, once we introduce the class-content of knowledge, it becomes possible to distinguish between capital's mental means of mental transformation and labour's mental means of mental transformation.

Table 1. Three categories of transformations

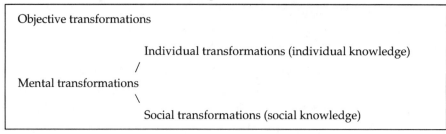

Objective transformations

                   Individual transformations (individual knowledge)

          /

Mental transformations

          \

                   Social transformations (social knowledge)

As mentioned in Chapter 1, Section 7, Marx distinguishes two stages of the production of knowledge, actually two stages of mental transformation (since as we shall see soon, the production of knowledge is always the combination of mental and objective transformations). The first is *observation*, the socially filtered sensory perception of the real concrete. The result is the *imagined concrete*, a 'chaotic conception of reality'. Subsequently, this imagined concrete is transformed through conception into the *concrete-in-thought*, which when compared to the imagined concrete, is a more structured and articulated view of the imagined concrete. This distinction, too, is analytical. In reality, observation requires a previous conceptual framework and conception requires a previous observation. However, at any given moment, we can start our conception on the basis of our previous observation or vice versa. For the present purposes, in what follows, no distinction will be made between observation and conception. Both will be considered to be mental transformations, productions of knowledge.

The distinction between objective and mental transformations is only analytical. In reality, objective transformations require mental transformations and vice versa. However, in dealing with objective transformations, we disregard the mental transformations needed for them, and vice versa in dealing with mental transformations – we disregard the needed objective transformations. The distinction between objective transformations and mental transformations is only the first step in the analysis. *Labour*, and thus a labour-process, is *always* the combination of *both* types of transformation. These two types of transformation cannot exist independently and can realise themselves as a labour-process, only conjointly and contemporaneously. But a labour-process, and thus labour, is *either* an objective labour-process or a mental labour-process *depending upon which type of transformation is determinant* (see relations (3) and (4) in Appendix 2).

Given that it is not possible to observe which of the two types of transformation is determinant during the labour-process, we can trace back the nature of this process by considering the outcome. Usually this nature is empirically given. Thus, in the production of a car, it is the objective aspect of the output that is empirically given (and, on this basis, we know that the production-process has been an objective one, one in which the objective transformation has been determinant) and, in the production of a concert, it is the mental aspect which is empirically apparent (so that we can deduce that it is the mental aspect which has been determinant). However, this rule is not always accurate. What decides the issue is the *social validation of the product*. This social validation occurs at the moment of exchange. Thus, for example, a book is produced and exchanged primarily because of its mental content and its objective features (it must be clearly printed, graphically attractive, with as few printing mistakes as possible, and so on) are necessary, but subordinate to (determined by) the mental content inherent in the book. Both aspects are potentially present in the outcome before exchange, but only one realises itself and becomes then the determinant aspect. As a short-cut, we can say that the outcome of an objective labour-process is an objective product (commodity) and that of a mental labour-process is new knowledge. But we should be aware that these are the determinant, and not the only aspects of that outcome.

We have seen in Chapter 2 that labour is both concrete (the expenditure of human energy in the specific modalities needed to produce the specificity of the products) and abstract (the expenditures of undifferentiated human energy, such as calories, needed to produce value and surplus-value). As a consequence, both concrete and abstract labour can be both mental and objective. For example, the labour of a researcher is mental labour, which is both concrete, according to the object and the outcome of her research, and abstract because it is at the same time the expenditure of undifferentiated human energy. The labour of a shoe-maker is objective labour. It too is both concrete and abstract. The relation between objective and mental, concrete and abstract labour is set out in Table 2 below.

Table 2. Four categories of labour

```
                    Concrete labour (material)
               /
    Objective labour
               \
                    Abstract labour (material)

                    Concrete labour (material)
               /
    Mental labour
               \
                    Abstract labour (material)
```

Two points of clarification are in order. First, with regard to Table 2, it is clear that abstract labour is not equivalent to mental labour: abstract labour is always material (an expenditure of material human energy in the abstract) and is an aspect of both objective and mental labour. The same holds for concrete labour which is also always material and an aspect of both objective and mental labour. This is in conformity with the results obtained in Chapter 2. Second, *within* labour-processes, either objective or mental transformations are determinant. The production of knowledge (mental transformations) is objectively determined (determined by objective transformations) only in the case of objective labour-processes (see relation (3) in Appendix 2) and not in the sense that mental transformations are always determined by objective transformations. At the level of society as a whole, a level of abstraction which comprises all labour-processes, both mental and objective, each labour-process is determined by *the whole* of the rest of society in the sense of what was clarified in Chapter 1 above. Thus, thinking is not determined by being (as if thinking were not being) nor is knowledge determined by material reality (as if knowledge were itself not a material reality). Rather, each labour-process, *including the production of knowledge*, is materially determined because it is determined by all other objective and mental labour-processes and thus by all other objective and mental transformations that are material processes. It is in *this* sense that the production of knowledge, besides being itself material, is materially determined.

Finally, the theory submitted above calls for a definition of material, that is, of what is matter. The concept of matter is a contentious question that goes back to the origin of philosophical thought. In what follows, it will be touched upon only tangentially. It will suffice to mention that matter should not be confused with anything physical, tangible. The identification of matter with physical, tangible reality goes back to Descartes. As McMullin recounts

> The Cartesian usage of the term 'matter' proved so useful in an age when mechanics was revealing its possibilities that soon the older, more technical senses were forgotten, save by philosophers. In this way, ' matter' passed into general use in Western languages, no longer as a clear-cut technical term, but rather as a vague practical label for a varied array of things that the physicist speaks about, one that does not commit the speaker to any particular theory about the nature of these things. This is the sense it retains in ordinary usage today.[25]

This notion is insufficient for the present purposes, not least because it leaves open the question as to whether knowledge and society are material. Consonant with the theory submitted above and from a truly materialist standpoint, *matter* is here defined as anything that can be proven to *exist*, that is, that can be proven to be (the outcome of) a *process*, physical, biological, neurological etc., that is, of *something that comes to be, develops and passes away within a spatio-temporal dimension*. From this perspective, matter is the only form of existence, that is, only matter is real. For example, the notion of God, a specific form of knowledge, is material because the outcome of a specific, material (mental) labour process. However, God is not material and thus does not exist because it cannot be proven that God is the outcome of a process, that is, that it came to be, developed and will eventually die. As for society, it too is material, given that individual and social relations are processes, interactions among individuals. The relation between relations and processes as was noted in Chapter 1 can now be seen to be a relation of determination between a specific type of process, individual and social relations, or human interactions, and the processes determined by those interactions.

This position could be criticised on the following grounds. First, as Lobkowicz submits, 'if *matter* is an all-embracing, absolutely universal concept, then the statement "everything is material" cannot be proven'.[26] The notion of matter submitted here is unscathed by this objection, since it requires an

---

[25] McMullin 1978, pp. 18–19.
[26] Lobkowicz 1978, p. 165.

empirical verification of the existence of a process. Second, 'if whatever exists, is material, what does this tell us of what exists? If nothing but matter exists, what are, then, the properties of whatever exists?'[27] This question is easily answered. Each form of existence of matter has its own specific features. Moreover, all forms of existence of matter share four specific features. Matter, being a process, is movement. Since movement implies space and time, these latter dimensions are also an essential feature of matter. But movement implies also change and change, in social reality, implies the contradiction of what has become realised and what exists potentially. Reality and thus matter implies both the realm of the realised and that of the potential. The four essential, general features of matter are thus space, time, the existent and the potential.

In this connection, it is intriguing that, for Lenin as well as for the Marxism-Leninism of the Stalin-era, consciousness was not thought to be material. Thus, in Lenin's famous definition

> the *sole* 'property' of matter with whose recognition philosophical materialism is bound up is the property of *being an objective reality*, of existing outside our mind.[28]

In this view

> Matter is a philosophical category denoting the objective reality which is given to man by his sensations, and which is copied, photographed and reflected by our sensations, while existing independently of them.[29]

Here, the status of material reality is ascribed only to objective reality, only to what exists outside us and independently of our perception and knowledge of it. In other words, for Lenin and Marxism-Leninism, knowledge and consciousness are not material. The problem with this approach is, if that is the case, what is the ontological status of knowledge and consciousness? If they are not material, what are they? This all-important question remains unanswered. It does not help to distinguish between the material *base* of consciousness and the *essence* of consciousness. This is the distinction made by Kol'banovsky

---

[27] Lobkowicz 1978, p. 160.
[28] Lenin 1972b, p. 311.
[29] Lenin 1972b, p. 145.

The material base of thinking and consciousness are the nervous processes that happen in man's brain; but the very essence of understanding and awareness that gives to man the possibility of abstracting from concrete objects and phenomena, the possibility to universalise them, to analyse and synthesise, to discover complex connections of the multiform phenomena of reality…this essence of thinking and consciousness consists of an ideal reflection of the objective world.[30]

This distinction cannot escape the question raised above: what is this 'very essence of understanding and awareness', if it is not material? Neither does it help to hold that, if material reality exists only outside us, psychic events, being subjective, cannot be material.[31] Here, too, the same question arises as to their ontological status.

The question is why Lenin and Marxism-Leninism denied materiality to consciousness, thus sliding into a theoretical cul-de-sac. Kol'banovsky uses a somewhat curious argument: given that 'the conflict of materialism and idealism' is the fundamental struggle in the history of philosophy, if consciousness were to be material this struggle would become meaningless and all philosophy would be pointless.[32] However, it is clear that it is just the recognition that knowledge and consciousness are material that delivers the decisive blow to idealism.

The reason for denying the ontological status of materiality to knowledge resides in the acceptance of reflection-theory. The reasoning seems to be that, if matter is only objective reality, a reflection of matter in our thoughts cannot be material. However, if one deems knowledge not to be material, one lapses into an idealist position. For Marxism-Leninism, idealism is a philosophical position in which matter, by being the objective material reflected in our knowledge of it, exists before ideas and thus somehow determines them. However, the denial of the primacy of ideas in relation to material reality is not sufficient to eradicate idealism. By denying materiality to ideas, Marxism-Leninism creates a much more idealistic position, the admission of something non-material. It is not sufficient to assert the primacy of matter in relation to

---

[30] Kol'banovsky, quoted in Lobkowicz 1978, p. 183.
[31] Lobkowicz 1978, p. 180.
[32] Lobkowicz 1978, p. 182.

ideas as if ideas were not matter; it is necessary to assert the materiality of ideas.

As seen above, modern developments in neuroscience show that knowledge is material. Knowledge is matter knowing itself. This is the only true materialist standpoint. There is no 'vulgar' materialism here, if by 'vulgar' materialism it is meant the *full* identification of consciousness with matter. It is one thing to argue that consciousness is material but it is another to reduce it only to its materiality. Consciousness and knowledge are indeed material but their materiality, that is, synaptic changes, is only what makes the emergence of new knowledge possible. Synaptic changes do not explain the specificity of the new knowledge emerging through these changes. What explains the specificity of the new knowledge emerging from these material processes is its dialectical, and thus class-determination, as expounded in Chapter 1 above. Stated differently, synaptic changes cause only an undifferentiated change in our knowledge, they can cause a change in our knowledge in many different directions. The knowledge actually emerging from this material process is the result of its social, and ultimately class-determination. This theoretical position hinges upon the theorisation of social knowledge and of its dialectical interaction with individual knowledge. This is the task of the next section. To anticipate, different concrete individuals have different views of reality, by definition. However, different concrete individuals have also common interests, something that aggregates them (as abstract individuals) into social groups. Thus, each concrete individual belonging to a social group shares potentially a common view of reality which becomes realised as and through the knowledge of its intellectual representative. These realised social knowledges are internalised and given a specific form by each concrete individual and emerge again concretely as individual knowledges. At this point, the process starts again when these individual knowledges aggregate again into social knowledges. Synaptic changes are the material processes that lend materiality to the social process through which the different (individual and social) views of reality constantly emerge, change and disappear. Like value, knowledge is both material and social.

A concise rendition of the process of production of individual knowledge can be found in Appendix 2.

4. Social knowledge

The key to conceptualise social knowledge is provided by the distinction between concrete and abstract individuals as was explained in Chapter 1, Section 3. This is concerned with neither the concrete individuals' different subjective views, nor with their simple summation. As a first approximation, we can say that social knowledge is a *commonly shared subjectivity that can reproduce itself irrespective of which concrete individuals share it*. This is a first definition. This commonly shared subjectivity defines a *knowledge-group*, a specific group of abstract individuals. The individuals sharing that knowledge are abstract individuals because abstraction is made of their specific way of internalising and reproducing that knowledge. Thus, social knowledge can also be understood as the view of reality from the perspective of knowledge-groups.

The question now is: how can concrete individuals, who produce an individual knowledge which is by definition different from any other individual knowledge, produce social knowledge? This is possible because concrete individuals undergo from the first moment of, and throughout, their life a process of internalisation of social phenomena. Through the concrete individuals' internalisation, a process that is different for each individual because it is a part of her personality, social phenomena are transformed from actually existing social phenomena into potential social phenomena existing in the concrete individuals' consciousness and individuality. If a certain social phenomenon is internalised by different individuals, inasmuch as different individuals internalise the same class-content, its class-content becomes the *common element* unifying the different consciousnesses. Subsequently, when concrete individuals engage in individual phenomena, they transfer to those individual phenomena the potentiality to actualise again social phenomena and thus the class-content inherent in those phenomena. It is this potentiality that becomes realised if individual relations become social relations, in other words, if concrete individuals become abstract individuals (replaceable) on the basis of some socially relevant common features. It is for this reason that, as elements of a concrete individuals' knowledge, social phenomena are amenable to being actualised again, possibly *in a different form, in a different realm of reality, and with a different class-content* due to the process of determination, as already discussed in Chapter 1 of this work. Knowledge is thus social (and this is a second and more precise definition) when it can reproduce itself irrespective of which concrete individuals share it, in the specific sense that different individuals share the class-content of that knowledge.

If all concrete individuals develop different forms of social knowledge, only some expand their individual knowledge into forms of knowledge that represent the interests of social groups. They transform those interests into their own view of reality. They become a social group's *intellectual representatives*. Their individual knowledge becomes then their specific, personal rendition of a social knowledge, it becomes the specific form of a manifestation of a generality. The importance of those concrete individuals' uniqueness is that it is suited to interpret collective interests and transform them into specific forms of knowledge. There may be many concrete individuals with those capacities. Which one of them becomes an actual representative is a matter of the conjunctural situation. In class-divided societies, only some concrete individuals have the possibility to become intellectual representatives, so that a group emerges whose specific (and often paid) function is that of being an intellectual representative. This function often requires a special system of rewards and status so that they develop vested interests in this specific function.

But the intellectual representatives do not think in isolation. On the basis of their social practice and their class-collocation, they interiorise the knowledge produced by the other members of that group and rework it to produce their own knowledge. This process is common to everybody. But, in the case of the intellectual representatives, the knowledge produced is, as it were, the *representative knowledge*, the knowledge accepted by other members of that knowledge-group even if each individual has his or her own interpretation of that knowledge. The emergence of the representative knowledge is the result of the interaction among all members of knowledge-groups, including the intellectual representative. There might be more than one intellectual representative for each objectively defined social group. It is a matter of chance, who among the many are potentially capable of becoming intellectual representatives of that group, and who actually do so.

Thus, social knowledge has a realised social content, namely, the representation of the interests of a specific knowledge-group. There is no ideologically neutral knowledge. The production (and reproduction) of social knowledge is at the same time the transformation of social interests into a commonly shared view of reality. The formation of social knowledge is also simultaneously an ongoing attempt by each group to impose its own view upon that of other groups through the knowledge developed by the intellectual representatives. This means that the knowledge produced by the intellectual representatives of a group can incorporate elements of different social knowledges (representing the interests of other groups), up to the point where possibly the social content of that social knowledge undergoes a radical change. At this point, that social knowledge has become the theoretical expression of a different group's or class's interests, so that those intellectuals become representatives of other groups. There is thus no automatic guarantee that a group develops a knowledge (through its intellectual representatives) which represents that group's interests and needs, in other words that a class becomes conscious of its real interests.

It follows that acceptance by the members of a knowledge-group of a representative knowledge is at the same time their *acceptance of the social, and thus class-content* of that knowledge, irrespective of differences between the individual representations and manifestations of that representative knowledge and irrespective of whether the members of a knowledge-group become conscious of the economic, political, and ideological interests represented by that knowledge. These individual knowledges are different in their personal forms, but are similar from the point of view of their social content. As a first approximation, social knowledge has been defined as a commonly shared subjectivity, or as knowledge whose reproduction is ensured by the principle of substitutability. As a second approximation, social knowledge has been defined as knowledge that can reproduce itself through the principle of substitutability, that is, irrespective of which concrete individuals share it, in the specific sense that different individuals share the class-content of that knowledge. The third and final definition is that *knowledge is social when it can reproduce itself irrespective of which concrete individuals share it, in the specific sense that different individuals share its contradictory class-content, as represented by the class-content of the representative knowledge, irrespective of the specific way each concrete individual internalises and reproduces that class-content.* Capitalist mass-media and the new methods of communication, like information-technology, are extremely influential in shaping collective consciousness by capital under contemporary capitalism. This is an area of research whose importance is vital and which has been the object of extensive research by other authors. However, the capitalist media are not all powerful in shaping individual consciousness and in aggregating them into forms of social consciousness. Rather, the power of the media is inversely proportional to labour's ability to produce an alternative conception of reality, both social and natural. And the latter is premised also upon labour's ability to develop a dialectical, class-theory of knowledge-production. And this, in its turn, is a necessary precondition for the development of a theory of crises and thus for a successful fight against capitalism.

It follows that the process of formation of social knowledge is a specific instance of a wider process, of the struggle between the two fundamental classes. This takes the form of the struggle amongst a myriad of phenomena, both individual and social, for the radical transformation in each of those phenomena of one type of rationality (class-content) functional for the reproduction of capitalism into the other, functional for its supersession, and vice versa; for the reduction of social phenomena to individual ones; and for the emergence of individual phenomena into social ones (for example, political parties). The two fundamental classes can be theorised at the highest level of abstraction in terms of the capitalist ownership-relation, so that labour is composed of all those who do not own the means of production. However, due to the two opposite rationalities inherent in the ownership-relation, these two classes' *form of manifestation* is highly fluid and dynamic; it is given by all the potential and realised social phenomena (individual beliefs, social consciousnesses, traditions, crystallisations of previous struggles, and so on) whose contradictory social content is functional for the reproduction of capitalism (in the case of the capitalist class) or for its supersession (in the case of the labouring class). Radically antagonistic movements (for example, women, racial, student, ecological) are indeed elements of labour as a class, just as much as radically antagonistic elements of blue-collar, industrial workers or highly skilled labourers or even isolated objective or mental producers are, inasmuch as they express an anticapitalist social content, one based on equality, co-operation and self-management. Classes are born at the level of production (of value and surplus-value), but their terrain of empirical manifestation is the result of their attempt to predominate over each other; it is nothing less than a struggle for the change in the class-content of each realised and potential individual and social phenomena. All these struggles are just as important for the development of class-consciousness and for the supersession of capitalism. Only the specific conjuncture will tell which one of them is, under those specific historical and social circumstances, the most decisive.

But the final supersession of capitalism requires the supersession of the ownership-relation.

Thus, other classes besides capital and labour, groups within classes (like women, foreign workers), or groups cutting across classes (homosexuals, ethnic and racial minorities, regional, religious, nationalist, ecological and other groups) are not just epiphenomena of little significance for the reproduction of society or for its supersession. Their specific type of oppression, their resistance against it, and the consciousness which emerges from these processes are ultimately determined by the capitalist ownership-relation because they have ultimately received their contradictory social content from it in a mediated way and in a transmuted form. Feminist literature, for example, has rightly stressed that women have specific interests because they are subjected by male workers to a specific form of oppression both within and outside the household. Their fight for the abolition of this form of oppression here and now is not only sacrosanct. It is also one of the conditions for the abolition of capitalism, because women's oppression by males is a specific manifestation of the struggle between capital and labour, even though it is not reducible to that struggle because of its own specific form of oppression and resistance. Women's oppression is the outcome of the successful attempt by capital to change the social content of the social relation between male and female workers. Labour is thus internally fragmented by capital and made internally contradictory. The productive worker is only a part of it and is itself internally fragmented and contradictory. However, capitalism can exist without racism or sexism, but not without the extraction and appropriation of surplus-value. Capital and *productive* labour are an indissoluble, dialectical, unity. To assert that capital cannot exist without labour but that labour can exist without capital is confusing because the supersession of capital implies also the supersession of labour *as shaped by* capital.

Similar considerations hold also for those social relations which have pre-existed the capitalist system, like racism. Having been immersed in a different (that is, capitalist) social context, they acquire a social content functional for the reproduction of ownership and thus production-relations (for example, lower wages and worse working and living conditions for minority and ethnic groups) or for its supersession: they become determined in their specific form by that relation. As such, they react upon and modify that relation and become historically specific forms of capitalism's reproduction or of radical change.

5. Labour's knowledge

Theories of the class-determination of knowledge are usually rejected with empirical arguments. This holds both for social consciousness and for the natural sciences. This chapter deals with the former, the next chapter will deal with the latter.

It is often pointed out that some labourers behave always according to their class-collocation, some others do so only at particular historical conjunctures, and others never do so. This could be taken to show that there is no class-determination of consciousness, that the choice by labourers of labour's rationality is a matter of chance or of non-structural factors. This is the age-old question of whether there is a necessary relation between class-location or position and class-consciousness.

The first consideration is that this necessary relation exists indeed in the case of capital and pro-capitalist consciousness. The capitalists cannot continue to be capitalists if they cease to conform to capital's rationality, that is, the exploitation of labour. For them, and for all those who perform the function of capital, their consciousness must conform to their class-collocation.[33] Some individual capitalists might hold at times a pro-labour rationality. However, this could never become one of capital's forms of *social* subjectivity. The capitalist class expresses different social subjectivities representing the interests of the different fractions within it. But it cannot express social subjectivities with pro-labour class-content, in other words, commonly accepted and self-reproducing forms of knowledge representing interests antithetical to those of capital.

The case is different for the labourers. They are exploited whether their individual subjectivities, and at times their social subjectivities, conform to the rationality inherent in their class-collocation or not. The defining element of the working class' subjectivity is neither a one-sided emphasis on class-struggle nor a one-sided emphasis on the production- (ownership-) relation nor a mechanical subjectivism (class-consciousness as a reflection, even if distorted, of the objective existence of class). Labourers are far from being, by definition, passive victims of capitalism or the passive bearers of social relations. Nor do

---

[33] As pointed out above, some agents of production might hold spurious positions so that they perform both the function of capital and the function of labour. This has consequences for their class-consciousness. See Carchedi, 1977 and 1987.

they develop automatically an anti capitalist class-consciousness. As concrete individuals, having internalised the contradictions inherent in the capitalist system, they are potentially able to resist and change it. Since individual and social subjectivities are determined by all other social phenomena and, in the last instance, by the ownership-relation, classes, other social groups and individuals attempt constantly to change the social content of the various social and individual phenomena, including forms of individual and social knowledge, to their own advantage. The outcome of the struggle is undetermined. However, the fact that labour can express anti-labour subjectivities is no argument against the determination of subjectivity by the ownership-relation.

These views can be set against Italian workerism [*operaismo*]. Even though this approach will be discussed at some length in Section 7 below, a brief comment can be made by way of comparison. In its first phase, workerism theorised that the factory, or the capitalist production-process, is either the exclusive or the privileged source of a radically antagonistic consciousness. However, in the 1980s, some workerist authors were forced to concede that this was too narrow a focus and that obviously other factors do play a role as determinants of class-consciousness. However, the relation between the key determinant (in the workerist perspective, the technical composition of capital or the organisation of the production-process) and these other determinants has remained an unsolved problem.

Just as for capital, labour's class-collocation makes itself known at the level of social consciousness. But it does that in a specific way. The capitalist system exhibits a tendency towards its reproduction or towards its own supersession (including a movement in the direction of self-destruction, of which the threat of nuclear wars or the impact of our ecological system are possible examples). If an objective movement must be represented at the level of consciousness, the movement towards self-supersession produces at the level of social consciousness the daily (re)production of ideas, theories, political and other practices, along with a plethora of social and individual phenomena, consciously as well as unconsciously aiming at this supersession, as well as by eruptions at critical historical junctures of conscious collective attempts to supersede the system. Just as the system oscillates between the movement towards reproduction and supersession, so does society's consciousness oscillate between the dominance of capital's rationality (expressing the reproducing counter-tendency which could possibly end in the system's self-destruction) and that of labour's rationality (expressing the superseding tendency).[34] While capital expresses consistently capital's rationality, labour expresses now labour's rationality and then capital's rationality, in one sector and then in another sector, in one place and then in another place. *There is always a correspondence between labour's class-collocation and labour's class-consciousness but in a contradictory way* (even in revolutionary moments labour's class-consciousness contains elements of inimical ideologies) *and only cyclically, at different times and in different places and not always for the working class as a whole.* Within capitalism, when capital's rationality prevails within labour, there are always knowledge-groups within labour representing labour's rationality (in their many manifestations). Vice-versa, when labour's rationality prevails within labour, there are always knowledge-groups holding procapitalist forms of social subjectivity. In short, *labour's pro-labour subjectivities are internally contradictory, sectoral, cyclical and tendential.* When they disappear as realised social phenomena, they are reduced to potential social phenomena, only to reappear again as realised social phenomena in a different form, in different sectors of labour, in different places and at a different time. The outcome is not only a struggle between capital and labour but also among different sectors of labour expressing different interpretations and different degrees of the two rationalities. The struggle between capital and labour manifests itself also within labour so that labour can produce different and contradictory types of class-consciousness. This is what the history of capitalism teaches us.

It is thus not true that there is no correspondence between labour's objective class-collocation (in terms of the ownership-relation) and its anti capitalist consciousness. This correspondence exists but, rather then being a general and constant phenomenon, it is sectoral, cyclical, and tendential. Social consciousness arises in the process of the dialectical determination of all social phenomena including the ownership-relation (which is ultimately determinant) as set forth in Chapter 1. Social consciousness is not determined by class-collocation *in spite of* all other social phenomena but *because* of all phenomena, including class-collocation, in their mutual determination. It is in this sense that the

---

[34] The argument for supersession as the tendency has been submitted in Chapters 2 and 3.

following should be understood: 'It is not consciousness that determines life, but life that determines consciousness'.[35]

The question then concerns the relation between changes in *social* 'life', where social life stands for *the whole of individual and social phenomena in their dialectical interrelation* as set forth in Chapter 1 of this work, and changes in labour's consciousness. *Changes in the 'social life' change the potential, contradictory, sectoral, tendential and cyclical manifestation of labour's contradictory forms of consciousnesses, but cannot prefigure their specific form, time of occurrence, and class-content.*

It is thus mistaken to conclude from the determination of the superstructure by the economic structure (and primarily by the ownership-relation) that knowledge (one element of the superstructure) is determined only by the economic structure. As stressed in Chapter 1, knowledge in all its manifestations is ultimately determined by the ownership-relation and thus by the economic structure, but the specific features of each form of knowledge are determined by the whole of society (social life) through the process of dialectical determination. In sum, the age-old antinomy – between economic determinism (the superstructure being just a reflection of the base) and mutual interrelation in which the economic base has no preferred role – fades away.[36]

A certain 'radical' sociology usually associated with analytical Marxism searches for the maximum degree of correspondence between objective factors (for example, class-collocation, status, education, income) and class-consciousness (for example, ideology and voting behaviour). This type of class-analysis defines classes variously, for example as occupational categories or in terms of levels of skills. It then chooses an indicator of class-consciousness, for example, voting behaviour. Subsequently, it uses statistical procedures to relate class-consciousness to objective factors. Finally, it concludes that that objective factor accounts for a certain proportion of those individuals sharing a certain class-consciousness. Often, an approach is judged to be better than another one if an objective factor accounts for a greater number of people sharing a certain class-consciousness. Erik Olin Wright is the prominent sociologist who has worked with this methodology within a Marxist perspective.[37]

---

[35] Marx and Engels 1970a, pp. 36–7.
[36] For a discussion of the theoretical quicksand in which the base and superstructure debate sank in the US Communist Party in Hollywood, see Ceplair 2008.
[37] Wright 1989; for a detailed critique, see Carchedi 1989.

There are many reasons why this is unsatisfactory. The first one is that this is a Weberian approach rather than a Marxist one.[38] Within the Weberian conception, there is a simple interrelationship between all variables without an ultimately determining factor (ownership-relation). Lacking this factor, the necessarily contradictory nature of the phenomena studied (and of capitalism, in the last analysis) remains unexplained. It can be observed, and even measured, but there is no reason to assume that this contradictoriness is the essence of this society. That is the class-content of this approach.

Second, there is also another reason why the content of this approach is pro-capital: it is a static approach. Statistical correlations do not explain why the same objective factors determine different forms of class-consciousness at different times. It relates statistically two or more sets of data at any given moment (a static relation). Empirical studies of the correlation between the same phenomena can be accomplished at different points in time. But consideration of successive static moments does not make this method a dynamic one. The reason is that it considers only realised (objective and subjective) factors, thus ignoring the potential aspects of reality. But it is just that potential that accounts for change. As stressed in the previous chapters, a theory that cannot explain movement and change has an inherently pro-capital class-content.

Third, this is an individualistic approach. Class (variously defined) is seen here as an *element affecting individual behaviour*. The ability to explain individual phenomena in terms of social ones is not a proof of the ability to explain social phenomena in their contradictory movement and thus capable of explaining society's laws of movement and change. While there are always very personal and unique causes accounting for each concrete individual's concrete manifestation of (a mix) of one of the two rationalities, at the level of society, there are always carriers of the two opposite types of rationality because of the opposite tendencies inherent in the capitalist system. What methodological individualism cannot account for is how and why *social determination in one realm of reality* (the necessary and constant aggregation of concrete individuals in two fundamental classes which *necessarily* express opposite types of rationality) *manifests itself as a number of chance-events in another realm of reality*, that of concrete individuals and, vice versa, why chance-events in one realm of reality (that of the

---

[38] Weber 1949.

individuals) manifest themselves as social regularities in another realm (that of social classes). *As far as the class-determination of knowledge is concerned, there is no irreconcilability of social determination and free-will.*

That is not to say that statistical correlations between realised objective determinants and realised determined social subjectivities are useless. On the contrary, they can be helpful and provide useful information, but only if they are part of a dynamic, dialectical approach which alone can explain determination and thus movement, change and ultimately the class-nature of capitalism. Outside this approach, they become tools of a conservative social science. This is in line with the relation between formal and dialectical logic highlighted in Chapter 1.

As an example of a Marxist analysis of the dialectical determination of social consciousness, let us consider the labour-aristocracy. The notion of a labour-aristocracy was born in England in the nineteenth century to designate a section of the working class enjoying higher wages, more stable work, better living conditions and a greater control of the labour-process due to these labourers' greater skills. These limited economic advantages had been made possible by England's role in international commerce and accounted not only for the internal segmentation of the English working class, but also for the social peace of the 1850s and 1860s after the class-struggles of the preceding decennia. Both the trade-unions and the capitalists tried to replace the social conflict with negotiations and conciliation within the legal framework. Marx analysed lucidly the labour-aristocracy in connection with the Irish question. In a letter he wrote to Sigfrid Mayer and August Vogt in 1870, he wrote

> Owing to the constantly increasing concentration of leaseholds, Ireland constantly sends her own surplus to the English labour market, and thus forces down wages and lowers the material and moral position of the English working class.[39]

As a consequence, he added:

> Every industrial and commercial centre in England now possesses a working class divided into two *hostile* camps, English proletarians and Irish proletarians. The ordinary English worker hates the Irish worker as a

---

[39] Marx 1973b, p. 668.

competitor who lowers his standard of life.... The Irishman pays him back with interest in his own money. He sees in the English worker both the accomplice and the stupid tool of the *English rulers in Ireland.*[40]

This was 'the secret of the *impotence of the English working class,* despite its organisation'.[41] These remarks are especially important because, besides their theoretical interest, they contain all the themes that were later developed by Engels and Lenin.

In 1883, in a letter to Bebel, Engels reaches basically the same conclusions: 'Participation in the domination of the world market was and is the basis of the political nullity of the English workers'.[42] Two years later, in 1885, in commenting on the economic crisis that hit England, America and France, Engels expresses his hope that 'it will make an end of the old trade unions here' and adds:

> These unions have peacefully retained the craft character which clung to them from the first and which is becoming more unbearable every day.... Whoever wants admission must be attached as an apprentice for a period of years (usually seven) to some worker belonging to the union. This was intended to keep the number of workers limited.[43]

In 1889, Engels remarks that the new trade-union movement is

> utterly different from that of the *old* trade unions, the skilled labourers, the aristocracy of labour. The people are throwing themselves into the job in quite a different way, are leading far more colossal masses into the fight, are shaking society much more deeply, are putting forward much more far-reaching demands: eight-hour day, general federation of all organisations, complete solidarity.[44]

And in 1890 he notes that

> these unskilled are very different chaps from the fossilised brothers of the old trade unions; not a trace of the old formalist spirit, of the craft exclusiveness of the engineers, for instance; on the contrary, a general cry

---

[40] Ibid.
[41] Marx 1973b, p. 669.
[42] Engels 1995, p. 55.
[43] Engels 1979, p. 377.
[44] Engels 1987b, p. 320.

for the organisation of all trade unions in one fraternity and for a direct struggle against capital.[45]

Lenin developed the international dimension of the labour-aristocracy already stressed by Marx and Engels and applied it to imperialism in the early 1900s. He stressed that the appropriation of international surplus-value is used by capital in the imperialist countries as the material basis for the formation of the labour-aristocracy with the aim of weakening the militancy and the solidarity of the working class as a whole:

> as a result of the extensive colonial policy, the European proletarian *partly* finds himself in a position when it is *not* his labour, but the labour of the practically enslaved natives in the colonies, that maintains the whole of society. The British bourgeoisie, for example, derives more profit from the many millions of the population of India and other colonies than from the British workers. In certain countries this provides the material and economic basis for infecting the proletariat with colonial chauvinism. Of course, this may be only a temporary phenomenon.[46]

Some authors see a contraposition between the notion of labour-aristocracy as an internal segmentation within the imperialist countries (for example, unionised versus non-unionised workers, as stressed by Engels) and a different notion stressing, as in Lenin, that in a way all workers in the imperialist countries benefit from the appropriation of international value. But there is no contraposition between the two theses, once it is realised that it is not those firms that appropriate international surplus-value that pay higher wages than other firms. They simply realise higher profits. Rather, the policy of higher wages is pursued by the states in the imperialist countries which appropriate (part of) that international surplus-value from those firms (for example, through taxation) and pursue pro-labour economic polices, as for example more favourable labour- (and wage-) legislation or infrastructures. Thus, it is the whole of the working class in the imperialist countries that profits from the appropriation of international surplus-value and not only privileged and relatively small sections of it. At the same time, it is also true that labour in the imperialist countries profits in various degrees from the appropriation

---

[45] Engels 1978a, pp. 340–41.
[46] Lenin 1972a, p. 77.

of international surplus-value according to each imperialist country's class-segmentation and differently in various phases of the cycle.[47] For example, with reference to the US-economy,

> the 'benefits' of increased profitability and growth due to imperialist investment [are not – G.C.] distributed equally to all portions of the working class...the racial-national and gender structuring of the labor market result in women and workers of color being concentrated in the labor-intensive and low-wage sectors of the economy.[48]

These notions are important for the theorisation of the relation between objectivity and labour's subjectivity. Nevertheless, they are insufficient. Three point points require further elaboration.

First, all the works on the labour-aristocracy ignore Marx's distinction in *Capital*, Volume III, between the function of labour and the function of capital (see Chapter 2). Synthetically, the former consists in the transformation of use-values (both objective and mental) into new use-values and thus in the creation of value and surplus-value, the latter in the extraction and appropriation of surplus-value. Originally, it was the owners of the means of production who performed the function of capital. However, as the complexity and the size of the labour-process has increased, the function of capital has been delegated to a bureaucratic and hierarchical structure spanning the gamut from Chief Executive Officers to the first line-supervisors. Those who are part of this structure are neither capitalists nor labourers. They are an extension of capital without being capitalists. This requires material privileges (whose size increases as one climbs the hierarchical structure) vis-à-vis those who are supervised.[49] This feature makes it impossible for these agents as a whole (that is, irrespective of changes in the consciousness of individual agents) to develop a radically alternative class-consciousness. Moreover, many positions comprise both functions[50] and with the introduction of new

---

[47] Thus Mandel's claim that 'the real "labor aristocracy" is no longer constituted inside the proletariat of an imperialist country but rather by the proletariat of the imperialist countries as a whole' (quoted in Post 2006) is unnecessarily one-sided.

[48] Post 2006.

[49] Within this structure, usually the same agent is both a supervisor at a certain level and supervised at a higher level. See Carchedi 1977.

[50] This is the objective basis of what I have called the new middle class. See Carchedi 1977.

technologies, the function of capital disappears in some positions (this is their proletarianisation, that is, the devaluation of their labour-power due to functional dequalification) while new positions arise comprising both or only one of these functions. This element of fluidity in the objective class-composition is fundamental because it establishes a changing relation between objectivity and subjectivity at the level of production. Those who perform the function of capital without being capitalists are a new way in which the proletariat is 'infected', to use Lenin's expression.

Second, it is usually held that it is the large firms in the imperialist countries that through barriers to entry reap higher profits and thus can pay higher wages than the smaller-size competitors. However, as Chapters 2 and 3 have argued, it is the technological innovators that reap higher profits through their higher productivity: 'More recent studies have confirmed the absence of a strong correlation between industrial concentration and higher-than-average profits and wages. Instead, profit- and wage-differentials were rooted in differences in labour-productivity and capital-intensity of production'.[51] In principle, these firms must give up a part of this international surplus-value to the state. The extra surplus-value that accrues to the imperialist countries derives not so much from the repatriation of profits made in the dependent countries as from the appropriation of international value through the innovators' higher productivity. The debate as to whether there is a real tendency towards the equalisation of the rates of profit or not is misplaced. Some argue that the monopoly- (or oligopoly-) stage of imperialism and the barriers to entry posed by large firms are an obstacle to the equalisation of the profit-rates. The oligopolistic sector presumably reaps higher profits which are then the source of labour-aristocracy's economic privileges. Whether the economy is segmented into an oligopolistic and a free-competition sector or not is immaterial for an analysis of the labour-aristocracy, given that (a) it is the state that collects and redistributes the international surplus-value to the labourers and (b) if there are wage-differentiations between, say, white and non-white workers, these differentiations are applied basically by all capitalists and not only by those who appropriate international surplus-value (supposedly, the oligopolistic sector).

---

[51] Post 2006.

Third, it follows from the above that national states retain an essential economic, political, ideological and military role for the appropriation of surplus-value. These are the conditions for the imperialist relations among states. Without them, there could be no appropriation of surplus-value by individual firms. But, in the present phase, the relations among states are shaped by their membership to antagonistic economic blocs, some of which have already emerged while others are at different stages of their constitution. In each bloc there are imperialist, or dominating, countries and dominated countries. Thus, the material base of the labour-aristocracy in the imperialist countries has a three-fold origin.

To begin with, within each bloc, the imperialist countries systematically expropriate surplus-value from the dominated countries within that bloc through instruments of economic policy common to it, including possibly a common currency which is that of the hegemonic country within that bloc.[52] A part of this surplus-value can then be used to finance the labour-aristocracy. Further, given the different levels of economic and financial development of the different blocs, there is also expropriation of the surplus-value produced by one bloc which is appropriated by the other.[53] This is a second source of financing of the labour-aristocracy. Finally, inasmuch as the imperialist countries as a whole have common interests antagonistic to those of the dominated countries, there is appropriation of surplus-value by the former from the latter. And this is a third source of financing the labour-aristocracy.

Along with these changes in the sources of financing the labour-aristocracy, there correspond changes in the way in which this appropriated international surplus-value is used to constitute the economic base of the labour-aristocracy. Higher wages and better living conditions are currently certainly still highly relevant. But perhaps even more important are other relatively more recent methods, such as the financing in the imperialist countries of Keynesian policies, both civilian and military, or of the welfare-state. Such policies would be impossible, or in any case much more difficult to finance, without the appropriation of international surplus-value. But this requires the active participation not so much of the workers themselves as of their unions and

---

[52] For the mechanism of seignorage associated with the emergence of the euro, see Carchedi 2001.

[53] See the example of the rivalry between the dollar and the euro in Carchedi 2001.

political representatives whose purpose is that of controlling the working class as a whole. They are indispensable for the corruption of the working class. Of course, this all is strongly dependent upon the phase of the economic cycle.

Thus, the position of privilege of the labour-aristocracy can be derived from (1) the negotiating power of the skilled labourers (both in the imperialist and in the dominated countries), (2) the function of capital, performed either exclusively or together with the function of labour, and (3) the above-mentioned three-dimensional redistribution of international surplus-value due to the modern features of present-day imperialism. The objective basis of the labour-aristocracy is thus quite diversified. The economic base of the labour-aristocracy, besides being so varied, is also subject to change. First, as mentioned above, new technologies erode the function of capital but can also have the opposite effect by creating new positions requiring just that function. Second, during depressions and crises, capital not only cuts Keynesian policies but also increases casual and temporary work, unemployment, exploitation, delocalisation, and so on. These developments cannot but erode the labour-aristocracy's material base and create one of the conditions for the emergence of new and antagonistic institutions and movements. While the labour-aristocracy analysed by Marx, Engels, and Lenin has been the object of exhaustive analyses, a new field of inquiry, which is just as important, concerns the effects on the working class' subjectivity, due to changes in the processes of the appropriation and distribution of the international surplus-value in a situation characterised by the clash among imperialist blocs.

It follows that the economic base of the labour-aristocracy does not result necessarily in practices functional for the reproduction of capitalism. There is no automatic relation between higher wages and reformism or outright right-wing ideology. In the twentieth century, anticapitalist or even revolutionary movements have emerged both in the imperialist and in the dominated countries. Procapitalist ideologies within the labouring class are determined by a range of factors that go well beyond material incentives. Nor is there an automatic relation between the appropriation of international surplus-value and higher wages. 'Rising profits and increased investment do not necessarily lead to higher wages for workers in the absence of effective working-class organisation and struggle.'[54] The notion of the labour-aristocracy can now be

---

[54] Post 2006.

extracted from the above analysis. It is that sector of the working class, both within the imperialist and within the dominated countries, whose political and ideological practices are functional for the reproduction of capitalism and are facilitated by the relatively stable but changing material privileges it enjoys vis-à-vis the rest of the working class. These material interests and privileges facilitate but do not determine the emergence of procapitalist ideologies. If the power-relations are favourable to the proletariat, even its economically privileged sectors can develop a class-consciousness antagonistic to capital. And, in the opposite case, a class-consciousness contrary to the interest of the proletariat can develop also in broad areas of the working class that not only have no economic privileges but have even sunk into poverty. If the differences between the labour-aristocracy and the rest of the working class shrink, the outcome can be a conservative, pro-capital, attachment to privileges, even if minimal, rather than an anticapitalist consciousness.[55]

6. Knowledge and value

We have now all the tools to tackle the question left unanswered in Chapter 2, namely, whether and under which conditions the production of knowledge is production of value and surplus-value. Two points should be mentioned. First, what follows applies to mental producers employed by capital, irrespective of whether their knowledge becomes a social phenomenon or not. Second, the object of analysis here is knowledge under capitalist production-relations. Topics such as 'tacit knowledge', knowledge that cannot be formalised, are not dealt with because the knowledge produced for capitalists must be saleable and thus cannot be tacit.

---

[55] Post questions the thesis of the labour-aristocracy by challenging the 'claim that super profits pumped out of workers in the global South underwrite a "bribe" in the form of higher wages for a minority of the working class in the global North' (Post 2006). The argument is that 'imperialist investment, particularly in the global South, represents a tiny portion of global capitalist investment', that only a tiny proportion of US-wages 'could have come from profits earned in Africa, Asia and Latin America' and that 'such proportions are hardly sufficient to explain the 37% wage differentials between secretaries in advertising agencies and "labor aristocracy" machinists working on oil pipelines, or the 64% wage differentials between janitors in restaurants and bars and automobile workers'. The problem with this critique is two-fold. On the one hand, it disregards the other source of appropriation of international value besides profit-repatriation, namely unequal exchange. On the other, it disregards the additional, numerous causes of wage-differentials, both economic and not.

(a) *Mental use-values*. If the production of value requires, as one of its conditions, the transformation of use-values into new use-values, the first question that naturally arises is: what is a mental use-value? Let us recall that the capitalist production-process is the combination of the labour-process and of the surplus-value producing process. This process is productive of surplus-value, if the labourers work for a time longer than that necessary to reconstitute their labour-power *and* if they transform existing use-values into new ones. For Marx, if the determining aspect of the labour-process deals with objective use-values without transforming them into new use-values (for example, purchase and sale of commodities) labour is objective but unproductive, even if the labourers are economically oppressed (unproductive labourers must work for a time longer than the time needed for the reconstitution of their labour-power). In this case, there has been a *formal* rather than a *real* transformation of objective use-values. Let us apply this principle to the production of knowledge. If knowledge, any knowledge, at whatever level of abstraction, is our perception, theorisation and thus comprehension of objective reality, in short our view of objective reality, *its use-value is the use to which that knowledge can be put*, that is, our perception, theorisation and comprehension of objective reality. The use-value of knowledge is a *mental use-value*. Accordingly, new knowledge (a mental transformation) is, by definition, a new mental use-value, because, by transforming our perception, theorisation and comprehension of objective reality, it transforms the use to which new knowledge can be put.

(b) *The production of knowledge as production of surplus-value.* It follows that any production of knowledge is at the same time the production of a new mental use-value and, if performed by mental labourers for the capitalists, is production of value and surplus-value as well.[56] But there are qualifications. First, capitalism requires the production of a certain type of knowledge that is necessary for the work of control and surveillance. It is needed in order to

---

[56] A capitalist process is not based necessarily on wage-labour in all segments of the labour-process. Schiller (1997, p. 111) argues that it is sufficient that wage-labour is the norm. The present work's perspective is that the capitalists can buy, for example, the produce of small independent farmers, or of artisans, as inputs of their production-process (see Carchedi 1991). When this takes place, the labour performed outside the capitalist production-relations counts as if it had been performed under those relations. Similarly, a writer selling her manuscript to a publishing company need not be a wage-labourer.

force or convince the mental labourers to work for a time longer than that necessary for the reproduction of their labour-power. If the function of capital cannot produce value, the same applies to the production of the knowledge needed for the performance of that function. If the knowledge needed for the performance of the function of capital cannot produce surplus-value, the same applies when the production of that knowledge detaches itself from the actual performance of that process and becomes a separate branch of the economy. On the other hand, in the production of value, the production of knowledge (mental transformation) is either determined by the objective transformations needed for that process or is determinant vis-à-vis the objective transformations, as, for example, research-institutions that develop new management-techniques. This requires objective transformations which, however, are determined by those mental transformations. Second, a similar approach holds (a) for a mental transformation determined by a formal objective transformation (purchase and sale of objective commodities, financial or speculative operations, etc.) or (b) for a mental transformation as the determinant aspect of a mental labour-process conceptualising formal objective transformations. The capitalist production-process based on this mental labour-process is unproductive of new value and surplus-value. Third, similar considerations hold also for the mental transformations that are the determined aspect of an objective labour-process destroying objective use-values or that is the determinant aspect of a mental labour-process conceptualising the destruction of objective use-values (value-destroying labour, both objective and mental).

The value and surplus-value accruing to these three processes (if carried out under capitalist production-relations) derives from the productive sphere. The mental workers employed in these three branches of activities do not produce new value and surplus-value, yet they are economically oppressed because they must work for a time longer than what is necessary for the reproduction of their labour-power. Their surplus-labour is the vehicle through which the capitalists running a mental labour-process of the three above mentioned types appropriate surplus-value from the productive spheres.

(c) *Knowledge and productivity.* Critics argue that it is impossible to measure value, productivity and exploitation in the case of knowledge-production. But, given that value is abstract labour under the capitalist production-relation, and given that the latter is the expenditure of human energy in the abstract, the value produced during the production of knowledge is measured by the intensity and length of the mental producer's abstract labour, given the value of her labour-power. Notice that it is not necessarily true that mental labourers (those who engage in a mental labour-process) produce more value than objective labourers (those who engage in an objective labour-process). It all depends on the value of their labour-power and on the time and intensity of their labour. If the value of a mental labourer's labour-power is less than that of an objective labourer, the value created by the former is less than that created by the latter, *ceteris paribus*. As for exploitation (or economic oppression that was discussed in the three above-mentioned cases), once the value produced (or appropriated, in the case of unproductive labour) and the value of labour-power are known, exploitation follows as the difference between the former and the latter. As for productivity, while in objective production the value produced can be subdivided into units of output so that productivity (output per unit of capital invested) can be easily (at least, conceptually) computed, the same is not possible in mental production. However, the type of knowledge we refer to if we refer to productivity is that developed in order to be applied to objective production, basically to produce more efficient means of production. Its productivity can be measured through the increased productivity of the means of production when it is incorporated in them or more generally when it becomes an element of the production-process.

(d) *Value and free knowledge.* It is also argued that nowadays the production of knowledge supposedly relies increasingly on free information (which has no value). In this view, given that only what has value can produce (in the case of labour-power) or transfer (in the case of the means of production) value,[57] how can an input that has no value create or transfer value? Also, 'free social knowledge is appropriated and turned into a source of private profit', so that 'direct exploitation is becoming less important as a source of profit'.[58] On both accounts, 'we have moved away from Marx's picture of classical capitalism'.[59]

---

[57] See Chapter 2.
[58] Morris-Suzuki 1997b, p. 64.
[59] Ibid. Davis and Stack reach the erroneous conclusion that 'With replacement of human labor by digitally rendered productive knowledge comes the beginning of the end of the distribution of the social wealth on the basis of time worked' (Davis and Stack (eds.) 1997, p. 137). The implication is that we move towards a fully automated economy in which not only objective products but also mental products are the outcome of the work of machines. The question then is: would machines (computers) produce value? This thesis has been refuted in Section 3 of Chapter 2 above. But, assuming machines do produce value, how would social wealth be distributed? To each according to her machines?

This argument is flawed. To begin with, it is not true that the production of information (an output) relies increasingly on free knowledge (as an input). If anything, the movement seems to go in the opposite direction. Suffice it to mention the privatisation of education, from kindergartens to universities, or the increasing use of intellectual property-rights. Secondly, Marx's 'classical picture' *can* take into account the free appropriation of knowledge (e.g. the appropriation of the knowledge imparted by parents to their children, who at a later date, will sell their labour-power; or the assimilation by workers of cultural and traditional elements, two cases Marx does not deal with explicitly) just as it takes into account the free appropriation of natural resources (something he does deal with explicitly). Both types of appropriation are a free gift for the capitalists, they increase their labourers' productivity, namely the production of *use-values* per unit of capital invested, but they do that without increasing the value produced (which depends only on human labour under capitalist production-relations). Just as in the case of improved techniques, this increased physical productivity makes possible a greater appropriation of value by some capitalists (those who benefit from these gifts) than by other capitalists.

(e) *Differences and similarities between objective and mental labour-processes concerning the production and appropriation of value.* First, knowledge as an output enters immediately, during the production-process, the mental labourer's labour-power. Thus, knowledge is *both* absorbed into the mental labourers' labour-power *and*, usually upon its incorporation in an objective shell, appropriated by the capitalist. Objective commodities, on the other hand, are only appropriated by the capitalists.

Second, similar to objective labour, it is the mental labourers who produce the knowledge appropriated by the capitalists. Capital's ideologists turn this upside down. For them, the employees' minds 'are repositories of knowledge accumulated over untold hours of listening and talking while not delivering any goods or services to paying customers...[they – G.C.] carry a share of the company's knowledge capital'.[60] But it is labour which produces both objective outputs and knowledge and which is exploited or economically oppressed by capital.

---

[60] Strassmann 1999.

Third, knowledge usually needs an objective shell. It is usually through this objective shell that knowledge, similar to objective commodities, can become an input of the next production-period. However, the difference is that new knowledge, as the output of a production-period, enters a subsequent production period also as a feature of the mental labourers' labour- (transformed) power.

7. The general intellect

Chapter 2 has argued against two of the major contemporary schools criticising Marx on grounds of inconsistency, the neo-Ricardian and the value-form school. A third influential current, workerism,[61] has not been dealt with in that chapter because, at that point, we did not yet have the tools to analyse it, such as the elements of a theory of knowledge that have been developed above in this chapter. Some commentators within this current have found aspects of a theory of knowledge in Marx's fragment on machines in the *Grundrisse*, a work that is supposedly 'in contradistinction to *Capital*'.[62] For these authors, the *Grundrisse* is superior to, and/or inconsistent with, *Capital*. It is within this perspective that they engage in a revision of Marx's notion of classes, of the class-determination of knowledge, and of the role of knowledge in what they believe to be a new class-composition. What follows will not review the workerist (and post-workerist) galaxy of approaches. Rather, the focus will be on some works that underline the major themes preoccupying the workerist school, with special emphasis on some epistemological points, that is, on the notions of classes, class-subjectivity, and knowledge.

Virno, for example, holds that Marx's fragment on machines contains a thesis that can be hardly called Marxian, namely that abstract knowledge (principally science) incorporated in the automatic system of machines tends to become the main productive force, thus marginalising the importance of direct labour and thus of fragmented and repetitive work. Due to the tendential pre-eminence of knowledge, the labourer steps to the side of the process of production rather than being its principal agent. Consequently, the law of value is eroded. The origin of crises is no longer, as in other writings by Marx,

---

[61] For a survey, see Wright 2002.
[62] Toscano 2007, p. 4.

to be found in the imbalance related to the working of the law of value, as for example, its relation to the tendential fall in the rate of profit (see Chapter 2). Rather, it should be sought in the contradiction between, on the one hand, production-processes that now rest directly and exclusively on science and, on the other, labour embodied as the unit of measure of wealth. According to Marx, Virno asserts, the development of this contradiction leads to the breakdown of capitalism and thus to communism. In post-Fordism, Virno continues, social knowledge, the general intellect (for example, knowledge, information, and epistemological paradigms) has indeed become, as anticipated by Marx, the immediate productive force because it is incorporated in the means of production and as a result, the production of value by direct labour has indeed become of marginal importance. But this evolution, rather than leading to communism, has resulted in the stable integration of science within capitalism's means of production (machines). Marx, Virno continues, should be criticised because of his neglect of the way in which the general intellect manifests itself as living labour. 'Thoughts and discourses function in themselves as productive "machines" in contemporary labour and do not need to take on a mechanical body or an electronic soul'. And, further, 'the labouring action of the general intellect presupposes the common participation to the "life of the mind" [and thus – G.C.] the end of the division of labour'.[63]

To evaluate this interpretation of Marx's fragment on machines, it is necessary to reproduce that fragment's salient passages.

> The exchange of living labour for objectified labour – that is, the positing of social labour in the form of the contradiction of capital and wage labour – is the ultimate development of the *value-relation* and of production resting on value. Its presupposition is – and remains – the mass of direct labour time, the quantity of labour employed, as the determinant factor in the production of wealth.[64]

Thus, the quantity of living labour employed, itself a consequence of the capital-labour contradictory relation, is and remains the only source of value.

> But to the degree that large industry develops, the creation of *real wealth* [emphasis added – G.C.] comes to depend less on labour time and on

---

[63] Virno 2001.
[64] Marx 1973a, p. 704.

the amount of labour employed than on the power of the agencies set in motion during labour time, whose 'powerful effectiveness' is itself in turn but depends rather on the general state of science and on the progress of technology, or the application of this science to production.[65]

The production of real wealth, in other words of *use-values* (as opposed to value), comes to depend increasingly on the means of production and thus on the science and technology incorporated in them and thus on the greater productivity ensuing from it.

> Real wealth manifests itself, rather – and large industry reveals this – in the monstrous disproportion between the labour time applied, and its product, as well as in the qualitative imbalance between labour, reduced to a pure abstraction, and the power of the production process it superintends.[66]

This is the contradiction, the increasing disproportion between an increasing quantity of use-values (real wealth) and a decreasing quantity of abstract labour (value) needed to produce that real wealth, where the value-creating labour encompasses the labour of superintendence (understood as co-ordination and unity) of the labour-process (of the production of use-values). The theory of crises developed in Chapters 2 and 3 rests on this contradiction. This type of labour increases in importance. In fact:

> Labour no longer appears so much to be included within the production-process; rather, the human being comes to relate more as watchman and regulator to the production process itself....He steps to the side of the production process instead of being its chief actor.[67]

As increasingly productive techniques are incorporated in the means of production, the labourer, instead of being the agent directly transforming the objects of labour into the finished products with the aid of the means of production, becomes the agent who supervises (in the technical sense) the working of machines, that is, an increasingly automated labour-process.

> In this transformation, it is neither the direct human labour he himself performs, nor the time during which he works, but rather the appropriation

---

[65] Marx 1973a, p. 705.
[66] Ibid.
[67] Ibid.

of his own general productive power, his understanding of nature and his mastery over it by virtue of his presence as a social body – it is, in a word, the development of the social individual which appears as the great foundation-stone of production and of wealth.[68]

The production of real wealth (use-values), thus, depends less and less on direct labour (labour directly transforming the inputs into the outputs) and more and more on the machinery's productive power and on the work of technical supervision of the labour-process. This presupposes a generalised knowledge of natural processes (natural sciences and techniques). In other words, the development of the social individual, the appropriation of natural sciences and techniques by the collective labourer, is the founding stone for the production of use-values and thus of value. Or, the value produced by the labourers is not the summation of the value of each of them independently of the others but it is the value produced collectively by them, by the collective labourer.

> As soon as labour *in the direct form* has ceased to be the great well-spring of wealth, labour time ceases and must cease to be its measure, and hence exchange-value [must cease to be the measure] of use-value [emphasis added – G.C.].[69]

At this point, we come to the crux of the matter. This passage has been read as if, as a consequence of these developments, labour-time ceased to be the measure of value and if the law of value would not longer apply under these conditions. However, what Marx says is that *what ceases to be the measure of value is not labour but labour 'in the direct form'*, the direct application of labour to machinery. Labour in the direct form is replaced by the labour of co-ordination and technical supervision of the labour-process. But labour, both as direct labour and as labour of co-ordination, decreases as the quantity of real wealth increases (see above). At this point, Marx considers the *tendential* outcome of this process:

> The *surplus labour of the mass* has ceased to be the condition for the development of general wealth, just as the *non-labour of the few*, for the development of the general powers of the human head.... The free

---

development of individualities, and hence not the reduction of necessary
labour-time so as to posit surplus labour, but rather the general reduction
of the necessary labour of society to a minimum, which then corresponds
to the artistic, scientific etc. development of the individuals in the time set
free, and with the means created, for all of them.[70]

This passage is extremely important but not for the reasons adduced by workerism. Marx depicts here the movement towards a generalised *labour-process*
(in its many facets) which is the substratum of a new society, communism.
In the new society, the surplus-labour of the collective labourer ceases 'to be
the condition for the development of general wealth' (use-values) because
that general wealth is produced by a system of machines in which human
labour is only of a supervisory nature and the non-labour (i.e. non-objective
labour, or mental labour) of the few (scientists, artists, etc.) ceases to be the
condition 'for the general powers of the human head', because those general
powers have become the feature of the collective labourer due to the fact that
there is no distinction any longer between mental and objective labour. The
result of the reduction of necessary labour-time is not any longer an increase
in surplus-value but an increase in the time during which individuals can
pursue freely the development of their potentialities. At this point,

production based on exchange-value breaks down, and the direct, material
production process is stripped of the form of penury and antithesis.[71]

In short,

Capital itself is the moving contradiction, [in] that it presses to reduce
labour-time to a minimum, while it posits labour-time, on the other side,
as sole measure and source of wealth.[72]

In other words,

Forces of production and social relations – two different sides of the
development of the social individual – appear to capital as mere means,
and are merely means for it to produce on its limited foundation. In fact,

---

[70] Ibid. This is a terminological inconsistency. For Marx, those who perform non-
labour are the capitalists and all those who perform the function of capital. The labour
of scientists, technicians, etc. is mental labour rather than non-labour.
[71] Marx 1973a, p. 706.
[72] Ibid.

however, they are the material conditions to blow this foundation sky-high.[73]

The contradiction between the social relations of capitalism and thus the decreasing quantity of surplus-value created, and the forces of production, that is, the increasing quantity of real wealth (use-values) produced thanks to the increasing power of science and technology incorporated in the means of production, this is the *moving* contradiction, the objective *condition* for the supersession of capitalism.

> The development of fixed capital indicates to what degree general social knowledge has become a *direct force of production,* and to what degree, hence, the conditions of the process of social life itself have come under the control of the general intellect and have been transformed in accordance with it.[74]

A few points become clear from the above. First, in this fragment, Marx was predicting neither the objective inevitability of communism (as Virno holds, see above) nor was he affirming that the production of value by labour has been replaced by the production of value by science and technique, that is, by the general intellect that does not reside in the factory any longer but is now ubiquitous in society at large.[75] The workerist reading rests on two misunderstandings. First, the fragment on machines *highlights what a collective labour-process would be in a communist society* as the outcome of a *tendential* movement inherent in capitalism itself. Second, this outcome is not inevitable, this is not an analysis of the inevitable and direct supersession of capitalism due to the moving contradiction between forces and relations of production.[76] Such a reading mutilates Marx's method, it separates the tendency from the counter-tendencies. For Marx, a movement is a contradictory and a tendential process. Therefore, it is clear that, in this context, *Marx considers only the tendential aspect of the process,* thus disregarding the counter-tendencies. The moving contradiction cannot lead inevitably to the advent of communism simply because of the counter-tendencies and because, even if capitalism tends to supersede itself, it is by no means certain that capitalism will be replaced by a socialist society. To extrapolate a real movement from the

---

[73] Ibid.
[74] Ibid.
[75] As in Hardt and Negri 2000, see below.
[76] See Panzieri 1961 and Turchetto 2001.

tendential aspects, while ignoring the counter-tendencies, absolutises one aspect of the process and reveals a formal logic rather than a dialectical logic. Lazzarato and Negri are aware of this objection. Their answer is that 'if evidence of a tendency cannot be confused with the analysis of the whole, on the other hand an analysis of the whole is valid only if clarified by the tendency that governs its evolution'.[77] Clearly, this evades the question: an analysis of the whole is valid only if clarified by the tendency *as well as* by the counter-tendencies that together govern its evolution.

Second, in this fragment, Marx stresses the class-nature of science and technique, a point stressed not only by Virno and workerism in general, but also in this work (see below). However, Virno and the workerist school radically misinterpret this fragment. A textual analysis of Marx's fragment is far from denying the pivotal importance of the moving contradiction between forces and relations of production, of which the tendential fall in the profit-rate is a manifestation rather than an alternative explanation as in Virno. And, as argued in Chapter 3, this contradiction is still alive and kicking in the present. There is therefore *no* contradiction between *Capital* and the *Grundrisse*. Neither is there in this fragment what Vercellone stresses, the supersession of the capitalist technical division of labour, that is, the supersession of the real subsumption of labour to capital:

> With the idea of the general intellect, he designates a radical change of the subsumption of labour to capital and indicates a third stage of the division of labour. It involves a tendential overcoming of the Smithian logic of the division of labour proper to industrial capitalism, and posits, in a new manner with respect to the other writings of Marx, the possibility of a direct transition to communism.[78]

Third, the thesis of the immateriality of labour is deeply erroneous.[79] As argued above, both 'material' (that is, objective) and mental transformations are material processes because they consist of expenditures of human energy. The difference is that *objective transformations* are the transformation of the objective world outside us while *mental transformations* are the transformation of our perception and knowledge of that outer world. The notions of

---

[77] Lazzarato and Negri 1991.
[78] Vercellone 2007.
[79] See, for example, Lazzarato and Negri 1991.

objective and mental labour rest on these epistemological foundation-stones and the distinction revolves around which one of the two types of transformations is determinant. Thus, immaterial labour does not exist: all labour (both objective and mental) is a material process because it is the expenditure of human energy both in the abstract (abstract labour) and as a specific activity (concrete labour). The opposite of mental labour is not material labour but objective labour. It has also been mentioned that one could justify the use of the category 'immaterial labour' by considering it as that labour which is material but whose outcome (for example, knowledge, information or even emotional responses) is immaterial.[80] Section 3 above, however, has rejected this view by emphasising that the material substratum of the new knowledge is the synaptic modification changing our perception of the world outside us and thus the capacity to transform it.

Fourth, let us consider the notion of the general intellect. As analysed by Virno and other workerist authors, this seems to be a disembodied, immaterial entity. As Vercellone puts it,

> The relation of capital to labour is marked by the hegemony of knowledges, by a diffuse intellectuality, and by the driving role of the production of knowledges by means of knowledges connected to the increasingly immaterial and cognitive character of labour. This new phase of the division of labour is accompanied by the crisis of the law of value-labour and by the strong return of mercantile and financial mechanisms of accumulation. The principal elements of this new configuration of capitalism and of the conflicts that derive from it are, in large measure, anticipated by Marx's notion of the general intellect.[81]

We have seen in the previous section that the law of value fits perfectly within the production of knowledge. For Marx, the general intellect is nothing else than the production of knowledge under conditions of what Marx calls in *Capital*, Volume I, the social division of labour, not only the social division between the collective objective and the collective mental labour,

---

[80] For example, Hardt and Negri 2000. For a good and detailed critique of the workerist notion of immaterial labour encompassing its many facets beyond knowledge, see Camfield 2007. However, this author also subscribes to the notion that immaterial labour and immaterial products do exist in contemporary capitalist society. See Camfield 2007, p. 32.

[81] Vercellone 2007, p. 16.

but also within the collective mental labour. *The general intellect is the production of knowledge by the increasingly mutually interpenetrating and interdependent single processes of mental production,* both individual and social. It is the internally articulated *collective mental labourer.* Some of this knowledge is produced outside capitalist relations. It cannot produce value but it affects the production of value because it is 'the great founding-stone' upon which that production rests, that is, because the greater and the more diffuse the knowledge produced outside the capital/labour relation, the more efficient the production of use-values and thus the greater the rate of profit of those capitalists for whom that knowledge is society's gift. The example has been mentioned of the knowledge transmitted by parents and the school-system and made their own by the potential labourers before they enter the capitalist production-relations.

Besides the knowledge produced by the general intellect, or collective mental labourer, outside the capitalist relations, there is also the knowledge produced by the collective labourer under those relations. In this case, there can be production of value under the shape of specific forms of knowledge, mental use-values, under the conditions specified above in Section 6. The general intellect under capitalism, rather than marking the end of the division of labour, is the whole make-up of the interconnected, hierarchically structured, complex mental labour-processes subjected to the rule of capital and thus, on the one hand, to a constant tendential de-skilling (the mental labourer's knowledge is incorporated in the machines, as for example, in the case of the computer in digital form, so that the mental labourers can ultimately be dispensed with) and concomitant devaluation of labour-power, and on the other hand, counter-tendential re-skilling and creation of new, qualified positions.[82] This is evident in virtual universities as capitalist enterprises that sell packaged knowledge (educational software) produced by instructors but appropriated by the enterprise (thanks to intellectual property-rights). Since, tendentially, the general intellect becomes increasingly a capitalist activity,

---

[82] 'Within the large restructured enterprises, the labor of the worker implies more and more and at different levels the ability to choose among different alternatives and thus the responsibility of certain decisions' (Lazzarato and Negri 1991). This is the re-skilling process, the counter-tendency, which is again absolutised. It is clear that the situation sketched by the authors was and has remained a myth.

the production of knowledge is increasingly production of value, *pace* the workerists and legions of other authors.

Lazzarato and Negri, on the other hand, hold that inasmuch as the labour-process comes to depend on the labourers' knowledge (needed to control the means of production rather than to use them as direct labour), inasmuch as labour has to be capable of taking independent decisions and responsibility but always within the confines posed by capital, capital has to organise and control labourers not only in their direct labour-time: it has to control their very subjectivity to allow them that amplitude of bounded choice and responsibility. Since subjectivity is formed during the whole day, this is the span of capital's control. Under the assumption that the effect of capital's controls is the production of surplus-value, surplus-value is produced in the space of the whole day. Or, as Hardt and Negri submit, 'As labor moves outside the factory walls, it is increasingly difficult to maintain the fiction of any measure of the working day and thus separate the time of production from the time of reproduction, or work time from leisure time.'[83] Consequently, 'The object of exploitation and domination tend not to be specific productive activities but the universal capacity to produce, that is, abstract social activity and its comprehensive power.'[84]

It is true that social and individual relations, knowledge, and more generally all individual and social phenomena are the necessary social background within which production takes place. This is not a new feature but is a constant of any society. But, contrary to the workerist thesis, these phenomena are the social *conditions* for production and *not* immediate *production*. The thesis that the ideological, political, and social control of labour is production of surplus-value is nothing more than an assumption lacking any theoretical and empirical substantiation. As pointed out by Callinicos,[85] the authors simply confuse exploitation in the Marxian sense with different forms of domination in different spheres of society. All these forms are ultimately determined by exploita-

---

[83] Hardt and Negri 2000, pp. 402–3.

[84] Hard and Negri 2000, p. 209. The extension of the time of exploitation to the whole working day has its roots in the workerist notion of social fabric as developed by Tronti in the early 1960s, that is, that capital subsumes the whole of society so that factory-discipline has to be imposed on society (Tronti 2006). It follows that all subordinate members of society are members of the 'social worker', a conclusion however reached not by Tronti but by Negri.

[85] Callinicos 2001.

tion and thus by the ownership-relation, because they are all conditions for the reproduction of that relation. The assumption that domination outside the production-process creates surplus-value, that surplus-value is created during the whole span of the day, is not only theoretically unproven. It is also belied by the empirical observation that capital strives continually to increase the length of the working day while decreasing the portion during which the labourers reconstitute their labour-power, which is a constant of capitalist society. This simple empirical falsification is sufficient to call into question the whole theory.[86] The authors' claim that Marx's value-theory (which they persistently grossly misunderstand) should be re-conceptualised is baseless.

For the workerist approach, the other side of the coin is that the formation of labour's subjectivity is, at the same time, their cultural self-valorisation, something that makes of labour a revolutionary force.[87] Knowledge workers must be creative and co-operative. 'The labour force becomes social and autonomous, capable of organising its own labour and its own relations with the enterprise.'[88] And this holds not only for skilled labourers but also for less skilled ones, at least tendentially. For them, this capacity is 'purely virtual ... still indeterminate, but it participates already in all the characteristics of the productive, post-industrial subjectivity'.[89] As Vercellone puts it, we witness the 'reappropriation of the cognitive dimensions of work by living labour'.[90]

First, such a view clashes with all empirical evidence and theoretical insights into capitalism. It is true that the new knowledge produced by mental labourers is retained by them, becomes part of their labour-power (see Section 6 above). However, under capitalism, this knowledge is appropriated by capital, which appropriates, as it were, a 'copy' of it (even if this appropriation is again a mental transformation).[91] Secondly, the mental workers work for capital. As Sections 8 and 9 below will demonstrate, they must produce

---

[86] Empirical evidence can be found in Camfield 2007, pp. 44 and ff.
[87] Negri, 1992.
[88] Lazzarato and Negri, 1991.
[89] Ibid.
[90] Vercellone 2007, p. 16.
[91] While value-form theory denies materiality to abstract labour, the autonomist school denies materiality to mental labour. Both are belied by medical science. The neo-Ricardians and more generally the physicalists are blissfully unaware of all this because theirs is a world in which only material commodities are produced and from which abstract labour is banned (see Chapter 2 above).

knowledge with a specific class-content. If this knowledge is pro-capital, the knowledge produced and incorporated into the labourers' labour-power is the contrary of what makes labour a revolutionary force. Third, for Lazzarato and Negri, de-skilling is not the tendency described in Marx. Rather, for these authors, the tendency is the creation of skilled labour, the transformation of labour from direct labour to 'knowledge labour'. This contains the possibility of a new sort of conflict between capital and labour as labour can use this bounded creativity and co-operation as the first step towards a reorganisation of the general intellect's alternative to capital's organisation.

This view is flawed in many ways. For example, as pointed out in Section 2 above, in the contemporary international social division of labour, the production of knowledge under capitalist production-relations is concentrated in the developed world, while objective production is shifted to the dominated countries, something which is arrogantly perceived as if objective production were disappearing. Or, as Camfield stresses,

> Hardt and Negri would have to argue persuasively that there really are significant degrees of qualitative commonality across the huge range of concrete labours that they would have us believe are all examples of immaterial labour. Instead, they simply assert that all labours whose products are immaterial, whether primarily intellectual-linguistic or affective, are part of the category of immaterial labour. This is unconvincing.[92]

But, even more importantly, the picture emerging from this line of thinking is that of a society tendentially and increasingly resting on the production of knowledge through a tendentially and increasing qualification of labour-power. Since more qualified and skilled labour-power produces more (surplus-) value, the tendency is towards a growing production of (surplus-) value and the increasing qualification of labour.[93] This is the opposite of Marx, who sees capitalism as tending towards crises (less production of value and surplus-value) and the de-qualification (de-skilling) of labour. It follows that labour's struggle is not the conscious manifestation of the system's objective tendency towards crises and de-qualification of labour but, similarly to the

---

[92] Camfield 2007, p. 34.
[93] The contrary thesis would imply the proof that a more qualified labour-power produces less (surplus-) value, an unenviable task that not by chance has not been attempted by anyone.

conclusion reached in the critique of physicalism, it merely becomes an act of voluntarism. This cannot but undermine that struggle.

The workerist revision of Marx's notion of classes and of labour's subjectivity has perhaps gained the widest resonance with Hardt and Negri's *Empire*. For a better evaluation of this issue, the authors' notions of Empire, crises, and classes will be first briefly assessed.[94]

(a) *Empire*. The authors' view is that we are witnessing an epochal change, from imperialism to Empire. While imperialism was 'an extension of the sovereignty of the European nation-states beyond their own boundaries', Empire is 'a series of national and supranational organisms united under a single logic of rule'.[95] It is a global network of power 'consisting of highly differentiated and mobile structures'.[96] Thus, Empire has no centre, 'center and margin seem continually to be shifting positions'.[97] In short, Empire 'can only be conceived as...a network of powers and counterpowers'.[98] The authors do not seem to realise that there is an inherent circularity here because 'Power can be constituted by a whole series of powers that regulate themselves and arrange themselves in networks'.[99] Moreover, there is power and power. It is true that even the dominant countries are now dependent on the global system. But they are dependent on it in quite a different way from the dominated countries are. Simply put, the former appropriate value from the latter. Empire does have a centre; it is the dominant capitals in the dominant imperialist countries.

But let us return to *Empire*'s theses. What are the fundamental reasons behind this change? Supposedly, the decline of sovereign nation-states. 'In a previous period, nation-states were the primary actors in the modern imperialist organisation of global production and exchange, but to the world market they appear increasingly as mere obstacles.'[100] Consequently, 'this border place no longer exists'. Due to this decline, 'Empire establishes no territorial center of power and does not rely on fixed boundaries or barriers. It is a *decentered* and *deterritorialising* apparatus of rule that progressively incorporates the entire

---

[94] Hardt and Negri 2000. For a critique, see Callinicos 2001, Panitch and Gindin 2002, and Carchedi 2003b.
[95] Hardt and Negri 2000, pp. xi–xii.
[96] Hardt and Negri 2000, p. 151.
[97] Hardt and Negri 2000, p. 39.
[98] Hardt and Negri 2000, p. 166.
[99] Hardt and Negri 2000, p. 162.
[100] Hardt and Negri 2000, p. 150.

global realm within its open, expanding frontiers.'[101] Nowadays, the transnationals are the 'fundamental motor of economic and political transformation'.[102] The objection to this thesis is that, aside from the fact that empirical evidence belies it, the assumption that the role of the state is fading away is of absolutely crucial importance for the architecture of *Empire*. One would then expect solid theoretical arguments and empirical evidence supporting this assumption. Instead, this assumption is simply stated as if it were the most obvious truth. Moreover, the thesis that nation-states are 'mere obstacles' is contradicted by the authors themselves when they state that 'Without the state, social capital has no means to project and realise its collective interest.'[103]

After the dealing with the nature of Empire, the authors consider its structure. They believe that the network-like structure of Empire does not deny the stratification of global power. At the pinnacle, they see the United States. On a second level, there is a group of nation-states and the organisations that bind them together. Finally, the third tier consists of groups that represent popular interests.[104] However, this hierarchy does not imply, according to the authors, that a country has a dominant position in it. The dubious and, again unproved, reason adduced by the authors is that 'when a power becomes monopolistic, the network itself is destroyed'.[105] The conclusion they reach is that 'The United States does not, and indeed no nation-state can today, form the center of an imperialist project.'[106] However, 'this is not to say that the United States and Brazil, Britain and India are now identical territories in terms of capitalist production and circulation, but rather that between them are no differences of nature, only differences of degrees'.[107] Are the differences between the exploiter and the exploited differences of degrees? Or, is this not yet another version of the apology of capital? The assertion that 'North and South no longer define an international order but rather have moved closer to one another'[108] is contrary to all empirical evidence and quite absurd.

---

[101] Hardt and Negri 2000, pp. xi–xii.
[102] Hardt and Negri 2000, p. 246. See also p. 304.
[103] Hardt and Negri 2000, p. 307.
[104] Hardt and Negri 2000, pp. 309–11.
[105] Hardt and Negri 2000, p. 173.
[106] Hardt and Negri 2000, p. xiii–xiv. See also p. 384.
[107] Hardt and Negri 2000, p. 335. See also 384.
[108] Hardt and Negri 2000, p. 336.

Moreover, the notion of Empire as a network leads the authors to conclude that, in terms of conflicts, Empire 'is organized not around one central conflict but rather through a flexible network of microconflicts...we have entered the era of minor and internal conflicts'.[109] This conclusion is a dangerous illusion. To mention just one example, the European Union might be militarily no match for the United States yet. But the potential rivalry between these two blocs and thus the possibility of a future major confrontation cannot be denied.[110] If, at present, there are no major conflicts in Empire the reason is not that power is everywhere and nowhere, distributed in a network. Rather, the reason is that it is heavily concentrated, as military power, in just one country, in the centre, the United States. The assertion that the 'United States is the peace police'[111] is quite astonishing.

Empire severely underestimates not only the economic aspects of imperialism but also the economic interest of its dominant core. The Gulf-War is seen basically as an exercise in the legitimation of the imperial order, 'of very little interest from the point of view of the objectives, the regional interests, and the political ideologies involved'.[112] This is sheer blindness to the geo-economic interests tied to the appropriation of oil and more generally blindness to the central role of the dominant imperialist countries' bloc and within it of the US. The US is 'called to intervene militarily...even if it were reluctant, the U.S. military would have to answer the call in the name of peace and order'.[113] In the name of peace and order? Who or what makes the call and who appropriates Iraq's oil? The network? Today, not only is imperialism alive and kicking, but old-fashioned colonialism, the fight for raw materials (oil, tropical natural resources, water, and so on) is becoming, if anything, more and more important. It co-exists with the new forms of imperialism but is still an extremely vigorous form of international exploitation.

(b) *Crises*. The authors hold that 'Since each worker must produce more value than he or she consumes, the demand for the worker as consumer can never be an adequate demand for the surplus-value.'[114] The inability to realise

[109] Hardt and Negri 2000, p. 201.
[110] Carchedi 2001.
[111] Hardt and Negri 2000, p. 181.
[112] Hardt and Negri 2000, p. 180.
[113] Hardt and Negri 2000, p. 181. See also p. 245.
[114] Hardt and Negri 2000, p. 222.

the surplus-value forces capital to invest in non-capitalist countries or sectors of the economy. But, sooner or later, this option comes to an end, if capital penetrates the whole globe. Thus, Empire is doomed to an inevitable collapse due to its internal, objective contradictions: 'The functioning of imperial power is ineluctably linked to its decline.'[115] However, if, on the one hand, the authors emphasise the objective causes of crises and of the inevitable demise of Empire, on the other they deny it by holding that 'history is a product of human action'.[116] The thesis now is that crises 'are best understood when seen as a *result* of the confluence and accumulation of proletarian and anti-capitalist attacks against the international capitalist system', that is, that they are determined basically by the struggles of the multitude.[117] The focus shifts from the accumulation of capital to the accumulation of the multitude's struggles. The former is the underconsumptionist thesis, the latter is basically the profit-squeeze theory. Aside from the untheorised relation between these two causes of the crisis, Chapter 3 above has amply refuted both of them.

Related to the above is a new theory of value and exploitation. In *Empire*, exploitation changes connotation radically. 'On the one hand, the relations of capitalist exploitation are expanding everywhere, not limited to the factory but tending to occupy the entire social terrain. On the other hand, social relations completely invest the relations of production.'[118] And further, 'As labor moves outside the factory walls, it is increasingly difficult to maintain the fiction of any measure of the working day and thus separate the time of production from the time of reproduction, or work time from leisure time.'[119] Consequently, 'The object of exploitation and domination tend not to be specific productive activities but the universal capacity to produce, that is, abstract social activity and its comprehensive power.'[120] Thus, 'The excess of value is determined today in the affects, in the bodies crisscrossed by knowledge, in the intelligence of the mind, and in the sheer power to act. The production of commodities tends to be accomplished entirely through language, where by language we mean machines of intelligence that are continuously renovated

---

[115] Hardt and Negri 2000, p. 361.
[116] Hardt and Negri 2000, p. 237.
[117] Hardt and Negri 2000, p. 261.
[118] Hardt and Negri 2000, p. 209.
[119] Hardt and Negri 2000, pp. 402–3.
[120] Hardt and Negri 2000, p. 209.

by the affects and subjective passion.'[121] Finally, 'Exploitation is the expropriation of cooperation and the nullification of the meanings of linguistic production.'[122] These are 'the postmodern relations of production'.[123] How do these new concepts of surplus and exploitation relate to underconsumption? What is the meaning of 'no adequate demand' for surplus-value conceived as 'determined today in the affects, in the bodies crisscrossed by knowledge, in the intelligence of the mind, and in the sheer power to act'? The point is not that this notion of exploitation renders the Marxian notion of exploitation obsolete. The point is not only that this thesis is based on the greatest theoretical obscurity and vagueness. The point is also, and most importantly, that if the factory as analysed by Marx has been replaced by the social factory; if, therefore, exploitation is a process that involves the whole of society, then, as held by workerism, exploitation is also a non-stop, twenty-four-hours-a-day process. Empirical evidence denies this notion, given that it is obvious to everybody that the capitalists attempt continuously to increase the time they force the labourer to labour and to decrease the time the labourers reconstitute their labour-power. If this is empirically false, the notion of the social factory and all that goes with it is proved also to be false.

(c) *Classes*. Empire is 'the center that supports' globalisation, that is, 'the globalization of productive networks' and 'yet it deploys a powerful police function against the new barbarians and the rebellious slaves who threaten its order', that is, against the multitude.[124] The basic contradiction is no longer between capital and labour but between Empire and the multitude. This is 'a broad category that includes all those whose labor is directly or indirectly exploited by and subjected to capitalist norms of production and reproduction'.[125] The multitude not only has 'called Empire into being'[126] since Empire 'is a *response* to proletarian internationalism',[127] it is also 'capable of autonomously constructing a counter-Empire'.[128] Why should the multitude be 'capable of autonomously constructing a counter-Empire'? The reason is

---

[121] Hardt and Negri 2000, pp. 365–6.
[122] Hardt and Negri 2000, p. 385.
[123] Hardt and Negri 2000, p. 210.
[124] Hardt and Negri 2000, p. 20.
[125] Hardt and Negri 2000, p. 52.
[126] Hardt and Negri 2000, p. 43.
[127] Hardt and Negri 2000, p. 51.
[128] Hardt and Negri 2000, p. xv.

supposedly that 'only the poor lives radically the actual and present being, in destitution and suffering, and thus only the poor has the ability to renew being'.[129] This is 'the discovery of postmodernity'.[130] But there is no discovery here, only the repetition of old-fashioned and obsolete concepts.

This is a distributive concept of class which, moreover, is internally contradictory. While the authors claim that 'the real revolutionary practice refers to the level of *production*', for them the multitude is defined in terms of poverty: 'the poor is [sic] destitute, excluded, repressed, exploited – and yet living! It is the common denominator of life, the foundation of the multitude'.[131] In short, the multitude is 'the common name of the poor'.[132] Or, 'Class struggle posed the problem of scarcity...that is, as the iniquity of the division of the goods of development.'[133] Moreover, why should destitution and suffering be the privileged life-experience that transforms a class into a revolutionary, conscious, agent? Certainly, the workers and students of the 1960s and 1970s who inspired autonomist thinking were Western societies' most conscious (that is, conscious of capital's contradictions) agents rather then being the most destitute sector of those societies. The authors sense this difficulty: 'One might object...with good reason, that all this is still not enough to establish the multitude as a properly political subject. This objection, however, is not an insuperable obstacle because the revolutionary past...cannot help revealing a telos, a material affirmation of liberation.'[134] It is true that it is warranted to expect the recurrence of an event if the causes have not changed. As long as poverty persists, the authors might be entitled to assume that revolution is possible also in the future. But the problem is that no justification is provided for the inherently revolutionary potential of the poor, of the multitude.[135]

---

[129] Hardt and Negri 2000, p. 157. See also p. 363.
[130] Hardt and Negri 2000, p. 158.
[131] Hardt and Negri 2000, p. 156.
[132] Hardt and Negri 2000, p. 158.
[133] Hardt and Negri 2000, p. 173.
[134] Hardt and Negri 2000, p. 359.
[135] I leave aside some of the most bizarre aspects of *Empire*, such as that the multitude's struggle requires that 'we need to change our bodies' (Hardt and Negri 2000, p. 216). The new body 'in addition to be radically unprepared for normalization,...must also be able to create a new life' (ibid.), something that seems to include potential metamorphoses breaking down the 'ambiguous boundary between human, animal and machine' (Hardt and Negri 2000, p. 218).

Having failed to establish *why* the multitude is the inherently revolution-ary force, the authors advance a hypothesis as to *when* the multitude becomes revolutionary: 'when it begins to confront directly and with an adequate con-sciousness the central repressive operations of Empire'.[136] This is not only triv-ial but also circular: the multitude becomes revolutionary when it starts acting in revolutionary manner. When, then do we know that the multitude starts acting, has become, revolutionary? The answer is: when it has advanced three demands. The first is the right to control its own movements, the second is a social wage and a guaranteed income for all, and the third is the right to re-appropriation of the means of production. The first two demands can be eas-ily part of any serious reformist programme. The question is: why these two demands and not others? The third demand does not relate so much to the physical means of production. Rather, given that 'the means of production are increasingly integrated into the minds and bodies of the multitude,... reap-propriation means having free access to and control over knowledge, infor-mation, communication, and affects – because these are some of the primary means of biopolitical production.'[137] Even if one were to agree with the bizarre notion that the physical means of production are integrated into our minds rather than our knowledge being integrated in the physical means of pro-duction, this demand is simply the demand to abolish Empire, or capitalism, immediately. But, then, if one decides to call for an end to capitalism (Empire) immediately and directly, why draw up a two-point social democratic pro-gramme?

To conclude, workerism is one more of the many 'improvements', 'cor-rections', 'updates' of Marx that deny, explicitly or implicitly, the essence of his theory, that is, that capitalism tends towards its supersession. They all unwittingly substitute the objective tendency of capitalism towards its own supersession with its tendency towards its reproduction. They all share this pro-capital class-content. Autonomist arguments are often self-contradictory, especially in their most well-known work, *Empire*, and expressed in an osten-tatious and obscure verbiage. Marx's theory, especially his epistemology, should be developed but the path is shown neither by value-form theory, nor by neo-Ricardian theory, nor by autonomist theory. Against this background,

---

[136] Hardt and Negri 2000, p. 399.
[137] Hardt and Negri 2000, pp. 406–7.

the following sections will attempt to develop a theory of knowledge in the tracks of Marx's theory and on the basis of the results reached in the previous pages.

8. Science, technique and alien knowledge

Let us recall two basic conclusions reached in Section 4 above. The first is that social phenomena are transformed from actually existing social phenomena into potential social phenomena existing in the concrete individuals' consciousness and individuality through the concrete individuals' internalisation. It is for this reason that, as elements of concrete individuals' knowledge, they are amenable to be actualised again in the social dimension in a different form and in a different realm of reality. The second conclusion was that not all concrete individuals create social knowledge. Only some concrete individuals develop forms of knowledge that represent the interests of social groups. They transform those interests in their own view of reality and transmit it to other concrete individuals who are the members of that knowledge-group. They become a social group's intellectual representatives. Their individual knowledge becomes then their specific, personal rendition of a social knowledge; it becomes the specific form of manifestation of a class-determined generality. These points can now be applied to the production of the natural sciences and techniques. The thesis will be that the natural sciences and technique, rather than being class-neutral, are class-determined and thus contain a class-content. They are not the result of a process of knowledge whose movement is detached from society and class-struggle, but are a specific result and sedimentation of that struggle. This point is of the greatest importance for a theory of transition, as the following two sections will argue.

If production is both objective and mental, the relations of production and thus the ownership-relation are also both objective and mental. Consider the relations of mental production. Section 3 has submitted that, in the process of mental production, it is the mental transformations that are determinant and that these latter are the transformation by labour-power of both subjective and objective knowledge. We can now introduce the class-dimension. Within this dimension, it is the capitalists who mandate the mental labourers to develop new knowledge. This means that the capitalists purchase and thus own the objective means of mental transformation (libraries, schools, research-institutes, computers, and so on) and can thus decide which means with what mental content (knowledge) to buy and (let) use in the mental labour-process. But the capitalists own also the mental labourers' labour-power. This means that the capitalists can decide, or let decide (see below), *which knowledge should be produced, how it should be produced, and for whom (in whose interest)*. The specific class-content of the natural sciences and techniques thus produced is that they must be functional for capital's *two major aims* in developing this type of knowledge: they must increase productivity (as the means for appropriation of surplus-value, see Chapter 3 above) and they must subjugate and contain labour. In Marx's words: 'It would be possible to write quite a history of the inventions made since 1830, for the sole purpose of supplying capital with weapons against the revolts of the working class.'[138] If the capitalists can decide, or let decide (see below), which knowledge should be produced, how it should be produced, and for whom (in whose interest), they *have the power to (let) define and (let) solve problems to their own advantage, in other word, they can direct the specific way the natural sciences and technique should be conceived and realised while satisfying capital's two above mentioned aims.*

David Noble has provided a classic example of the class-determination of numerically controlled machines. This author has shown that the choice of numerically controlled machines, instead of the alternative technique of record-playback, was due not to some ineluctable technological imperative but to two orders of motives. First of all, it favoured large firms rather than small ones. In fact, since the market for this technique was initially created by the Air Force, the builders of numerically controlled machines had no incentive to develop a type of less expensive machine which could be acquired by smaller firms. Moreover, since the Air Force favoured a certain type of program (APT) needed to run the machines, and since this program required expensive computers and experienced programmers, those who could not afford this program (basically, smaller firms) were deprived of government (Air Force) commissions. Secondly, numerical control was chosen instead of record-playback because, in this latter method, the machine repeated the motions of the machinist which were recorded on a magnetic tape. The preparation of the magnetic tape thus implied that the machinist retained control over the machine and thus over production. Numerical control, on the other

---

[138] Marx 1967a, p. 436.

hand, allowed far greater management, as opposed to workers', control, by transferring the knowledge needed to operate the machines from the shopfloor to production-engineers and managers. This was achieved by translating the specification needed to make a part into a mathematical representation of that part, then into a mathematical description of the path of the cutting tool, and finally in a large number of instructions which could be read by the machine. This type of knowledge was outside the reach of the machinist and became the prerogative of the planning office.[139]

This general result must be qualified. The first two qualifications will be considered in this section. The third one will be considered in the following section.

First, the capitalists, of course, do not have the knowledge necessary to direct the development of science and technique. This is the task of the mental collective labourer, or the general intellect in Marx's sense (see Section 7 above), as opposed to the objective collective labourer. The mental labourers composing the collective mental labourer develop science and technique not individually, but collectively, on the basis of a mental labour-process highly articulated and differentiated in different branches and in a number of different tasks. Similar to objective labourers, mental labourers are those who collectively engage in mental production for capital. The bridge between the collective mental labourer and capital is given by those mental labourers who become the intellectual representatives of capital in the sphere of science and technique. They are those scientists and technicians who formulate the general lines of what the rest of the mental labourers have to further develop and give specific form.[140]

The bridge between science and capital, that is, between scientists and the class-content of the natural sciences and techniques they produce, is then given by *internalisation*. In order to pursue capital's two aforementioned aims (the increase in productivity and the subjugation of labour), in other words, in order to conceive, plan, and direct the production of knowledge

---

[139] Noble 1978.

[140] This type of mental production is either carried out by business as 'in-house' research or as a business in itself. Universities too increasingly adopt a more commercial approach to their research by seeking research-contracts with industry, by patenting inventions, by licensing technologies, by forming joint-ventures with the business-world and by offering training courses for industry. Governments also shift funds to research of more strategic value to business.

with a specific pro-capital, social, class-content, the intellectual representatives must internalise capital's aims as their own aims and pursue them either
consciously or not. An example of an unconscious internalisation of capital's
aims is the internalisation and thus perception of a view of capitalism as the
economic and social system most consonant with human nature and of capitalism's expansion and domination as if they were the road towards progress.
It is on this basis that these mental labourers represent and realise capital's
interests by posing and solving problems which they perceive as obstacles on
the road to progress. Since the development of capitalism is identified with
the course of progress, any new theory or technique which makes possible the
further development of capitalism is perceived as a further step in scientific
progress, and this might just as well be the basic motive and satisfaction
behind those natural scientists' mental production. The motivation for natural
scientists may be their personal 'dreams', but these latter arise from a culture
which at the same time also draws the limits of what is perceived to be desir-
able. Selection, recruitment and training of mental labourers with the 'right
attitude', that is, willing to allow their unique behaviour as concrete individuals to be moulded and standardised, can be an important preliminary for the
production of the 'right' knowledge. Also, a system of institutions providing
status, monetary and other rewards (or threatening disciplinary measures,
such as unemployment), research-facilities, the prerogatives associated with
professionalisation and technical education, and the ideology of technical
'progress', is needed to stimulate the production by concrete individuals as
intellectual representatives of a type of knowledge which is ultimately consonant with capital's interests. This is how, as Marx puts it forcefully, 'the
accumulation of knowledge and skill, of the general productive forces of the
social brain ... [are] absorbed into capital'.[141]

Notice that this holds also for those scientists and technicians who do not
work directly for capital or who produce their knowledge in isolation from
other scientists:

> when I am active *scientifically*, etc. – when I am engaged in activity which
> I can seldom perform in direct community with others – then I am *social*,

---

[141] Marx 1976a, p. 694. Raniero Panzieri (1961) was the first to bring again to the
fore Marx's emphasis on the class-character of natural sciences and techniques in
post-WWII Italy.

because I am active as a *man*. Not only is the material of my activity given to me as a social product (as is even the language in which the thinker is active): my *own* existence *is* social activity, and therefore that which I make of myself, I make of myself for society and with the consciousness of myself as a social being.[142]

The production of knowledge, then, even if it is the result of a concrete individual's activity, is never disassociated from society because the objective and mental inputs of that activity are socially given and because the concrete individual has been formed through a process of socialisation. The process of internalisation described above is a logical development of what Marx only hints at in the passage above. Examples will be provided shortly.

Second, just as in the case of the objective collective labourer, the mental collective labourer is subjected to the capitalist technical division of labour. This internalisation is necessary for those mental labourers who are the intellectual representatives, who translate capital's interests into scientific questions and answers. It is not strictly necessary for the other mental labourers who compose the rest of the mental collective labourer. The application of the capitalist technical division of labour to the production of knowledge – that is, the fragmentation of the process into a (great) number of different tasks and the recomposition of these different segments into a body of knowledge – is the way the individual labourers who are not the intellectual representatives produce collectively, and possibly without being aware of it, a class-determined knowledge.

Clearly, different models of technical divisions of mental labour are dictated by different types of knowledge to be produced. They need not be strictly Tayloristic. It might be possible or even necessary to delegate a certain measure of independent inventiveness and responsibility to individual labourers or groups (teams) of labourers as, for example, in case of unpredicted turns in the research. The degree of independence and responsibility varies with the nature of the mental labour-process, with the type of capitalist organisation to which it is subjected as a surplus-value-producing process, and with the position of the labourers in the collective production of knowledge. It usually increases with the proximity to those positions where the general features

---

[142] Marx 1971, p. 137.

of the knowledge required are conceived and where the separate elements of knowledge are recomposed (the intellectual representatives' task). Other mental labourers have only a limited, partial, and isolated exposure to the collective process of the production of knowledge because of the technical division of labour within the process of production of knowledge. For them, the internalisation of capital's needs is not a prerequisite. Some, usually in the lower echelons of the hierarchical structure, might contribute to the production of that knowledge even against their will, for example purely because of economic reasons.

To make the argument less abstract, let us provide some examples of the pro-capital class-content of the natural sciences and techniques. A first case in point is medical science which, due to the pharmaceutical industry's economic interests, de-emphasises prevention and alternative medicines and medical techniques. This is the framework within which medical researchers might think of their work as a contribution to the eradication of illnesses. This is not to deny medical sciences' contributions to the welfare of humanity. It is only meant to stress that the general lines of development of these sciences have been drawn by capital's interests and aims, and that a different type of society or a different dominating class could impart a different direction to them. One example could be the development of acupuncture in China. Just to mention one example, as the World Health Organisation reports, 'the proportion of chronic pain relieved by acupuncture is generally in the range 55–85%, which compares favourably with that of potent drugs (morphine helps in 70% of cases)'.[143]

Another example is physics. Hessen's classic study highlighted the social determination and social content of Newton's theory. As I argue in my 1983 work, based on Hessen's 1931 analysis,[144]

> It is Hessen's merit to have shown, in his classical study of Newton's 'Principia', that both the new technological needs and the non-teleological view of science . . . were functional for (determined by) the rise and development of capitalism. Hessen shows very clearly how Newton's work addresses itself to solving those technical problems whose solution was a necessary condition for the development of manufacture and merchant

---

[143] World Health Organisation 2003, subsection 1.2.
[144] Hessen 1931 in Bukharin (ed.) 1931.

capital, and that the solution to those problems (Hessen analyses the three areas of communication, industry, and war) required a new type of science, a science based on the knowledge of causes, that is, a science able to reproduce phenomena experimentally and thus industrially.[145]

Moreover,

since most of these problems were of a mathematical nature, the image used by Newtonian science was that of our planetary system as a huge mechanism. Often the basic features of the determinant instance impress themselves on the determined one (in this case the new natural sciences) translated, as it were, in the language of the latter, that is, in this case as mechanicism. But, as Hessen stresses, the interpretative scheme in the 'Principia' is both mechanicist and religious and these two aspects are inseparable: a mechanism can be set in motion only by external forces, that is, by God. Newton embodies the philosophical view of the English bourgeoisie of his time which waged ideological class struggle in the form of religion (ibid.)....The social effects of Newton's theory consists thus in reinforcing the capitalist production relations not only on the economic level, because it fostered a tremendous growth in the capitalist productive forces, but also on the ideological level because – aside from the legitimation of those relations through the growth of these forces – belief in the existence of God, a belief which is a condition of class domination also under capitalism, seemed now to be grounded in the most advanced form of science.[146]

More recently, Baracca has remarked that

modern science has adopted, applied and developed in extremely efficient ways the fundamental attitude of the relation with nature that characterises capitalist society; in other words, the exploitation of natural resources, the artificial transformation of nature according to the needs of capitalist production, of profit, of the market.[147]

---

[145] Carchedi 1983, pp. 65–7. For another example, that of the social determination of the development of physics and chemistry at the turn of the nineteenth century, the reader is referred to the work of Baracca (in Carchedi 1983, Appendix to Chapter 1).

[146] Carchedi 1983, pp. 66–7.

[147] Baracca 2000, pp. 171–2.

Particularly relevant for the thesis of the class-content of the natural sciences and techniques is the class-content of the *new technologies*. Let us first consider the computer. The computer shares with all other machines three features. First, it increases labour's productivity (either immediately, if applied to objective transformations, or subsequently, if applied to mental transformations when they will be incorporated into computers applied to objective transformations). Second, it increases tendentially de-skilling and thus capital's control over labour. Third, it intermediates relations between people (like the telephone).

In considering the computer's social content, it could be argued that this, as other natural sciences and technique, is a socially neutral form of knowledge and that it is capital's use that determines labour's subjugation. A number of examples could be mentioned. Consider telecommuting. When people work from their homes on their computers, great savings are realised by capital not only on fixed capital (for example, lower costs for office-buildings) but also on variable capital (no medical benefits and no vacation-allowances, higher labour 'flexibility', and so on). Another example is virtual reality. In this case, it is the computer that perceives for and with us. The perception of reality is both extended and restricted to only what can be processed through a computer. Virtual reality might be the first step towards the fusion between humans and machines. Another step in the same direction is given by thought-controlled devices, that is, devices which can be controlled by brain-waves.

> The brain produces electrical signals which are known as electroencephalograms. In the 1960s, it was shown that subjects could modify one type of brain waves known as the alpha rhythm by closing their eyes and relaxing. This is the basis of biofeedback. Electrodes are attached to the subject's scalp and by using relaxation techniques they can be taught to move an on-screen cursor or activate a buzzer.[148]

This is the beginning of a line of research into 'certain types of electronic equipment [which – G. C.] seem to be susceptible to mental intervention'.[149] Researchers hope that, in twenty to fifty years, it will be possible to use these

---

[148] *Financial Times* 1995.
[149] Ibid.

techniques to move, for example, artificial limbs. But the possibility to control human brains through these techniques is the other side of the coin.

These and other similar techniques are so many steps towards the fusion of people and machines, thus creating a *positive* image of Robocop-like 'humans'. Further, they extend the reach of communication, while at the same time restricting both the content of that communication and creating the 'digital divide'. And, finally, they promise an easy and equal access for everybody to an increasing quantity of information, while they foster the increasing concentration of the mass-media and of information-technology in a few hands. All this, it could be argued, concerns the capitalist use of these machines and techniques and it could be avoided if the computer were to be used differently. This is true. The social content of these machines and techniques, however, is quite another story.

First, the computer separates the workers from each other, thus bringing the process of isolation and seclusion one step further. For example, telecommuting increases the extension of communication, but also the separation, between workers. Second, it has been argued that the increasing role played by the computer in the early formative years may allow the acquisition of new skills and forms of knowledge but, at the same time, it may imperil the development of the child's social skills.[150] This contributes to the formation of a collective worker whose individual components, as concrete individuals, lose those social skills which are necessary for them to acquire consciousness of their social position and function. Third, the real, qualitative difference between the social content of the old technologies and the new, computer-based technologies can be more easily grasped if we focus on the precursor of the computer, Turing's machine, first theorised by Turing in 1936. It can replicate the behaviour of any human 'worker' who is following (consciously or not) any fixed, definite decision procedure, whether it involves manipulating numbers, discrete physical objects or well-defined, publicly identifiable environmental conditions.[151] In short, it is 'capable of computing any function a human...can compute'.[152] This machine, then, mimicks the working of the

---

[150] Baran 1995.
[151] Caffentzis 1997, p. 51.
[152] Caffentzis 1997, p. 49.

human brain; it mechanises thinking through programming, a new feature and itself a commodity.[153]

Thus, while old technologies force human functions to adapt to the motion of machines (think of the conveyor-belt), new, computer-based technologies replicate human functions in a machine-like fashion and thus replicate in a machine-like manner both bodily movements and the production of knowledge, including the self-reflexivity of thought (think of robots). The social content of these technologies is that they mechanise human thought, human creativity, and human life itself so that these latter can be replicated (cloned) and better controlled. This mechanisation, as Morris-Suzuki has aptly put it, 'catches only fragments of the original cosmos of meaning'.[154] Consequently, these new technologies make possible the substitution of humans not only by machines (as in previous techniques) but also by *human-like machines*. The ideological ramifications are all-pervasive. These machines *propagate a view of humans as highly skilled machines* and elevate the machine-like mimicking of human functions to the ideal and most complete form of these functions. Since these machines can perform computational tasks that are impossible for humans, they propagate the notion that machines are the most perfect form that can be reached by humans (and by human intellect). In the end, they secrete the notion that *a perfect human is a machine-like human, that is, a machine.*

Incidentally, this is no gloomy picture. It is essential to realise that these attempts by capital to control labour are ultimately self defeating. In spite of the important differences with old, pre-computer-age techniques, the substitution of people with machines, whether human-like or not, undermines the production of value and surplus-value and thus tendentially pushes the capitalist economy towards crises and its own supersession. However, the outcome of this societal and radical change is open ended. But let us return to the main theme.

If the perfect human is a machine, nature is a machine too and thus subject to mechanical reproduction. The mechanical reproduction of human life achieves its greatest success with biotechnology and genetic engineering

---

[153] Kenney submits that, in Marx's time, workers were called machine-minders, something that implied that machines had no mind (Kenney 1997, p. 90). This changes with the Turing-machine which has a mind, even though a mechanised one.

[154] Morris-Suzuki 1997b, p. 69.

(agribusiness, pharmaceutical chemical, medical business, animal and human cloning, and so on). The reason is two-fold. First, as Yoxen aptly puts it, bio-technology views 'nature as programmed matter'.[155] That is, nature becomes a Turing-machine. Second, mechanisation means standardisation of proce-dures and thus of products. In biotechnology, it means the standardisation (through the replication) of biological make-ups. The threat for humanity from human cloning is immense. However, human cloning, while being perhaps the ultimate form of capital's control of labour, shipwrecks against capital's insurmountable contradiction, the need to compete by introducing new tech-nologies and thus by ejecting humans, whether cloned or not, thus inevitably proceeding towards crises and its own supersession. Capital's ultimate dream might be the production of humans without critical potentialities, unable to resist their exploitation and dehumanisation, unable to give a subjective form to capital's tendency towards its own supersession. But capital needs human creativity, which it must appropriate if it has to create new technologies as means for individual capitals to compete.

The concrete form taken by biotechnology and genetic engineering under capitalism is many-shaped and its development uncertain. It might be, for example, human cloning for profit, or the standardisation and patenting of human biological make-ups, or the creation of parts of the human body for sale. Or, it might be the genetically engineered manipulation of our biologi-cal make-up to produce humans moved by fixed and programmable decision procedures (imparted, of course by capital), who (which?) can then by substi-tuted for real humans. Or, it might be some sort of a productivity-enhancing fusion of machines and human life. As King puts it,

> As our understanding of biochemical processes increases, organisms will be used to produce molecular machines as sophisticated as electronic components.... In the longer run, these developments will end the separation between the self-replicated, self-assembled products of organisms, and the mechanical, electronic, and plastic products of human manufacture.[156]

A first step has already been made by the development of protein-based com-puter chips.[157] Or, it might be some sort of mixed form of life, both human

---

[155] Yoxen, quoted in Schiller 1997, p. 114.
[156] King 1997, p. 48.
[157] Davis and Stack (eds.) 1997, p. 138.

and non-human. In 2000, patent EP 380646 was granted by the EU Patent Office to the Australian enterprise Amstrad for the creation of 'chimaeric animals', that is, beings made up of human and animal cells.

These (and other similar) techniques might never become actualised. But this is irrelevant within this context. What counts is that capital, through their scientists, is seriously considering them, that is, they have become part of capital's dream. Its dream is the standardisation and the mechanisation of human life and thought. It is the Turing-machine brought to its perfection. It is, in short, the perfect monstrosity. The social content of this standardisation and mechanisation of human life is that it makes possible the perfect subjugation of life (labour) to capital.[158]

Nowhere is this clearer than in the transhuman and posthuman movements. They should not be taken too seriously. But it is worthwhile pointing out the social content of these 'dreams'. These movements posit that, through the development and use of techniques such as biotechnology, cybernetics, robotics, nanotechnology, and so on, human beings are in a state of transition towards a posthuman condition where our physical and biological limits (and perhaps even death, through cyber-immortality) will be overcome. Humans will be able to 'upgrade' themselves and their offspring by choosing sex, skin-colour, and other features, and more generally by consciously and freely redefining and redesigning themselves.[159] The social content of these and similar possible developments is that, as Rikowski rightly points out, they abstract from the social conditions within which these techniques have developed and thus from the social content of these technologies. If the posthuman society is a prolongation of capitalism, something which seems to be taken for granted by these movements, if it is a different technological world based upon the same social (ownership-) relations, only those forms (techniques) of 'self-expansion' will be allowed that will be functional for capitalism's reproduction. Individuals will be able to choose among *those and only those* forms.

---

[158] 'The capacity to rewrite the "code of life" has been applied to agricultural, food production and plant breeding to produce new strains of plants, new forms of food and new types of fertiliser.... As in other areas of capitalist technological development, these innovations have to be understood not simply as means to increase productivity, but as tools to change social relations.... Harry Cleaver has described how the "Green Revolution" was used to break down forms of rural community resistant to capitalist modernisation.' Dyer-Witheford 1999, p. 222.

[159] Rikowski 2003.

Moreover, just as the organisation of production based on the capitalist technical division of labour first fragments the labour-process in its constituent elements and then recomposes them in order to produce identical and cheaper products and thus, through the production of relative surplus-value, cheaper labour-power, similarly, capitals' need to generate profits implies that genetic engineering seeks the basic elements of life so that they might be recomposed in life-forms which are amenable to be reproduced in identical and cheaper copies (clones). In short, these forms of life would have a built-in biological impoverishment (euphemistically called 'specialisation'). This would bring the capitalist technical division of labour into life itself thus impeding the free and full development of those life-forms. This impossibility would be built into those life-forms themselves. True, biotechnology has therapeutic advantages. But never before have these therapeutic qualities become inextricably intertwined with de-humanising potentials, as is indeed the case today.[160]

9. Trans-epochal and trans-class knowledge

The two most common objections to the thesis of the class-determination and content of science and technology are that it supposedly cannot explain why the science and technique developed in one society and by one class can be used in other societies (the trans-epochal elements of knowledge) and by other classes (the trans-class elements of knowledge).[161]

Consider first the *trans-epochal elements of knowledge*. The principle needed to deal with this question can be found in the *Grundrisse*, for example in the following passage which is an extremely synthetic, yet extraordinarily evocative, rendition of the notion of dialectical determination developed in Chapter 1 of this work:

> In all forms of society there is one specific form of production which predominates over the rest, whose relations thus assign rank and influence

---

[160] Some feminist critiques advance the idea, correctly, that inherent in this project there is the possibility to expropriate women of their reproductive power by creating, for example, artificial wombs (see Heymann 1995). Artificial wombs would be strikingly apt to be produced industrially and could produce life also industrially, possibly for profit.

[161] These issues are dealt with in greater detail in Carchedi 1977, 1983, 1991.

to the others. It is a general illumination which bathes all the other colours and modifies their particularity. It is a particular ether which determines the specific gravity of every being which has materialised within it.[162]

Agriculture is a case in point:

> Among peoples with a settled agriculture…as in antiquity and in the feudal order, even industry, together with its organisation and the forms of property corresponding to it, has a more or less landed-proprietary character; is either completely dependent on it, as among the earlier Romans, or, as in the Middle Ages, imitates, within the city and its relations, the organisation of the land…. In bourgeois society it is the opposite. Agriculture more and more becomes merely a branch of industry, and is entirely dominated by capital.[163]

Agriculture becomes production for profit, it becomes determined by the capitalist ownership-relation (this relation becomes its condition of existence) and become a condition of reproduction of that relation and thus of capitalist society as a whole. *Its class-content changes.* This principle can be applied also to that specific type of social phenomenon that is knowledge, that is, to those elements of knowledge that survive from previous modes of production. The class-content of those elements of knowledge changes as they cross the societal boundaries. But when and why do certain elements of knowledge cross those boundaries and other do not?

The reason why certain forms of social knowledge can exist in different epochs of society's development is that they can be functional for the further-ance of the interests of classes and social groups in different types of societies. However, these elements of knowledge are applicable to different societies because the different social context (social relations) *change their social content,* because they are amenable to become elements furthering the reproduction or supersession of different social relations based on different ownership-relations. In this way, they become determined by that different social context. The trans-epochal nature of these elements of knowledge is explained not in spite of, but thanks to, their social determination. Gramsci reached similar conclusions in 1930:

---

[162] Marx 1973a, pp. 106–7.
[163] Marx 1973a, p. 107.

In the study of the superstructures, science occupies a privileged position since its reaction on the structure has a character of major extension and continuity of development, especially from 1700 onwards, when science obtained a position on its own in the public esteem. That science is a superstructure is also demonstrated by the fact that it has had whole periods of eclipse, obscured as it was by another dominant ideology, religion, which claimed that it had absorbed science itself; thus the science and technology of the Arabs seemed pure witchcraft to the Christians. Science never appears as a naked objective notion; it always appears in the trappings of an ideology. In concrete terms, science is the union of the objective fact with a hypothesis or system of hypotheses which go beyond the mere objective fact. It is true however that in this field it has become relatively easy to distinguish the objective notion from the system of hypotheses by means of a process of abstraction that is inherent in scientific methodology itself, in such a way that one can appropriate the one while rejecting the other. In this way one class can appropriate the science of another class without accepting its ideology. This is why one social group can appropriate the science of another group without accepting its ideology.[164]

Let us provide an example, the notion of the number 'one'.[165] For the ancient Greeks, 'one' was not a number. Since 'one' generates both odd and even numbers, they argued, it must stand above this dichotomy and thus cannot be a number. But it can also be argued, as it is indeed nowadays, that precisely because 'one' generates both odd and even numbers it must itself be a number. As Bloor remarks, both lines of argument are internally consistent. For the ancient Greeks, the world was a well-ordered arrangement of things. The order of numbers, then, was a succession of discrete entities. It was then natural to conceive of numbers as *numbers of some things*, as discrete, concrete, numbers that could be ordered and counted. Given their discrete nature, numbers could be represented as dots and thus ordered in triangular, square, or other shapes. Accordingly, the Greeks developed the notion of

---

[164] Gramsci 1975b, Q 4, §7; cf. Q 11, §38; written in May 1930. I thank Peter Thomas for having brought this passage to my attention. For a further analysis see Thomas 2009.

[165] What follows has been taken from Carchedi 1983, pp. 16–20, which in its turn relies on Bloor 1976 and Klein 1968. Carchedi 1983 provides also the example of the class-determination of the notion of inertia (pp. 27 and ff).

shaped numbers (for example, triangular). Numbers had 'visible and tangible bodies'. Moreover, since numbers could be ordered, their position revealed their being and nature, things had arithmetical properties and these properties concerned the being of things. The classification of numbers was then a means to grasp the meaning of life. In this view, a number's relation to its prior or posterior concerned not only its being but also the order of its being. Within this context, an abstract idea of numbers was incompatible with the ancient Greeks' ontology. Accordingly, the unknown solution to a specific problem was a specific number to be determined, not a variable.[166]

The modern interpretation of 'one' arises in the sixteenth century, the birth of capitalism, through the work of Simon Stevin, the Dutch mathematician. With the advent of capitalism, numbers came to perform a new function by indicating the properties of moving, active processes of change. For example, number and measurement became 'central to an intellectual grasp of ballistic, navigation and the use of machinery'.[167] The point is not only that Stevin was an engineer and that he was interested in applied mathematics and in the solution of practical problems. His theoretical preoccupations were also those upon which the development of capitalism depended. But this required the search for general relations, which, in turn, required that numbers had to become abstract numbers, separated from the things they measure. This implies that numbers be likened to a continuous straight line of homogeneous entities, rather than to a succession of discontinuous and heterogeneous dots. If the whole is homogeneous, its constituent parts (numbers) must all have the same nature and, therefore, one must also be a number. There is thus a connection between the development of capitalism, of sixteenth-century technology, of symbolic algebra, and of the notion that one is a number. Capitalism required a new notion of the number 'one'. Or, this notion, as well as the notion of numbers in general, survived the advent of capitalism only because it could become an element of a view of reality with a mutated social, class-content.

Consider next the *trans-class elements of knowledge*. Up to here, the class-content of natural sciences and techniques has been analysed as if it were functional only for the realisation of capital's aims and interests. This was

---

[166] Bloor 1976, p. 106.
[167] Bloor 1976, p. 104.

necessary to rebut the thesis of the neutrality of science. But this is only half the story. If science and technique are developed by the collective mental labourer and, to begin with, by the intellectual representatives within it, they are the outcome of neither the capitalists nor the labourers in isolation from society but *by* mental labourers *for* capital. *They are thus inherently contradictory,* just as the production and ownership-relations from which they emanate, are inherently contradictory and just as all other social phenomena are internally contradictory (see Chapter 1). If the producers of knowledge were the capitalists, they would produce a knowledge with only a pro-capital class-content. If they were labourers free from capital, they would produce a knowledge with only a pro-labour content. But, since the producers of knowledge are labourers working for capital (and the same applies to mental labourers, like scientists working independently within a capitalist context as argued above), they are socialised within a web of contradictory social relations and thus produce a knowledge which can be functional both for capital's domination and for labour's resistance against that domination. The specific way concrete mental labourers (and, to begin with, the intellectual representatives) produce this internally contradictory knowledge is that, by internalising a myriad of internally contradictory social phenomena in the course of their life, they internalise not only the needs and rationality of capital, but also those of labour in various ways and mixes and in various concrete and specific manifestations and forms of knowledge. As argued above, these social phenomena are reduced to a potential state in the concrete individuals' consciousnesses and can emerge again as social phenomena, in a transmuted form, in this case as knowledge, if these forms of knowledge are accepted by a number of people sufficiently large to ensure that knowledge's reproduction, irrespective of who adheres to it or not (according to the principle of substitutability). This explains a number of important features. It explains the possibility for some of these mental products to be used in a period of transition, by different classes, as we shall see in the next section. It explains also why mental labour can produce different types of sciences and techniques with different class-contents. It explains, finally, that capital's aims can be internalised *as if* they were the aims of labour as well. Capital can displace the terrain of conflict from capital versus labour to within labour itself.

Let us recall from Section 3 above that a mental transformation is the transformation of knowledge, the transformation by the mental labourers' labour-power of the knowledge contained in the mental labourers' labour-power (self-transformation) as well as of objective knowledge, such as the knowledge contained in the objective means of mental transformation. That section, however, did not consider the class-content of knowledge, the double and contradictory nature of knowledge in terms of class-rationality, that is, capital's rationality and labour's rationality. Given that capital and labour are the subjective and collective personifications of the tendency the capitalist system has towards its reproduction (in the case of capital), and at the same time towards its supersession (in the case of labour), and thus of the personification of the resistance against capital's rule, knowledge can be functional for capital's domination over labour as well as for labour's resistance against that domination. The specificity of knowledge, which also includes natural sciences and technique, whether in its fluid state as a process of self-transformation or as settled in the objective means of mental transformation, is revealed by the fact that its many specific forms of manifestation are so many concretisations of three different types of class-content.

i) One kind of knowledge has been conceived by mental labourers (who are, in this case, capital's intellectual representatives within the production of knowledge) to be used *only by capital* (for example, Taylorism or, more generally, management-techniques) and *for capital*. In this circumstance, it is capital (or those who perform the function of capital in the production of knowledge) that decides which knowledge to produce, for whom (capital itself), and how (with which techniques). The specificity of the production of this type of knowledge is that, in it, capital's rationality (based on exploitation, inequality and egoism) has been perceived, consciously or not, to be only positive and labour's rationality (based on co-operation, solidarity, and equality) as only negative, something to be avoided. This knowledge has been produced by labour, but can only be used to oppress labour (that is, used by capital) and thus cannot be used creatively. Labour cannot use its own rationality in the creation of this knowledge and this rationality is not allowed to manifest itself, that is, this knowledge cannot be used to resist capital's domination. This knowledge's class-nature forbids its use by labour. Those individuals who use this knowledge become carriers of capital's rationality (they become agents of capital), independently of whether they are the owners of the means of production or not, independently of whether they are objectively labourers or not.

ii) Another kind of knowledge has been conceived by mental labourers to be used only *by labour for labour*. Here, it is labour that decides which type of knowledge to produce, for whom (labour itself) and how. This is the case, for example, of a theory or system of competition among workers, but on the basis of mutual help, that is, in which those who can perform a certain task better teach and help the other to perform equally well, or, in which all improve their own condition together with, rather than at the expense of, the other.[168] Its specificity is that, in its production, capital's rationality has been seen as only negative and labour's rationality as only positive. This knowledge's class-nature forbids its use by capital. Thus, those individuals who use this knowledge become carriers of labour's rationality independently of their class-position. This type of knowledge goes beyond capitalist (production-) relations and is a prefiguration of a socialist form of knowledge.

iii) Finally, there is a kind of knowledge that has been conceived by mental labourers to be used *both by capital and by labour and to the advantage of both capital and labour*. This knowledge has been produced under capitalist production-relations, that is, in its production it has been capital that has decided what type of knowledge to produce, for whom, and how. This knowledge, thus, can be used by capital to dominate labour. However, the rationality of labour, based on co-operation, solidarity and equality, plays an important role in its conception, even though it is subordinated to capital's rationality in the sense that it is permeated, penetrated and shaped by it. Labour's rationality can reveal itself, and thus can be used by labour to resist capital's domination, but only in the forms and within the limits mentioned above. This knowledge *contributes to reproduce capital and its rationality even when it is used by labour to resist capital's domination*. This explains why and how this knowledge, which has been conceived by labour for capital, can be used by labour to resist capital's domination and why and how this use by labour cannot cancel this knowledge's capitalist nature and thus contributes at the same time to the reproduction of capital's domination upon labour. Its use by labour has this double and contradictory effect. This knowledge, thus, has a double and contradictory class-nature and thus a double and contradictory effect for labour's struggle against capital. The possibility of its being used by both classes is not

---

[168] It is thus incorrect to hold that, in a socialist system, there would be no competition and no creativity.

due to its class-neutrality. On the contrary, the possibility of its being used by both classes is due precisely to its class-character, to its being the product of two opposite rationalities of which one dominates the other. This is that type of knowledge that is erroneously thought to be class-neutral, simply because of its being used by both classes.

At this point, the question arises as to why capital should allow labour to conceive and apply a type of science that fosters capital's domination, but also, simultaneously, allows labour to resist that domination (even though this resistance is shaped by capital itself), while it is nevertheless possible to develop a knowledge, that of the first type, that excludes labour's use to resist its domination by capital. The point is that the first type of knowledge, if it can be used only by capital, can be used only to dominate (and thus exploit) labour rather than to stimulate labour to create new and ever greater quantities of use-values. The use of this type of knowledge stifles labour's creativity rather than stimulating it. However, capital needs labour's creativity above all because of technological competition, which is the motor of capital's dynamism, and which requires the development of the sciences and technologies that can be applied to the labour-process. Labour's creativity, thus, must be stimulated but, as seen above, only in the forms and within the limits imposed by capital. Basically, only that type of science and technique is stimulated that can lead directly or indirectly to the reproduction of capitalism.

This third category of knowledge is probably by far the most common. It is this category, and in particular, as it concerns the natural sciences and techniques, that is mistaken as being class-neutral due to their uses by different classes. But there are no class-neutral natural sciences and techniques, nor are there, more generally, class-neutral social phenomena. Their use by different classes and their contradictory effects in terms of class-struggle can and should be explained in terms of their class-determination and content rather than in terms of their class-neutrality. The notion of the class-determined nature of natural sciences and techniques took time before it finally emerged. In discussing the Luddites, Marx states: 'it took time and experience before the workers learnt to distinguish between machinery and its employment by capital, and transfer their attacks from the material instruments of production to the form of society which utilises these instruments'.[169] The realisation of

---

[169] Marx 1976a, p. 554.

the class-content of machines marked a leap forward for the maturity of the early nineteenth-century English working class. The contemporary working class, or collective objective and mental labourer, by ignoring or even denying the class-determination of machines and more generally of science and technique, has made a giant leap backwards in its collective maturity, something which is bound to have grave repercussions for its struggle against capital.

To conclude this section, an example will be provided of an element of knowledge that is both trans-epochal and trans-class: the notion of time.[170] Our perception of time is determined by the type of society in which we live. Previous societies' concept of time was cyclical – that is, tied to nature's cycles, as the succession of days, seasons, and years – and concrete, or qualitative, that is, tied to the specific tasks pertaining to the different parts of the day, of the week, of the month, of the season, and of the year. Whether constituted by hunters or land-tillers, those societies were strictly tied to these and other recurrent and specific events. While hunting societies were regulated by biological events, agricultural societies found in the constellation of planets and stars their reference-points to compute time. If the notion of the clock had existed, nature would have been their clock.[171] Under capitalism, on the other hand, time has become linear – that is, proceeding from past through the present to a future which is not a repetition of the past, as if flowing along a straight line – and abstract, that is, quantitative because time-periods are no longer associated with specific activities: any activity can be performed during any period of time.[172] Time is thus divisible into increasingly small parts. It is only within this notion of time that the concept of progress could arise, something unthinkable within traditional religions and world-views which stress the cyclical repetition of history. The future is no longer fixed in advance and a repetition of the past but rather is open-ended.

Of fundamental importance for the emergence of this new perception of time was the clock. The clock splits time into hours, minutes, seconds and fractions of seconds. The mechanical clock was introduced by the Benedictine

---

[170] Much of what follows on this point has been received from Rifkin 1989.

[171] Rifkin 1989, pp. 64–5.

[172] It has been argued that the notion of concrete time is abstract too, because it is the result of human abstraction. This is trivially true. But concrete vs. abstract here refers to time to be spent for specific activities versus time which can be spent on any activity.

order in the seventh century after Christ. The Benedictines differed from other religious orders, in that they were expected to pray and pursue religious activities every moment of the day. Time was scarce and could not be wasted. There was a time to pray, a time to eat, a time to bathe, a time to work and a time to sleep. The Benedictines re-introduced the hour as a unit of time (as a unit of time the hour was little used in medieval society). Every activity was tied to a specific hour. For example, the first four hours of the day were reserved for the necessary activities. The following two hours were devoted to reading, and so on. This could be interpreted as if the modern notion of time already existed in the Benedictine monasteries. But these hours were still hours of concrete time: each hour was to be used only for a specific task. Under capitalism, it has become irrelevant which specific activities are carried out in which specific hours: time has become abstract.

It is within this context that the clock was discovered. It is because it introduced a mechanical rhythm in daily life that the clock could be used later on under capitalism, when the rhythm of the machines began informing people's daily work and life. Marx's notion of abstract labour, an idea which emerges in the capitalist system, that is, the expenditure of human energy irrespective of the specific labour carried out, finds its corresponding notion in the notion of abstract time. It is not by chance that the clock achieved regularity of movement and precision only after Galileo discovered pendular motion in 1649, whose practical applications for the clock were perfected by Huygens in 1656. Minutes and seconds become part of daily experience when they appeared on the dial of the mechanical clock. The social content of this notion of time and thus of the clock, that is, their functionality for the reproduction of the capitalist economy and society, can now be discerned. The increasingly complex commercial and industrial activities could now be profitably organised thanks to a restructuring of the day in abstract time units so that each activity, no matter which, could be squeezed in increasingly smaller units of time, just like money. Time became money. The economy had become an economy of time too. People's lives, and to begin with the working people's lives, began to be ruled by the rhythm of the mechanical clock first and then by the machines, whose rhythm was as regular as that of the clock. The biological and cosmic notions of time had been replaced by the formal and empty ticking of the clock.

But this notion of time at least referred to periods which could still be experienced. The computer introduces units of time which cannot be experienced any longer, nanoseconds, that is, billionths of a second. This notion of time is unrelated to human experience and can be 'perceived' and counted only by machines (nanoseconds). As was submitted above, the social content of this notion is characterised by the introduction of a new ideal of perfection, a machine-like human or a human-like machine able to perceive time just as a computer can. Whatever remains of human life is standardised, impoverished, suitable to manipulation through genetic engineering and, ultimately, completely and irrevocably subjected to capital. This is the potential inherent in the contemporary development of the natural sciences and techniques.

Even the last residue of the cyclical notion of time, the dial in which the two hands make a recurrent complete revolution every 12 hours, has been replaced by digital clocks and watches indicating only the present time which can be read as numbers. Any reference to the past and to the future is erased in the digital watch. Only the present exists. At the same time, the ticking of the mechanical clock is now being replaced by the pulse of the electronic watch. As Rifkin rightly remarks, the digital clock is a fitting metaphor for a society in which the past and the future exist only functionally for the present: the past is a collection of information which can be retrieved from data banks and the future is any of the many possible combinations of those bits of information. The future is not the realisation of what is potentially present in realised reality but is the recombination of elements of already realised reality. The universe is not seen any more as an immense clock, as in the Newtonian tradition, but is now perceived by many scientists as a sort of immense self-developing information-system, a sort of gigantic computer. Life itself is now perceived as a code of billions of information bytes which can be re-arranged at will for the purpose of producing new life forms. These are the cultural roots of genetic engineering.

Thus, due to social phenomena's inner contradictoriness, this notion of time can be incorporated into conceptualisations functional both for capitalist domination and for resisting that domination. But, even in this latter case, resistance against that domination depends concurrently on a notion of time functional for the continuation of that domination. Labour is forced to use this notion of time to resist capital's domination, but, at the same time, it uses a notion determined by capital and with a pro-capital class-content, therefore simultaneously reproducing and displacing capital's rule over labour.

10. **Knowledge and transition**

The question of the use of the productive forces developed under capitalism for the struggle for socialism and for the period of transition is of paramount importance. The thesis of the class-neutrality of knowledge regarding the natural sciences and techniques and consequently the organisation of the labour-process as well, has had disastrous consequences for the struggle for socialism. For example, this thesis was an important ideological element in the restoration of capital's rule in the factories and working places in post-WWII Italy, a restoration favoured by the Italian Communist Party (PCI). As Steve Wright notes, 'True children of the Comintern, for whom the organisation and form of production were essentially neutral in class terms, the PCI leadership saw no great problem in conceding – in the name of a "unitary"' economic reconstruction – the restoration of managerial prerogative within the factories.'[173] This belief had deep theoretical roots. Both Lenin and Gramsci subscribed to the neutrality-thesis. This made it possible for the former to theorise the socialist use of Taylorism[174] and for the latter to theorise the use of coercion in the labour-process,[175] that is, the extension of the proletarian condition under capitalism to the whole society rather than the supersession of that condition.[176] As Kicillof and Starosta point out, 'the true critique of the crude materialism of orthodox Marxism does not consist in giving primacy to social relations over productive forces (the common "Western"-Marxist critique), but in grasping the essentiality of the latter in their qualitative historical specificity'.[177] In the present work, the primacy of social relations (their determinant role) and the historical specificity of the productive forces (their class-character) are two sides of the same coin, because the class-content of the latter derives from the class-content of the former.

---

[173] Wright 2002, p. 9.
[174] Lenin 1968, pp. 594–5; 1964, pp. 152–4; 1965, pp. 235–77; and 1969, pp. 68–84.
[175] Gramsci 1971, p. 301.
[176] Gramsci 1975a, p. 412. See also Linhart 1976.
[177] Kicillof and Starosta 2007a, p. 15.

On the basis of the analysis of the class-nature of science and technique, it follows that, in a transition-period, it is of the utmost importance to distinguish those elements of knowledge (especially of the natural sciences and techniques) that can express only capital's rationality from those expressing only labour's rationality and from those expressing both types of rationality. The first should be abandoned immediately, the second should be strengthened to the maximum and the third, whose use will be necessary for a period, can be used to foster labour's rationality. However, labour should be conscious that their pro-capital nature keeps operating even when used by labour to resist and weaken capital's domination, that this pro-capital nature is still present as a negative factor slowing down the progress towards socialism. Ultimately, this type of knowledge should be replaced by a knowledge developed by labour, to be used by labour, for labour.

A radically different type of natural science and technique will originate only from a radically different type of society, based on different production-relations. Both Marx's theory and the past and present struggles of the international collective labourer indicate that these would be egalitarian production-relations, in the sense that each and everybody would have the same chances to realise their potentialities to the fullest. It is, of course, impossible currently to prefigure what these new types of science and technique will be, even if the radical-science movement of the 1970s offers some indications.[178] Competition generates inequality, while egalitarianism implies co-operation and self-management because this is the only real basis for freedom. Egalitarianism, co-operation, and self-management are the conditions for a free association of producers who themselves decide what to produce, for whom, why and how. It implies the abolition of production for profit and its replacement by an economy based on the production of use-values for the satisfaction of human needs, as defined by the producers themselves. This society implies also a different concept of human nature. While the notion fostered by capitalism pushes 'specialisation' to its extreme and makes of people caricatures of themselves, the alternative, egalitarian, notion stands for the largest possible development of the individual, for the unfolding of all the facets of the indi-

---

[178] In the 1970s, the radical-science movement in many countries engaged in the critique of existing science and technology while intertwining with a variety of other social movements. See Werskey 1975. In its short life, this movement could only produce a preview of some radically different types of science and technique.

vidual's personality together with, rather than at the cost of, everybody else. This thesis has been challenged on a variety of grounds. Let us mention four of them.[179]

First, there is the question of the presumed impossibility to achieve a different, egalitarian division of labour. This objection rests on a carefully cultivated and endlessly repeated misunderstanding: the impossibility, it is said, for everybody to be able to do everything.[180] However, the question is not the abolition of any form of technical division of labour. Rather, the question is how to restructure the division of labour in such a way that all positions (jobs) are 'balanced' in the specific sense that they all, while requiring different tasks, offer roughly the same possibility for self-realisation (including a balanced 'mix' between objective and mental labour).[181] This new structure of positions should be complemented by their flexible nature (the internal composition of positions should be changed whenever the exigencies of the individuals so require) and by the possibility for individuals to move from one position to another (again, whenever the exigencies of the individuals so require). Maximum possible balancing within positions, flexibility of positions, and rotation among positions should be the *three basic principles of an egalitarian technical division of labour*. This implies constant re-qualification of labour. It is on this basis that first the new techniques and then new natural sciences can be developed.

Second, it is argued that if 'specialisation' enhances 'productivity', less specialisation also implies less production and productivity. The question then would become one of a trade-off between production, productivity and specialisation, on the one hand, and human self-realisation on the other. But it is just the opposite that is true. Productivity will increase if the producers are really in charge of their own lives rather than having to be either forced or convinced to do unrewarding and alienating jobs. Moreover, as far as production is concerned, an egalitarian society would do away with the gigantic

---

[179] For a refutation of other tangentially similar objections, see Mobasser 1987.
[180] In observing that nearly a decade after the fall of 'Communism' no 'Western style' capitalism has been created in the former 'Communist' countries, A. Greenspan, a former Chairman of the Fed, discovered that 'much of what we took for granted in our free market system and assumed to be human nature was not nature at all, but culture' (Hoagland, 1997). What, for a first-year sociology-student, is a plain fact, becomes, for the neoclassical economist, a revelation.
[181] See Albert and Hahnel 1981, 1991a, 1991b.

waste inherent in the capitalist mode of production, for example, in advertising, in the production of weapons, in economic crises and unemployment, in the public and private institutions of repression, and in speculative activities. This would free up sufficient labour-power and time for the production of a quantity of use-values adequate for all to satisfy their socially determined needs.

Third, it is also argued that specialisation enhances the possibilities for human self-realisation. For example, Taylor, the father of 'scientific management', submitted that

> the frontiersman had to be not only a surgeon, but also an architect, house-builder, lumberman, farmer, soldier, and doctor, and he had to settle his law cases with a gun. You would hardly say that the life of the modern surgeon is any more narrowing, or that he is more of a wooden man than the frontiersman. The many problems to be met and solved by the surgeon are just as intricate and difficult and as developing and broadening in their way as those of the frontiersman.[182]

In this example, the task of the surgeon has indeed replaced all other activities, but, at the same time, it has been greatly expanded, not narrowed. The Tayloristic division of labour, on the other hand, implies that the surgeon would be reduced to, say, manning a machine which has incorporated the surgeon's qualities so that the surgeon would have been reduced to an unskilled labourer performing a disqualified, repetitive task. Moreover, there is absolutely no reason why, in an egalitarian society, the surgeon could not perform also (some of) these other duties, with the exclusion of course of settling his law cases with a gun. More generally, under capitalism, as opposed to an egalitarian society, specialisation is time-saving but, aside from counter-tendencies, the extra free time is used neither to reduce the working day nor to increase the possibilities for self-realisation of those operating those machines.[183]

---

[182] Taylor 1985, pp. 125, 126.

[183] In considering whether the working day has been shortened or not, it is the collective labourer on a global scale (with situations in the Third World reminiscent of the English Industrial Revolution) which should be considered, rather than only the labourers of the developed capitalist countries.

Fourth, the critics submit, undesired tasks will always exist, also in an egalitarian society. Thus, it will always be necessary to force somebody to perform those tasks, even if on a rotation-basis. The answer resides not only in the above principles of balanced positions and flexibility of positions, whereby it is on this basis that rotation can be meaningful for an egalitarian society. It resides also on a type of social interaction, to begin with at the level of production, based on altruism, as opposed to the egoism inherent in the capitalist production-relations.

In conclusion, it is possible to argue that, for Marx, 'another world' is a socio-economic system based on co-operation (solidarity), egalitarianism, and self-management in planning, allocation, production, distribution, and consumption in harmony with nature. The specific forms of this radically alternative system cannot be forecast. They will emerge from each country's specific history, including the history of its struggle to move from a capitalist society to an egalitarian one. However, just as there are general principles of capitalism which apply to all specific capitalist countries, so there are general principles which should apply to all egalitarian countries. If labour does not use this compass, it will never achieve its liberation from capital. Faced with these questions, labour needs answers; it needs them badly and it needs them sooner rather than later. But to get the right answers it must ask the right questions. To this end, it would do well to revert to Marx's epistemology and value-theory and develop them rather than denying them in a constant but vain pursuance of ever new fads.

Appendix One
The Building Blocks of Society

A social phenomenon can be symbolised as

(α) A = {A^r, A^p} and, similarly, a different social phenomenon can be symbolised as {B^r, B^p}

where the curly brackets indicate unity and the superscripts refer to the realised and the potential state.

Three points follow. First, {A^r, A^p} indicates the *unity of identity and difference*. A^r is identical to itself but also different from itself, as A^p. {A^r, A^p} is the synthetic rendition of the 'affirmative recognition of the existing state of things [and] at the same time, also the recognition of the negation of that state' (*Capital*, Volume I, quoted in Zelený 1980, p. 87). It is only by considering the realm of potentialities that the otherwise mysterious unity of identity and difference makes sense. Second, {A^r, A^p} indicates also the *unity of opposites*, inasmuch as the potential features of a phenomenon are opposite (contradictory) to its realised aspects. Third, {A^r, A^p} indicates the *unity of essence and appearance* (the form of the manifestation of the essence): A^p is the essence of A, that which can manifest itself in a number of different realisations, while A^r is its (temporary and contingent) appearance, the form taken by one of the possibilities inherent in A's potential nature. Notice however, that

274 • Appendix One

the essence is not immutable but subject to continuous change. Notice also the temporal dimension: at a certain moment, A^r contains within itself A^p and *subsequently* A^p manifest itself as (a different) A^r. The realised phenomenon is temporally prior to the realisation of the potential one. This first principle, then, contains within itself a *temporal dimension*.

On this basis, we can consider mutual determination. Take two phenomena, A and B. Let => symbolise determination and let the direction of the arrow indicate which is the active and which the passive element in that relation. Consequently, when two phenomena are given, A and B, A => B indicates that A is the determinant and B the determined phenomenon, that is, A is the realised condition of existence B and transfers its contradictory social content to B. Let A <= B symbolise the determination of A by B, that is, B is the realised condition of reproduction or supersession of A because its social content, which it received from A, reacts upon A's social content, thus reproducing A or superseding it. Therefore, the relation of mutual determination is indicated by A <=> B. Given that there is a temporal difference between A => B and A <= B, the relation of mutual determination becomes

(β) A^{t_1} <=> B^{t_2}

where the superscripts t1 and t2 indicate two points in time. The time-dimension is essential. At t1, A determines B. At t2, B determines A. Dialectical determination takes place within a temporal setting. Given that A is {A^r, A^p} and B is {B^r, B^p}, if we substitute (α) into (β) we have

(γ) {A^r, A^p}^{t_1} <=> {B^r, B^p}^{t_2}.

Two points should be stressed. First, due to the action of B on A, A can reproduce itself but it does so *in a changed form* and not at t2 (even less at t1) but at a subsequent point in time, t3. Thus, if A reproduces itself, {A^r, A^p}^{t_1} ≠ {A^r, A^p}^{t_3}. After the mutual determination has taken place, the process starts again with {A^r, A^p}^{t_3} <=> {B^r, B^p}^{t_4}. Second, at t1, before its realisation at t2, B^r is contained in A^r as one of the many possible A^p. At t2, one of the many possible A^p becomes realised as B^r and this B^r contains within itself a range of B^p. The new B^r and the new B^p form a new unity, {B^r, B^p}^{t_2}. It is this new unity, {B^r, B^p}^{t_2}, that is a condition of reproduction or supersession of {A^r, A^p}^{t_3}. The typical example is capital that calls into existence labour as the condition of reproduction or of the supersession of capital.

Up until this point, we have considered social phenomena. We shall now also consider individual phenomena. If <=> indicates reciprocal determination as in relation (γ)

Concrete individuals <=> individual phenomena
Abstract individuals <=> social phenomena

If B^i indicates the individual phenomenon as a potential social phenomenon, a formless potential social phenomenon, relation (γ) above becomes

(δ) $\{A^r, A^p\}^{t_1} <=> \{B^r, B^p, B^i\}^{t_2}$.

This relation expresses the relation between social phenomena both as determinant and determined, both as realised and as potential, both as emerging from social phenomena and from individual phenomena. Relation (δ) is the *most concise rendition of dialectical determination* in social reality. It represents *from a dialectical, class-, perspective* the *building block of society*, the cell out of which the constantly changing social structure is made. This is in line with the commodity being 'the economic cell-form" of bourgeois society (Marx, 1976a, p. 90). The commodity is a specific instance of the general cell-form as in relation (δ) given above. The former is contained in the latter.

Appendix Two
Objective and Mental Labour-Processes

Define

O^T = objective transformations

M^O = means of objective transformations

O^O = objects of objective transformations

L^O = labour-power's capacity to transform objective reality

and

M^T = mental transformations, or transformtions of knowledge

K^S = subjective knowledge

K^O = objective knowledge

L^K = labour-power's capacity to transform knowledge

Then,

(1) $O^T = (L^O \to M^O, O^O)$

(2) $M^T = (L^K \to K^S, K^O)$

where $\to$ indicates labour-power's transformative action; the parentheses indicate unity in transformation; and M^T is both observation and conception. The outcome of M^T is the new knowledge produced. Thus, relation (1) says that an objective transformation is the transformation of the objects and of the means of objective transformation by labour-power. Similarly, relation (2) says that a mental transformation, whose outcome is new knowledge, is the transformation by labour-power of the knowledge which is an element of the individual labourer's labour-power (subjective knowledge) and of that contained in the other labourers' labour-power and in objective means of mental transformation (objective knowledge).

Transformations are combined in labour, both objective and mental. Then, if => indicates determination, so that the element to the left of the arrow is the determinant element and that to the right the determined one and if the curly brackets indicate unity in determination

(3) $OLP = \{O^T => M^T\} = P^O$

(4) $MLP = \{M^T => O^T\} = P^K$

Relation (3) says that an objective labour-process (OLP) is the unity in determination of objective transformations (determinant) and mental transformations (determined) whose outcome is an output in which the objective aspect is determinant relative to the knowledge contained in it (P^O). Relation (4) says that a mental labour-process (MLP) is the unity in determination of mental transformations (determinant) and objective transformations (determined) whose outcome is an output in which the objective aspect is determined by the knowledge contained in it (P^K). Some mental labour-processes, like a concert, do not need a material shell.

If relations (1) and (2) are inserted in relations (3) and (4), we obtain

(5) $OLP = \{O^T => M^T\} = \{(L^O \rightarrow M^O, O^O) => (L^K \rightarrow K^S, K^O)\} = P^o$

(6) $MLP = \{M^T => O^T\} = \{(L^K \rightarrow K^S, K^O) => (L^O \rightarrow M^O, O^O)\} = P^K$.

Relations (5) and (6) become *the most concise representation of the production of individual knowledge both for an objective labour-process* and *for a mental labour-process.*

Appendix Three

Marx's Mathematical Manuscripts[1]

Further validation for the view of dialectics submitted in Chapter 1 can be found in Marx's Mathematical Manuscripts.

Usually, commentators focus on the Mathematical Manuscripts in order to inquire into Marx's own method of differential calculus from the perspective of the history of mathematics.[2] One of the questions raised by the commentators is why Marx embarked on such a study. As is well known, Marx was motivated explicitly by his interest in calculus because he recognised that his knowledge of it was insufficient for his elaborations of the principles of economics. Alcouffe holds that Marx liked mathematics as such because of its 'rigor and intellectual gymnastics'[3] and that the recreational, playful and philosophical aspects of mathematics were, for him at least, as important as his preoccupation with economics. On the other hand, Yanovskaya, the most important commentator of the Manuscripts, remarks that the

---

[1] This Appendix is a modified version of Carchedi 2008a and of Carchedi 2008c. These two previous versions have benefited from comments by Hans van den Bergh, professor of mathematics at the University of Wageningen, by Joseph Dauben, Distinguished Professor of History and History of Science, The City University of New York, and by Alain Alcouffe, Professor of Social Sciences, Toulouse University. The usual caveat applies. See also Carchedi 2008b.

[2] See Alcouffe 1985 and 2001; Antonova 2006; Blunden 1984; Engels 1983 and 1987; Gerdes 1985; Yanovskaya 1969 and 1983; Kennedy 1977; Lombardo Radice 1972; Smolinski 1973.

[3] Alcouffe 1985, pp. 40–1.

Manuscripts offer no answer as to what prompted Marx to move from the pursuit of algebra and commercial arithmetic to that of differential calculus.[4] Marx was probably stimulated by more than one interest so that Alcouffe's thesis does no necessarily exclude Marx explicitly stated reason. But there might be yet another reason, a more philosophical one. As will be seen below, Marx's critique of differential calculus and the development of his own method of differentiation focus on the *ontological nature of the infinitesimals*. The thesis of this Appendix is that Marx, in studying differential calculus, was seeking both support and material for the further development of his method of social analysis. Seen from this angle, the Manuscripts are vastly more significant for the social scientist than for the mathematician or for the historian of mathematics.

The first evidence of Marx's interest in mathematics is contained in a letter to Engels from 1858 in which he wrote: 'In working out economic principles I have been so damned delayed by mistakes in computation that out of despair I have begun again a quick review of algebra. Arithmetic was always foreign to me. By the algebraic detour I am shooting rapidly ahead again.'[5] In 1863, he wrote again to Engels: 'In my free time I do differential and integral calculus.'[6] Most interestingly, in another letter to Engels ten years later (1873), he provides an example of what economic principles he had in mind:

> I have been telling Moore about a problem with which I have been racking my brains for some time now. However, he thinks it is insoluble, at least *pro tempore*, because of the many factors involved, factors which for the most part have yet to be discovered. The problem is this: you know about those graphs in which the movements of prices, discount rates, etc. etc., over the year, etc., are shown in rising and falling zigzags. I have variously attempted to analyze crises by calculating these ups and downs as irregular curves and I believed (and still believe it would be possible if the material were sufficiently studied) that I might be able to determine mathematically the principal laws governing crises. As I said, Moore thinks it cannot be done at present and I have resolved to give it up for the time being.[7]

---

[4] Yanovskaya 1969, p. 23.
[5] Marx 1978.
[6] Marx 1974.
[7] Marx 1976.

In light of the fact that 'the principal laws governing crises' are, as all social laws, tendential and contradictory, 'to determine mathematically' the laws is an impossible task. First, mathematics is a branch of formal logic. As seen above, premises in formal logic cannot be contradictory. However, to account for the laws of movement in society one has to start from contradictory premises (in the sense of dialectical contradictions as explained in Chapter 1 above) and this is why the laws of movement are tendential. Second, even if all the 'factors involved' were known, it would be practically impossible to consider all of them. This is why econometric models, even large ones involving thousand of relations, have such a dismal record as tools of prediction. But if it is impossible to determine the laws of crises purely in terms of mathematics, it is certainly possible to analyse the cyclical movement of economic indicators (the ups and downs) by using 'higher mathematics'. This was Marx's intuition.

At this juncture, two further questions arise. First, why did Marx make no use of differential calculus in his work? According to Smolinski

> For him [Marx, G.C.] the key fact is that a commodity has value or does not have it, labor is productive or is not, a participant in the economic process is a capitalist or a proletarian, society is capitalist or socialist. For this polarized universe a binary calculus might be a more suitable tool than differential calculus.[8]

However, Alcouffe remarks that the reproduction-schemes and the tendential fall of the profit rate are amenable to be treated with the mathematics developed by Marx. For example, differential calculus can be used to compute the instantaneous rate of change in the profit-rate.[9] Both perspectives seem to have an element of truth. Differential calculus is indeed applicable to some aspects of Marx's economic theory, but the question is whether this would be relevant. Rather, the relevant question is not how the rate of profit changes instantaneously, but how it changes due to the dialectical interplay between the tendency and the counter-tendencies.[10] A more probable explanation is that Marx, given that he finally mastered calculus towards the end of his life,

---

[8] Smolinski 1973, p. 1199.
[9] Alcouffe 1985, p. 37.
[10] This point differs from Alcouffe's view that a formal mathematical treatment of the law of the tendential fall in the profit-rate would be 'particularly welcome' (ibid.).

did not have the time and opportunity to write an analysis of the quantitative aspects of economic life (for example, of the economic cycle, the 'zigzags' as he puts it in the letter above).

The second question is how Marx would have applied calculus had he had the time and opportunity to do so. This question cannot be settled by considering how mathematics has been applied in economic planning by the formally centrally planned economies. As Smolinski reports, 'According to a widely held view, it was Marx's influence that has delayed by decades the development of mathematical economics in the economic systems of the Soviet type, which, in turn, is said to adversely affect the efficiency with which they operate.'[11] But, as the author rightly points out, and as the Manuscripts show, Marx was far from being ignorant of calculus and was greatly interested in its application to economics. It is true that

> The planners' 'mathematicophobia,' to use L. Kantorovich's apt expression, led to a substantial misallocation of resources through nonoptimal decisions....The intellectual cost of the taboo in question was also high: reduced to a status of a 'qualitative,' dequantified science, economics stagnated....[Oskar Lange – G.C.] pointed out that Soviet economics degenerated into a sterile dogma, the purpose of which became 'to plead the ruling bureaucracy's special interests and to distort and falsify economic reality.' These processes led to 'a withering away of Marxism.... Marxist [economic] science was replaced by a dogmatic apologetics'.[12]

There is considerable confusion here. While Marx cannot be held responsible for the insufficient application of mathematics in Soviet-type economies, and while this insufficiency was certainly an obstacle to the efficient functioning of an economic system, the reasons for the demise of the USSR and other Soviet-type centrally planned economies should be sought elsewhere. In short, in spite of its specific features, including the absence of the market, the USSR had become a system where the political/managerial class was performing the function of capital. The application of planning techniques was meant to mirror the market as an allocation-system but, at the same time, would have weakened the position of the bureaucrats and strengthened that of the tech-

---

[11] Smolinski 1973, p. 1189.
[12] Ibid.

nocrats. Nevertheless, aside from this, the application of planning techniques in those economies was opposite to a system based on the labourers' self management of the economy and society. Contrary to Smolinski's view, the planners' choice was often mistaken not because they 'reflected the mistaken labor theory of value'[13] but because an inherently capitalist system needed the market as an allocation-system rather than any other type of allocation-system. The optimal allocation *for capital* can only be achieved through the market. The system was thus inherently weak and unable to compete with fully developed capitalist countries.[14]

As for Marx, the important question here is not whether and how Marx would have applied differential calculus to his economic theory. This is scarcely important. Rather, the point is that even though the Manuscripts do not deal with the relation between dialectics and differential calculus, *Marx's method of differentiation provides key insights into what was Marx's dialectical view of reality*. This point has escaped the commentators of the Manuscripts. Yet, it is these insights rather than Marx's own original method of differentiation that are the really important aspect of the Manuscripts.

Let us begin by considering how 'Leibniz arrived at the notion of derivative...from geometric considerations.'[15] Let $y_1 = x_1^3$. Starting from $dx = x_1 - x_0$ and $dy = y_1 - y_0$:

(1) $y_1 = x_1^3 = (x_0 + dx)^3 = x_0^3 + 3x_0^2 dx + 3x_0 (dx)^2 + (dx)^3$

---

[13] Smolinski 1973, p. 1190.

[14] Carchedi 1987. According to Dauben, 'Study of Marx's *Mathematical Manuscripts* had a major impact on Soviet research in the history and philosophy of mathematics, beginning in the 1930s. This was especially true in philosophy of mathematics, where virtually all of the work published between 1930 and 1950 dealt with the manuscripts. The history of mathematics, however, also received considerable stimulation due to what Marx had written....Thus the significance of the discovery and study of the mathematical papers of Karl Marx in the Soviet Union may be assessed in several different ways. To the extent that editorial work on the manuscripts promoted study in the 1930s of the history of mathematics, its effect was positive. In particular, the manuscripts provided a strong rationale for serious examination of the history of analysis. It also followed that to appreciate Marx fully, it was necessary to study the history of mathematics in general. Unfortunately, where foundations of mathematics are concerned, Marx and the manuscripts have had a largely negative impact. This has been due primarily to the tendency of foundational research to focus almost exclusively on dialectical interpretations of mathematics according to Marx's fundamental doctrines. As for the technical, internal development of mathematics itself, Marx's manuscripts do not seem to have played any appreciable role, positive or negative'. Dauben 2003, pp. 2–3.

[15] Gerdes 1985, pp. 24–30. See also Struik 1948, pp. 187 and ff.

And given that $y_0 = x_0^3$

(2) $y_1 = y_0 + 3x_0^2dx + 3x_0(dx)^2 + (dx)^3$

so that

(3) $y_1 - y_0 = dy = 3x_0^2dx + 3x_0(dx)^2 + (dx)^3$

and dividing both members by dx we obtain

(4) $dy/dx = 3x_0^2 + 3x_0dx + (dx)^2$.

At this point, following Leibniz, we can cancel dx on the right given that dx is infinitely small. Thus, we obtain

(5) $dy/dx = 3x_0^2$ or more generally $3x^2$.

The problem, according to Marx, is twofold. First, the derivative $3x_0^2$ already appears in equation (1), i.e. *before the derivation*, before dx is set equal to zero. Thus, to get the derivative, 'the terms which are obtained in addition to the first derivative $[3x_0dx + (dx)^2$ – G.C.]…must be *juggled away* to obtain the correct result $[3x_0^2$ – G.C.].'[16] This is necessary 'not only to obtain the true result but any result at all.'[17] Marx calls this the 'mystical' method. Second, if dx is an infinitesimally small quantity, if it is not an ordinary (Archimedean) number, how can we justify the use of the rules for ordinary numbers, e.g. the application of the binomial expansion to $(x_0+dx)^3$? More generally, what is the theoretical and ontological status of infinitesimally small quantities?

In dealing with these difficulties, Marx develops his own method of derivation. Basically, Marx's method is as follows. Given a certain function, such as y=f(x), Marx lets first x_0 become x_1. Both x and y increase by a *finite* quantity, Δx and Δy (so that the rules for ordinary numbers can be applied here). The ratio $\Delta y/\Delta x = [f(x1)-f(xo)]/(x1-xo)$ is what he calls the provisional or preliminary derivative. Then, he lets x_1 return to x_0 so that $x_1-x_0=0$ and thus $y_1-y_0=0$ therefore reducing this limit-value to its absolute minimum-quantity. This is called the definitive derivative, dy/dx (so that the derivative appears only after the process of differentiation).[18] 'The quantity x_1, although originally obtained from the variation of x, *does not disappear; it is only reduced to* its

[16] Marx 1983a, p. 91.
[17] Ibid.
[18] For a mathematically more precise formulation of Marx's method, see Marx 1983a, note 7, pp. 195–6.

minimum limit value = x.'[19] Let us then see how Marx computes the derivative of y = x³.

If x_0 increases to x_1, y_0 increases to y_1. Given that $x_1-x_0 = \Delta x$ and $y_1-y_0=\Delta y$

(1) $\Delta y/\Delta x = (y_1-y_0)/(x_1-x_0) = (x_1{}^3-x_0{}^3)/(x_1-x_0)$.

Given that

(2) $(x_1{}^3-x_0{}^3) = (x_1-x_0)(x_1{}^2+x_1x_0+x_0{}^2)$

we substitute (2) into (1)

(3) $\Delta y/\Delta x = [(x_1-x_0)(x_1{}^2+x_1x_0+x_0{}^2)]/(x_1-x_0)$

and we get the provisional derivative

(4) $\Delta y/\Delta x = x_1{}^2+x_1x_0+x_0{}^2$.

To get the definitive derivative, x_1 goes back to x_0 so that $\Delta x = dx = 0$ and $\Delta y = dy = 0$. Equation (4) becomes

(5) $dy/dx = x_0{}^2+ x_0{}^2 +x_0{}^2 = 3x_0{}^2$.

The definitive derivative is thus the 'preliminary derivative reduced to its absolute minimum quantity.'[20] The two methods are thus conducive to the same results but there are differences between them. First, 'the starting points...are the opposite poles as far as operating method goes.'[21] In one case it is $x_0+dx = x_1$ (the 'positive form'); in the other (Marx) it is x_0 increasing to x_1, i.e. $x_1-x_0 = \Delta x$ (the 'negative form'[22]). 'One expresses the same thing as the other: the first negatively as the difference Δx, the second positively as the increment h.'[23] In the positive form 'from the beginning we interpret the *difference* as *its* opposite as a *sum*.'[24] Second, the procedures differ too: the fraction $\Delta y/\Delta x$ is transformed into dy/dx and the derivative is obtained after the derivation, after x_1 is reduced to its absolute minimum quantity. In the positive method (form) 'the derivative is thus in no way obtained

[19] Marx 1983a, p. 7; emphasis added.
[20] Ibid.
[21] Marx 1983a, p. 68.
[22] Marx 1983a, p. 88.
[23] Marx 1983a, p. 128.
[24] Marx 1983a, p. 102.

by differentiation but instead simply by the expansion of f(x+h) or y_1 into a defined expression obtained by simple multiplication.'[25]

It could be argued that these differences are insignificant given that both use only elementary algebra and divide the increment of a quantity, y, that depends on another quantity, x, by the increment in x.[26] Moreover, from a mathematical viewpoint, Marx's method is of limited applicability 'because it is often impossible to divide $f(x_1)-f(x_0)$ by x_1-x_0.'[27] Yet, it could also be argued that Marx's method is of historical significance. His procedure allows him to realize that dy/dx is not a ratio between two zero's but a *symbol* indicating the procedure of first increasing x_0 to x_1 (and thus y_0 to y_1) and then reducing x_1 (and thus y_1) to their minimum values, x_0 and y_0. Marx's discovery that dy/dx is an operational symbol anticipated 'an idea that came forward again only in the 20th century'.[28] Marx's stress on dy/dx as being an operational symbol, the 'expression of a process' and the 'symbol of a real process' is a real achievement, an outstanding critique of the 'mystical' foundations of infinitesimal calculus, of the metaphysical nature of infinitely small entities which are neither finite nor null.[29]

Be that as it may, these considerations are only of marginal interest for the present purposes. The point is that the analysis of this method offers important insights into Marx's notion of dialectics as submitted above.[30] Let us then see how these principles emerge implicitly from the Manuscripts.

First, for Marx, the notion of an infinitesimally small quantity, of an infinite approximation to zero, of something that is neither a number nor zero, should be rejected as 'metaphysical', as a 'chimera'. In his method, first x_0 is increased to x_1 (i.e. by dx) and then x_1 is reduced to x_0 so that x_1 does not disappear but is reduced to its minimum limit-value, x_0. Thus, dx, rather than being *at the same*

---

[25] Marx 1983a, p. 104.

[26] I owe this point to Hans van den Berg in a private communication.

[27] Gerdes 1985, p. 7.

[28] Kolmogorov, quoted in Gerdes 1985, p. 75. According to Lombardo Radice, Marx did not know the critical foundations of analysis, from Cauchy to Weierstrass, something which emphasises his 'geniality' in criticising autonomously the 'mystical' foundations of calculus (Lombardo Radice 1972, p. 274).

[29] Lombardo Radice, quoted in Ponzio 2005, p. 23.

[30] This view differs from Alcouffe's interpretation that 'the formalization of a social, and in particular of a critical science' should be sought in Hegel's *Science of Logic* (Alcouffe 1985, p. 104). As argued above, especially in Chapter 1, it should be sought in and extracted from Marx's own work.

time zero and not zero, is *first* a real number and *then* is posited equal to zero. This is the theorisation of a *temporal, real process*. In this way, Marx escapes the 'chimerical' notion of derivative. The notation dx=0 and dy=0 are the symbols of this process, not real numbers divided by zero.[31]

Second, in the 'positive' form, motion is the result of a (small) quantity (dx) added to x_o, which is a *constant*. Implicitly, x_o remains constant throughout, so that movement and change affect only a *limited section* of reality.[32] The starting point is a constant, a lack of movement and of change, to which change is added only as an appendix. This is a view of a *static reality* only temporarily disturbed by a movement that moreover applies only to an infinitesimal part of reality. The analogy with equilibrium and disequilibrium (temporary deviations from equilibrium) in the social sciences and with marginalism in economics is clear. Dx is added to x *from outside* x. Movement is not powered by the internal nature of the structure but is *the result of external forces*. Behind the 'positive form' lays a static interpretation of reality, behind the latter a dynamic view.

For Marx 'x_1 is the increased x itself; its growth is not separated from it....This formula distinguishes the increased x, namely x_1, from its original form prior to the increase, from x, but it does not distinguish x from its own increment.'[33] In Marx's method, it is *the whole*, x_o that *moves*, that grows to x_1 by dx. The movement from x_o to x_1 (Marx's starting point) and back (the end point) indicates *a change in the whole of reality, even if caused by a minimal part of it*. X_o cannot increases by Δx (or dx) without changing into x_1; the change in a part of reality (however small) changes the whole of it due to the interconnection of all of reality's constituent parts. This is a dynamic view in which absence of movement and change play no part. X_o can grow to x_1 only because x+dx is inherent in x *as one of its potentialities*. Then, Marx's method implies

---

[31] A similar point is made by Yanovskaya. According to Gerdes, 'some scientists explained the infinitesimals or infinitely small quantities in terms of the dialectical nature of opposites – at the same time equal to zero and different from zero. Yanovskaya called these scientists "*pseudo-Marxists*" because they forgot that dialectical materialism does not recognize static contradictions (=0 and $\neq$0), but only contradictions connected with motion.' (Gerdes 1985, pp. 115–16.)

[32] In a letter to Marx dated 1882, Engels writes: 'the fundamental difference between your method and the old one is that you make x change into x', thus making them really vary, while the other way starts from x+h which is always only the sum of two magnitudes, but never a variation of a magnitude.' Engels 1983, p. xxix.

[33] Marx 1983a, p. 86.

that x contains potentially *within* itself x+dx, that this latter realises itself as x+dx, and that if x +dx returns to x it becomes again a potential inherent in x. Even though not explicitly stated by Marx, his method presupposes that aspect of dialectics submitted here that distinguishes between the realised and the potential.[34] The fact that this might not be the way modern mathematics conceptualises dx is irrelevant for these purposes.

There is one point, however, that could be discordant with the notion of dialectics developed here. Marx mentions in passing (only once) that his two-step approach to the derivative is an example of the negation of the negation: 'The whole difficulty in understanding the differential operation (as in the negation of the negation generally) lies precisely in seeing *how* it differs from such a simple procedure and therefore leads to real results.'[35] This seems to be a fairly thin basis for arguing that 'Marx is interested above all to show how the negation that is at work in differentiation, if rid of its metaphysical approach, turns out to be a dialectical negation.'[36] Alternatively, one would be tempted to consider it as an example of Marx coquetting with the mode of expression peculiar to Hegel. But Marx wrote that he had been coquetting with Hegel's terminology in 1873 while the Manuscript under consideration was written in 1881.

The quotation above can be interpreted in two different ways. First, it could be that Marx was thinking that the negation of the negation is a concept valid for both the natural and the social sciences. This would be discordant with the theory put forth in this work in the sense that it would focus only on formal similarities. One can think, for example, of x_0 being negated by x_1 and this latter in its turn being negated by x_0. But this double negation is quite different from that in social reality. This movement is (1) only a quantitative change from x_0 to x_1, and vice versa, that is, there is no qualitative change; and (2) no account is given of the forces inherent in x_0 that cause it to change to x_1 and vice versa. In society, the negation of the negation accounts for the possibility that due to their contradictory nature, social phenomena supersede themselves through the creation of their own conditions of supersession. This is

---

[34] In social reality, on the contrary, a social phenomenon can decrease in size up until the point when it becomes an individual phenomenon, a potential social phenomenon. But in social reality the notion of infinitesimally small is nonsensical.

[35] Marx 1983a, p. 3.

[36] Ponzio 2005, p. 33. See also Kennedy 1977, p. 311.

not the case for derivation. If this were Marx's position, he would agree with Engels, for whom the laws of dialectics are 'valid just as much for motion in nature and human history and for the motion of thought'.[37] However, if the question is to explain contradictions, contradictory change, there is no negation of the negation in the process of derivation just as there is no negation of the negation in mathematics.

Mathematical reasoning is based on formal logic, a logic that excludes contradictions and thus contradictory movement. Marx agrees that mathematics can account for movement: 'the algebraic method ... [is] the exact opposite [of] the differential method'[38] because the former is the analysis of static quantities while the latter analyses changing quantities. However, in spite of this difference, both branches of mathematics share a characteristic, that of dealing only with quantities and thus with quantitative change which cannot be qualitative, contradictory change. If mathematics deals only with quantity, it deals only with the realm of realisations (i.e. not with the realm of potentials). Then, it cannot deal with dialectical contradictions and thus with qualitative change. Mathematics abstracts away concrete reality. Thus, its concepts can be applied to *any* realm of *quantifiable* reality and for this reason, it does not seek confirmation in the real concrete. On the other hand, dialectical logic is a theoretical concentrate of concrete reality (see Chapter 1, Section 7). For this reason, it seeks validation in that reality. But it is also possible that Marx meant that the negation of the negation, both in the natural and in the social sciences, share the feature of leading to 'real results', in spite of their differences. In this case, there would be agreement with the present theory of dialectical determination.

In any case, the important conclusion is that Marx *differentiates with the eyes of the social scientist, of the dialectician.* His method of differentiation mirrors a process that is real, temporal, in which a realised instance (a real number) cannot be at the same time a different realised instance (zero) and in which movement affects the whole rather than only the part and is the result of the interplay of potentials and that which is realised. Marx's method of differential calculus is consonant only with a dynamic and temporal approach (and inconsistent with an approach in which time does not exist, as in simulta-

[37] Quoted in Gerdes 1985, p. 88.
[38] Marx 1983a, p. 21.

neism in economics) and, more generally, with the notion of dialectics as submitted here. This conclusion is highly relevant for the debate between those Marxists who hold that, in Marx's theory, time is the essential coordinate of a dynamic, non-equilibrium system and those who adhere to a theory in which time and movement are absent (see Chapter 2 above). The question is not whether Marx's method (in any case, correct within its limits) is relevant for mathematics or for the history of mathematics.[39] The question is rather that the Manuscripts are highly relevant for the social scientists interested in uncovering and further developing Marx's own notion of dialectics as a method of social research and as a tool of social change.

---

[39] Dauben draws attention to the link between non-standard analysis and Marx's Mathematical Manuscripts in China: 'Nearly a century after Marx, Chinese mathematicians explicitly linked Marxist ideology and the foundations of mathematics through a new program interpreting calculus using infinitesimals, as Marx had advocated, but now on the rigorous terms of nonstandard analysis, the creation of Abraham Robinson in the 1960s. During the Cultural Revolution (1966–1976), mathematics was suspect in China for being too abstract, aloof from the concerns of the common man and the struggle to meet the basic needs of daily life in a still largely agrarian society. However, when Chinese mathematicians discovered the mathematical manuscripts of Karl Marx, these seemed to offer fresh grounds for justifying abstract mathematics, especially concern for foundations and critical evaluation of the calculus' (Dauben 2003, p. 328). Notice that this would seem to provide no answer to what was essentially Marx's question, i.e. the ontological nature of infinitely small or large numbers. The hypothesis that there is a 'cloud' of hyperreal numbers floating infinitesimally close to each number on the * R line leaves Marx's question unanswered.

References

Alberro, Jose and Persky Joseph 1981, 'The Dynamics of Fixed Capital Revaluation and Scrapping', *Review of Radical Political Economics*, 13, 2: 21–37.

Albert, Michael and Robin Hahnel 1981, *Socialism Today and Tomorrow*, Boston: South End Press.

—— 1991a, *Looking Forward. Participatory Economics for the Twenty-First Century*, Boston: South End Press.

—— 1991b, *The Political Economy of Participatory Economics*, Princeton: Princeton University Press.

Alcouffe, Alain 1985, *Les Manuscrits Mathématiques de Marx*, Paris: Economica.

—— 2001, 'Economie et mathématiques dans les travaux de Marx', *MEGA Studien*, IMES Amsterdam: 142–65.

Antonova, Irina 2006, 'Einige Methodologische Aspekte der Wechselwirkung von Sozial- und Natuurwissenschaften bei Marx', *Beiträge zur Marx-Engels-Forschung, Neue Folge*: 162–77.

Arthur, Christopher 2001, 'Value, Labour and Negativity', *Capital and Class*, 73: 15–39.

—— 2004a, 'Value and Negativity, a Reply to Carchedi', *Capital and Class*, 82: 17–22.

—— 2004b, *The New Dialectic and Marx's 'Capital'*, Historical Materialism Book Series, Leiden: Brill.

Bank of England 2009, *Financial Stability Report*, available at: <http://www.bankofengland.co.uk/publications/fsr/2009/fsr25sec1.pdf.>

Baracca, Angelo 2000, 'Contribución para una análisis marxista de las ciencias de la naturaleza y del papel de la "Corporación Scientifica"', *Papeles de la FIM*: 165–76.

Baran, Nicholas 1995, 'Computers and Capitalism: A Tragic Misuse of Technology', *Monthly Review*, 47: 40–6.

Baran, Paul 1968, *The Political Economy of Growth*, New York : Monthly Review Press.

BBC 2007, *The Downturn in Facts and Figures*, 21 November, available at: <http://news.bbc.co.uk/2/hi/business/7073131.stm>.

Bell, Franklin 2005, 'The New Dialectic and Marx's *Capital*', *Capital and Class*, 85: 149–51.

Bernstein Jared, Mishel Lawrence and Shierholz Heidi 2006–7, *The State of Working America*, Washington: Economic Policy Institute.

Blackburn, Robin 2008, 'The Subprime Crisis', *New Left Review*, II, 50: 63–106.

Bidet, Jacques 2005, 'The Dialectician's Interpretation of *Capital*', *Historical Materialism*, 13, 2: 121–46.

Bloor, David 1976, *Knowledge and Social Imagery*, London: Routledge & Kegan Paul.

Blunden, Andy 1984, 'Dialectics and Mathematics', *Labour Review*, available at: <http://home.mira.net/~andy/works/dialectics-mathematics.htm>.

Board of Governors of the Federal Reserve System 2006, *Flows of Funds Accounts of the United States, Historical Series and Annual Flows and Outstandings, Fourth Quarter 2005*, available at: <http://www.federalreserve.gov/releases/Z1/Current/>.

Bradley, Raymond and Norman Swartz 1979, *Possible Worlds, an Introduction to Logic and its Philosophy*, Oxford: Basil Blackwell.

Braverman, Harry 1974, *Labor and Monopoly Capital*, New York: Monthly Review Press.

Brenner, Robert 2002, *The Economics of Global Turbulence*, London: Verso.

Bukharin Nikolai (ed.) 1971 [1931], *Science at the Crossroads*, London: Taylor & Francis.

Burkett, Paul and John Bellamy Foster 2008, 'The Podolinsky Myth: an Obituary. Introduction to "Human Labour and Unity of Force" by Sergei Podolinsky', *Historical Materialism*, 16, 1: 115–61.

Business Week 2008, 'The Fed Bails Out AIG', 16 September, available at: <http://www.businessweek.com/bwdaily/dnflash/content/sep2008/db20080916 _387203. htm?chan=top+news_top+news+index+−+temp_top+story>.

Caffentzis, George 1997, 'Why Machines Cannot Create Value; or Marx's Theory of Machines', in Davis, Hirschl and Stack (eds.) 1997.

Callinicos, Alex 2001, 'Toni Negri in Perspective', *International Socialism Journal*, 92, available at: <http://pubs.socialistreviewindex.org.uk/isj92/callinicos.htm92>.

Camfield, David 2007, 'The Multitude and the Kangaroo: A Critique of Hardt and Negri's Theory of Immaterial Labour', *Historical Materialism*, 15, 2: 21–52.

Carchedi, Guglielmo 1977, *On the Economic Identification of Social Classes*, London: Routledge and Kegan Paul.

—— 1983, *Problems in Class Analysis*, London: Routledge and Kegan Paul.

—— 1984, 'The Logic of Prices as Values', *Economy and Society*, 13, 4: 431–55.

—— 1987, *Class Analysis and Social Research*, Oxford: Basil Blackwell.

—— 1989, 'Class and Class Analysis', in *The Debate on Classes*, edited by Erik Olin Wright, London: Verso,

—— 1991, *Frontiers of Political Economy*, London: Verso.

—— 1996, 'Non-Equilibrium Market Prices', in *Marx and Non-Equilibrium Economics*, edited by Alan Freeman and Guglielmo Carchedi, Cheltenham: Edward Elgar.

—— 2001, For *Another Europe. A Class Analysis of European Economic Integration*, London: Verso.

—— 2003a, 'A Note on Chris Arthur's "Dialectics of Negativity"', *Capital and Class*, 81: 25–31.

—— 2003b, 'Il valore e l'imperialismo: sono ancora attuali per un'analisi del capitalismo contemporaneo?', in *Il Piano Inclinato del Capitale, Crisi, Competizione Globale e Guerre*, edited by Luciano Vasapollo, Milan: Jaca Books.

—— 2003c, 'Il declino dello stato keynesiano', *Proteo*, May–December: 148–52.

—— 2005a, 'On the Production of Knowledge', *Research in Political Economy*, 22: 267–304.

—— 2005b, 'Sapiens nihil affirmat quod non probat', *Review of Political Economy*, 17, 1: 127–39.

—— 2006a, 'The Fallacies of Keynesian Policies', *Rethinking Marxism*, 18, 1: 63–81.

—— 2006b, 'Tsakalotos on Homo Economicus: Some Additional Comments', *Science and Society*, 70, 3: 370–5.

—— 2008a, 'Dialectics and Temporality in Marx's Mathematical Manuscripts', *Science and Society*, 72, 4: 415–26.

—— 2008b, 'Logic and Dialectics in Social Science, Part I', *Critical Sociology*, 34, 4: 495–523.

—— 2008c, 'Logic and Dialectics in Social Science, Part II', *Critical Sociology*, 34, 5: 631–56.

—— 2009, 'The Fallacies of "New Dialectics" and Value-Form Theory', *Historical Materialism*, 17, 1: 145–69.

—— forthcoming, 'From Okishio to Marx through Dialectics', *Capital and Class*, 99: 59–79.

Ceplair, Larry 2008, 'The Base and Superstructure Debate in the Hollywood Communist Party', *Science and Society*, 72, 3: 319–48.

Chote, Robert 2008, 'Financial Crisis: Someone Will Have to Dig Us Out of All this Debt', *Telegraph*, 8 October, available at: <http://www.telegraph.co.uk/finance/comment/3161595/Financial-Crisis-Someone-will-have-to-dig-us-out-of-all-this-debt.html>.

Corriere della Sera 2000, 'Clonazione, Londra dice sì alla Ricerca sugli Embrioni Umani', 20 December.

Council on Foreign Relations 2008, *Economic Report of the President*, Washington.

Cullenberg, Stephen 1994, *The Falling Rate of Profit*, London: Pluto.

Dauben, Joseph 2003, 'Mathematics, Ideology, and the Politics of Infinitesimals: Mathematical Logic and Nonstandard Analysis in Modern China', *History and Philosophy of Logic*, 24: 327–63.

Davis Jim, Thomas Hirschl and Michael Stack (eds.) 1997, *Cutting Edge, Technology, Information Capitalism and Social Revolution*, London: Verso.

Davis Jim and Stack Michael 1997, 'The Digital Advance', in Davis, Hirschl and Stack (eds.) 1997.

Dmitriev, Vladimir Karpovich 1974 [1898], *Economic Essays on Value, Competition and Utility*, Cambridge: Cambridge University Press.

Durkheim, Émile 1966 [1895], The *Rules of Sociological Method*, New York: The Free Press.

Dyer-Witheford, Nick 1999, *Cyber-Marx: Cycles and Circuits of Struggle in High Technology Capitalism*, available at: <http://www.fims.uwo.ca/people/faculty/dyerwitheford/index.htm>.

Engels, Friedrich 1978a [1890], 'Engels an Hermann Schlüter in New York', *Marx Engels Werke*, Band 37, Berlin: Dietz Verlag.

—— 1978b [1889], 'Engels an Friedrich Adolph Sorge in Hoboken', *Marx Engels Werke*, Band 37, Berlin: Dietz Verlag.

—— 1995 [1883], 'Engels to August Bebel in Borsdorf near Leipzig', *Marx Engels Collected Works*, Volume 47, Moscow: Progress Publishers.

—— 1979 [1885], 'Engels an August Bebel in Plauen bei Dresden', *Marx Engels Werke*, Band 36, Berlin: Dietz Verlag.

—— 1983 [1882], 'Engels to Marx in Ventnor', in Marx 1983.

—— 1987 [1873–82], *Dialectics of Nature*, in Karl Marx and Frederick Engels, *Collected Works*, Volume 25, Moscow: Progress Publishers.

Ernst, John 1982, 'Simultaneous Valuation Extirpated: a Contribution of the Critique of the Neo-Ricardian Concept of Value', *Review of Radical Political Economics*, 14, 2: 85–94 .

Ferretti, Francesco 2004, 'E se lasciassimo a casa il cervello?', *Il Manifesto*, 9 January.

Financial Times 1995, 'When It's All in the Mind', 26 September.

Fine, Ben (ed.) 1986, *The Value Dimension*, London: Routledge and Kegan Paul.

—— and Laurence Harris 1976, 'Controversial Issues in Marxist Economic Theory', *The Socialist Register*, London: Merlin Press.

Foley, Duncan 1986, *Understanding 'Capital': Marx's Economic Theory*, Cambridge, MA., Harvard University Press.

—— 1999, 'Response to David Laibman', *Research in Political Economy*, 17: 229–33.

—— 2000, 'Response to Freeman and Kliman', *Research in Political Economy*, 18: 278–84.

Foster, John Bellamy and Fred Magdoff 2008, 'Financial Implosion and Stagnation. Back to the Real Economy', available at: <http://monthlyreview.org/081201foster magdoff.php#fn33b>.

Freeman, Alan 1999, 'Between Two World Systems: a Response to David Laibman', *Research in Political Economy*, 17: 241–48.

—— 2008, 'Simultaneous Valuation vs. the Exploitation Theory of Profit: A Summing Up', *Capital and Class*, 94: 107–17.

—— n.d. 'What Makes the US Profit Rate Fall?', Unpublished.

—— and Guglielmo Carchedi (eds.) 1996, *Marx and Non-Equilibrium Economics*, Cheltenham: Edward Elgar.

—— and Andrew Kliman 2000, 'Two Concepts of Value, Two Rates of Profit, Two Laws of Motion', *Research in Political Economy*, 18: 243–68.

Geras, Norman 1983, *Marx and Human Nature: Refutation of a Legend*, London: Verso.

Gerdes, Paulus 1985, *Marx Demystifies Calculus*, Minneapolis: Marxist Educational Press.

Giacchè, Vladimiro 2001, 'Perché la guerra fa bene all'economia (I)', *Proteo*, 3: 111–16.

—— 2008, 'Scene da un patrimonio…Che non c'è più: banche e non solo', *La Contraddizione*, October–December: 46–55.

Giussani, Paolo 2005, 'Capitale fisso e guruismo', unpublished, available at: <http://www.countdownnet.info/archivio/analisi/altro/326.pdf>.

—— and Antonio Pagliarone 2004, 'Come i Morti anche le Mode ogni tanto Ritornano', available at: <http://www.countdownnet.info/archivio/Analisi_storico_politica/165.pdf>.

Gold, Gerry and Paul Feldman 2007, *A House of Cards*, London: Lupus Books.

Goldstein, Matthew 2008, 'Bear Stearns' Big Bailout', *Business Week*, March 14, available at: <http://www.businessweek.com/bwdaily/dnflash/content/mar2008/db20080314_993131_page_2.htm>.

Gowan, Peter 2009, 'Crisis in the Heartland', *New Left Review*, II, 55: 5–29.

Gramsci, Antonio 1971 [1929–35], *Prison Notebooks*, edited and translated by Quintin Hoare and Geoffrey Nowell Smith, New York: International Publishers.

—— 1975a [1919–20], *L'Ordine Nuovo*, Torino: Einaudi.

—— 1975b, *Quaderni del Carcere*, Torino: Einaudi.

Guidi, Carlo 2000, 'Le chimere diventano realtà: purché si paghi', *Il Tempo*, 1 December.

Guthrie, Douglas 1967, *Storia della Medicina*, Milan: Feltrinelli.

Hardt, Michael and Antonio Negri 2000, *Empire*, Cambridge, MA.: Harvard University Press.

Harman, Chris 2009, 'The Slump of the 1930s and the Crisis Today', *International Socialism*, 121: 21–48.

Heinrich, Michael 2004a, 'Relevance and Irrelevance of Marxian Economics', *The New School Economic Review*, 1: 83–90.

—— 2004b, 'Ambivalences of Marx's Critique of Political Economy as Obstacles for the Analysis of Contemporary Capitalism', *Historical Materialism,* Annual Conference, 10 October, London, revised paper.

Hessen, Boris 1931, 'The Social and Economic Roots of Newton's "Principia"', in Bukharin (ed.) 1971.

Heymann, Dagmar 1995, 'Frankenstein und die Schopfungstraume der Naturwissenschafler', *Wechselwirkung*, October/November: 62–5.

Hoagland, Jim 1997, 'Looks Who Says Capitalism Needs Government', *International Herald Tribune*, 28 August.

Holton, Robert 1992, *Economy and Society*, London: Routledge and Kegan Paul.

Hunt, Ian 2005, 'The Economic Cell-Form', *Historical Materialism*, 13, 2: 147–66.

Kennedy, Hubert 1977, 'Karl Marx and the Foundations of Differential Calculus', *Historia Mathematica*, 4: 303–18 .

Kenney, Martin 1997, 'Value Creation in the Late Twentieth Century: The Rise of the Knowledge Worker', in Davis, Hirschl and Stack (eds.) 1997.

Keynes, John Maynard 1964 [1935], *The General Theory of Employment, Interest and Money*, New York: Harcourt, Brace and World.

Kicillof, Axel and Guido Starosta 2007a, 'On Materiality and Social Forms: a Political Critique of Rubin's Value-Form Theory', *Historical Materialism*, 15, 3: 9–43.

—— 2007b, 'Value Form and Class Struggle, a Critique of the Autonomist Theory of Value', *Capital and Class*, 92: 13–40.

King, Jonathan 1997, 'The Biotechnology Revolution: Self-Replicating Factories and the Ownership of Life Forms', in Davis, Hirschl and Stack (eds.) 1997.

Kircz, Joost 1998, 'Engels and Natural Science: A Starting Point', *Science and Society*, 62, 1: 62–78.

Klein, Jacob 1968, *Greek Mathematical Thought and the Origin of Algebra*, Cambridge, MA.: M.I.T. Press.

Kliman, Andrew 1996, 'A Value-Theoretic Critique of the Okishio Theorem', in Freeman and Carchedi (eds.) 1996.

—— 1999, 'Sell Dear, Buy Cheap? A Reply to Laibman', *Research in Political Economy*, 17: 235–40.

—— 2001, 'Simultaneous Valuation vs. the Exploitation Theory of Profit', *Capital and Class*, 73: 97–112.

—— 2007, *Reclaiming Marx's 'Capital': A Refutation of the Myth of Inconsistency*, Lanham: Lexington Books.

—— 2009, 'The Destruction of Capital and the Current Economic Crisis', available at: <http://akliman.squarespace.com/crisis–intervention/>.

—— and Alan Freeman 2000, 'Rejoinder to Duncan Foley and David Laibman', *Research in Political Economy*, 18: 285–94.

—— 2006, 'Replicating Marx: A Reply to Mohun', *Capital and Class*, 88: 117–26.

Laibman, David 1982, 'Technical Change, the Real Wage and the Rate of Exploitation: The Falling Rate of Profit Reconsidered', *Review of Radical Political Economics*, 14, 2: 95–105.

—— 1999a, 'Okishio and his Critics: Historical Costs Versus Replacement Costs', *Research in Political Economy*, 17: 207–27.

—— 1999b, 'The Profit Rate and Reproduction of Capital: A Rejoinder', *Research in Political Economy*, 17: 249–54.

—— 2000a, 'Two of Everything: A Response', *Research in Political Economy*, 18: 269–78.

—— 2000b, 'Numerology, Temporalism, and Profit Rate Trends', *Research in Political Economy*, 18: 295–306.

—— 2001, 'Rising "Material" vs. Falling "Value" Rates of Profit: Trial by Simulation', *Capital and Class*, 79: 79–96.

—— 2009, 'The Onset of the Great Depression II: Conceptualizing the Crisis', available at: <http://www.scienceandsociety.com/editorial_july09.pdf>.

Lazzarato, Maurizio and Toni Negri 1991, 'Travail immatériel et subjectivité', available at: <http://multitudes.samizdat.net/Travail-immateriel-et-subjectivite>.

Lefebvre, Henri 1982, *Logique formelle en logique dialectique*, Third edition, Paris: Terrains/Editions Sociales.

Lenin, Vladimir 1964 [1914], 'The Taylor System – Man's Enslavement by the Machine', in *Collected Works*, Volume 20, Moscow: Progress Publishers.

—— 1965 [1918], 'The Immediate Tasks of the Soviet Government', in *Collected Works*, Volume 27, Moscow: Progress Publishers.

—— 1968 [1913], 'A Scientific System of Sweating', in *Collected Works*, Volume 18, Moscow: Progress Publishers.

—— 1969 [1918], 'Original Version of the Article 'The Immediate Tasks of the Soviet Government', in *Collected Works*, Volume 42, Moscow: Progress Publishers.

—— 1972a [1907], 'The International Socialist Congress in Stuttgart', in *Collected Works*, Volume 13, Moscow: Progress Publishers.

—— 1972b [1908], *Materialism and Empirio-Criticism*, in *Collected Works*, Volume 14, Moscow: Progress Publishers.

Likitkijsomboon, Pichit 1995, 'Marxian Theories of Value-Form', *Review of Radical Political Economics*, 27, 2: 73–105.

Linhart, Robert 1976, *Lénine, les paysans, Taylor*, Paris: Seuil.

Lobkowicz Nicholas 1978, 'Materialism and Matter in Marxism-Leninism', in McMullin (ed.) 1978.

Lombardo Radice, Lucio 1972, 'Dai "Manoscritti Matematici" di K. Marx', *Critica Marxista-Quaderni*, 6: 273–7

Mandel, Ernest 1978, *Late Capitalism*, London: New Left Books.

Marx, Karl 1967a [1867], *Capital*, Volume I, New York: International Publishers.

—— 1967a [1894], *Capital*, Volume III, Progress Publishers: Moscow.

—— 1967b [1894], *Capital*, Volume II, New York: International Publishers.

—— 1967c [1894], *Capital*, Volume III, International Publishers: New York.

—— 1969a [1868], 'Marx to Kugelmann in Hanover', in Karl Marx and Frederick Engels, *Selected Works*, Volume II, Moscow: Progress Publishers.

—— 1971 [1844], *The Economic and Philosophic Manuscripts of 1844*, New York: International Publishers.

—— 1973a [1939], *Grundrisse*, Harmondsworth: Penguin Books.

—— 1973b [1870], 'Marx to Sigfrid Meyer and August Vogt In New York', in *Marx Engels Werke*, Band 32, Berlin: Dietz Verlag.

—— 1974 [1863], 'Letter to Engels 6 July', in *Marx/Engels Werke*, Volume 30, Berlin: Dietz Verlag.

—— 1976 [1873], Letter to Engels 31 May, in *Marx/Engels Werke*, Volume 33, Berlin: Dietz Verlag.

—— 1976a [1867], *Capital*, Volume I, Harmondsworth: Penguin Books.

—— 1976b, 'Results of the Immediate Process of Production', in *Value: Studies by Karl Marx*, edited by Albert Dragstedt, London: New Park Publications.

—— 1977 [1859], *A Contribution to the Critique of Political Economy*, Moscow: Progress Publishers.

—— 1978 [1858], 'Letter to Engels 11 January', in *Marx/Engels Werke*, Volume 29, Berlin: Dietz Verlag.

—— 1983a [1881], *Mathematical Manuscripts of Karl Marx*, New York: New Park Publications

—— 1983b [1858], 'Letter to Engels 16 January', in *Marx Engels Collected Works*, Volume 40, Moscow: Progress Publishers.

—— 1988 [1861–3], 'Economic Manuscript of 1861–63', in *Marx and Engels Collected Works*, Volume 30, Moscow: Progress Publishers.

—— 1992 [1863–7], 'Ökonomische Manuskripte 1863–1867', *MEGA*, Amsterdam: Internationales Institut für Sozialgeschichte.

Marx, Karl and Friedrich Engels 1970a [1845–6], *The German Ideology*, edited by Chris Arthur, New York: International Publishers.

—— 1975a, *The Holy Family*, in *Marx and Engels Collected Works*, Volume 4, Moscow: Progress Publishers.

Marshall, Alfred 1920, *Principles of Economics*, London: Macmillan.

May, Christopher 2000, 'Knowledge Workers, Teleworkers, and Plumbers', available at: <www.ciaonet.org/isa/mac01>.

McKie, Robin 1997, 'Scientists Clone Adult Sheep', *The Observer*, 23 February.

McMullin Ernan 1978, 'Introduction: The Concept of Matter in Transition', in McMullin (ed.) 1978.

McMullin, Ernan (ed.) 1978, The *Concept of Matter in Modern Philosophy*, Notre Dame: University of Notre Dame Press.

Mihevc, John 1995, *The Market Tells Them So*, London: Zed Books.

Milios, John 2009, 'Rethinking Marx's Value-Form Analysis from an Althusserian Perspective', *Rethinking Marxism*, 21, 2: 260–74.

Mobasser, Nilou 1987, 'Marx and Self-Realization', *New Left Review*, I, 161: 119–28.

Mohun, Simon 2003, 'On the TSSI and the Exploitation Theory of Profit', *Capital and Class*, 81: 85–102.

—— and Roberto Veneziani 2007, 'The Incoherence of the TSSI', *Capital and Class*, 92: 139–45.

Morris-Suzuki, Tessa 1997a, 'Robots and Capitalism', in Davis, Hirschl and Stack (eds.) 1997.

—— 1997b, 'Capitalism in the Computer Age', in Davis, Hirschl and Stack (eds.) 1997.

Moseley, Fred 1977a, 'The Rate of Profit and the Future of Capitalism', *Review of Radical Political Economics*, 29, 4: 23–41.

—— 1997, 'The Rate of Profit and Economic Stagnation in the US Economy', *Historical Materialism*, 1: 161–74.

—— 2000, 'The "New Solution" to the Transformation Problem: A Sympathetic Critique', *Review of Radical Political Economics*, 32, 2: 282–316.

—— 2008, 'The "Macro-Monetary" Interpretation of Marx's Theory: A Reply to Ravagnani's Critique', *Review of Radical Political Economics*, 40, 1: 107–18.

Murray, Patrick 2000, 'Marx's "Truly Social" Labour Theory of Value. Part I, Abstract Labour in Marxian Value Theory', *Historical Materialism*, 6: 27–65.

—— 2005, 'The New Giant's Staircase', *Historical Materialism*, 13, 2: 61–84.

Negri, Toni 1992, 'Infinité de la communication – finitude du désir', available at: <http://multitudes.samizdat.net/Infinite-de-la-communication>.

New York Times 2009, 'The US Financial Crisis: the Global Dimension and Implications for the US Policy', 12 February, available at: <http://topics.blogs.nytimes.com/2009/02/12/the-us-financial-crisis-the-global-dimension-with-implications-for-us-policy/>.

Noble, David 1978, 'Social Choice in Machine Design: The Case of Automatically Controlled Machine Tools and a Challenge for Labor', *Politics and Society*, 8, 3–4: 313–47.

Ollman, Bertell 1993, *Dialectical Investigations*, New York: Routledge.

Okishio, Nobuo 1961, 'Technical Changes and the Rate of Profit', *Kobe University Economic Review*, 7: 85–99.

Pagliarone, Antonio 2008, *Mad Max Economy*, Milano: Sedizioni.

Panitch, Leo and Sam Gindin 2002, 'Gems and Baubles in Empire', *Historical Materialism*, 10, 2: 17–43.

Panzieri, Raniero 1961, 'L'uso capitalista delle macchine nel neocapitalismo', *Quaderni Rossi*, 1: 53–72.

Paolucci, Paul 2006a, 'Classical Sociological Theory and Modern Social Problems: Marx's Concept of the Camera Obscura and the Fallacy of Individualistic Reductionism', *Critical Sociology*, 27,1: 77–120.

—— 2006b, 'Assumptions of the Dialectical Method', *Critical Sociology*, 27,3: 116–46.

Perez, Manuel 1980, 'Valeur et prix: un essai de critique des propositions néo-ricardiannes', *Critiques de l'Economie Politique*, Nouvelle Série, 10: 122–49.

Ponzio, Augusto (ed.) 2005, *Karl Marx, Manoscritti Matematici*, Milano: Spirali.

Post, Charles 2006, 'The Myth of the Labor Aristocracy', Part 1, *Solidarity*, available at: <http://www.solidarity-us.org/node/128#R25>.

Ramos, Alejandro 1998–9, 'Value and Price of Production: New Evidence on Marx's Transformation Procedure,' *International Journal of Political Economy*, 28, 4: 55–81.

—— 2004, 'Labour, Money, Labour-Saving Innovation and the Falling Rate of Profit', in *The New Value Controversy and the Foundations of Economics*, edited by Alan Freeman, Andrew Kliman and Julian Wells, Cheltenham: Edward Elgar.

Ravagnani, Fabio 2005, 'A Critical Note on Moseley's "Macro-Monetary" Interpretation of Marx's Theory', *Review of Radical Political Economics*, 37, 1: 85–96

Resnick, Stephen and Richard Wolff (eds.) 2006, *New Departures in Marxian Theory*, London: Routledge.

Reuten, Geert 2004, 'Zirkel Vicieu or Trend Fall? The Course of the Profit Rate in Marx's *Capital III*', *History of Political Economy*, 36, 1: 163–86.

Rifkin, Jeremy 1989, *Time Wars*, New York: Simon & Schuster.

Rikowski, Glenn 2003, 'Alien Life: Marx and the Future of the Human', *Historical Materialism*, 11, 2: 121–64.

Robinson, Joan 1963, *An Essay on Marxian Economics*, 2nd Edition, London: Macmillan.

—— 1972, 'Ideology and Analysis', in *A Critique of Economic Theory*, edited by Jesse Schwartz, Harmondsworth: Penguin Books.

Rovelli, Carlo 2006, *What Is Time? What Is Space?*, Rome: Di Renzo Editore.

Shaikh, Anwar 1978a, 'Political Economy and Capitalism: Notes on Dobb's Theory of Crisis', *Cambridge Journal of Economics*, 2, 2: 233–51.

—— 1978b, 'An Introduction to the History of Crises Theories', *US Capitalism in Crisis*, URPE: New York.

—— 2003, 'Who Pays for Welfare in a Welfare State? A Multicountry Study', *Social Research*, 70, 2: 531–50.

Schiller, Dan 1997, 'The Information Commodity: A Preliminary View', in Davis, Hirschl and Stack (eds.) 1997.

Screpanti, Ernesto 2005, 'Guglielmo Carchedi's *The Art of Fudging* Explained to the People', *Review of Political Economy*, 17, 1: 115–26.

Smolinski, Leon 1973, 'Karl Marx and Mathematical Economics', *Journal of Political Economy*, 81, 5: 1189–204.

Stålenheim, Petter, Catalina Perdomo and Elisabeth Sköns 2008, *SIPRI Yearbook 2008*, Summary, available at: <http://yearbook2008.sipri.org/05/>.

Steedman, Ian 1977, *Marx after Sraffa*, London: Verso.

Stockholm International Peace Research Institute 2002, *SIPRI Yearbook 2002*, available at: <http://editors.sipri.se/pubs/yb02/pro2.html>.

——2004, *SIPRI Yearbook 2004*, available at: <http://editors.sipri.se/pubs/yb04/aboutyb.html>.

Strassmann, Paul 1999, 'Calculating Knowledge Capital', available at: <www.strass
mann.com/pubs/km/calc-km.html>.
Struik, Dirk Jan 1948, 'Marx and Mathematics', *Science and Society*, 12, 1: 181–96.
Sweezy, Paul 1970 [1942], *The Theory of Capitalist Development: Principles of Marxian
Political Economy*, New York: Monthly Review Press.
Sweezy, Paul (ed.) 1973, *Karl Marx and the Close of his System*, Fairfield: Kelley Publishers.
Taylor, Frederick Winslow 1985 [1911], *The Principles of Scientific Management*, New
York: Harper.
Thomas, Peter D. 2009, *The Gramscian Moment: Philosophy, Hegemony and Marxism*, His-
torical Materialism Book Series, Leiden: Brill.
Ticktin, Hillel 2008, 'Editorial', *Critique*, 46, available at: <http://www.metamute.org/
en/content/notes_on_the_last_few_months#sdfoo tnote5sym>.
Toscano, Alberto 2007, 'From Pin Factories to Gold Farmers: Editorial introduction to
a Research Stream on Cognitive Capitalism, Immaterial Labour, and the General
Intellect', *Historical Materialism*, 15, 1: 3–11
Tronti, Mario 2006 [1966], *Operai e Capitale*, Rome: DeriveApprodi.
Tsakalatos, Euclid 2004, 'Homo Economicus, Political Economy, and Socialism', *Sci-
ence and Society*, 68, 2: 137–60.
Turchetto, Maria 2001, 'Dall' operaio massa all'imprenditorialità comune: la scon-
certante parabola dell'operaismo italiano', available at: <http://www.intermarx
.com/temi/oper.html>.
Tuszynski Jack (ed.) 2006, *The Emerging Physics of Consciousness*, Heidelberg: Springer.
Vlachou, Anna (ed.) 1999, *Contemporary Economic Theory: Radical Critiques of Neo-
Liberalism*, Basingstoke: Macmillan.
Vercellone, Carlo 2007, 'From Formal Subsumption to General Intellect: Elements for
a Marxist Reading of the Thesis of Cognitive Capitalism', *Historical Materialism*, 15,
1: 13–36.
Virno Paolo 2001, 'General Intellect', in *Lessico Postfordista*, Milan: Feltrinelli, English
translation available at: <http://www.generation–online.org/p/fpvirno10.htm>.
Von Böhm-Bawerk, Eugen 1973 [1896], 'Karl Marx and the Close of his System', in *Karl
Marx and the Close of his System*, edited by Paul Sweezy, Fairfield: Kelley Publishers.
Von Bortkiewicz, Ladislaus 1971 [1906], 'Calcolo del valore e calcolo del prezzo nel
sistema marxiano', in *La Teoria Economica di Marx*, Turin: Einaudi.
—— 1973 [1907], 'On the Correction of Marx's Theoretical Construction in the Third
Volume of Capital', in *Karl Marx and the Close of his System*, edited by Paul Sweezy,
Fairfield: Kelley Publishers.
Weber, Max 1949 [1903–17], *The Methodology of the Social Sciences*, New York: The Free
Press.
Werskey, Gary 1975, 'Making Socialists of Scientists: Whose Side is History On?', *Radi-
cal Science Journal*, 2, 3: 13–50.
Woolf, Nancy 2006, 'Microtubules in the Cerebral Cortex: Role in Memory and Con-
sciousness', in *The Emerging Physics of Consciousness*, edited by Jack Tuszynski,
Heidelberg: Springer.
Wolff, Richard 1999, 'Limiting the State versus Expanding It: a Criticism of this Debate',
in *Contemporary Economic Theory: Radical Critiques of Neo-Liberalism*, edited Anna Vla-
chou, Basingstoke: Macmillan.
World Health Organization 2003, *Acupuncture: Review and Analysis of Reports on Controlled Clinical Trials*, Geneva, available at: <http://apps.who.int/medicinedocs/
en/d/Js4926e/>.
Wright, Erik Olin (ed.) 1989, *The Debate on Classes*, London: Verso.
Wright, Steve 2002, *Storming Heaven, Class Composition and Struggle in Italian Autonomist Marxism*, London: Pluto Press.
Yanovskaya, Sofia Alexandrovna 1969, 'Karl Marx's *Mathematische Manuskripte*', *Sow-
jetwissenschaft, Gesellschafts-wissenschaftliche Beiträge*, I.
—— 1983, 'Preface to the 1968 Edition', in Marx 1983.
Zelený, Jindrich 1980, *The Logic of Marx*, Oxford: Basil Blackwell.

Index

Werskey, Gary   268, 298
Wolff, Richard   180, 298
Woolf, Nancy   194, 298
Work of co-ordination and unity   80, 82
Work of control and surveillance   71, 76, 79, 82–3, 191, 221
Workerism   209, 225–43

Wright, Erik Olin   211–31, 292
Wright, Steve   267, 298

Yanovskaya, Sofia Alexandrovna   279–80, 287, 298

Zelený, Jindrich   6, 43, 273, 298